Angles on Otherness in Post-Franco Spain

Cristina Fernández Cubas. Photo courtesy of Jerry Bauer.

Angles on Otherness in Post-Franco Spain

The Fiction of Cristina Fernández Cubas

Jessica A. Folkart

Lewisburg
Bucknell University Press
London: Associated University Presses

©2002 by Rosemont Publishing & Printing Corp.

All rights reserved. Authorization to photocopy items for internal or personal use, or the internal or personal use of specific clients, is granted by the copyright owner, provided that a base fee of $10.00, plus eight cents per page, per copy is paid directly to the Copyright Clearance Center, 222 Rosewood Drive, Danvers, Massachusetts 01923.[0-8387-5486-4/02 $10.00 + 8¢ pp, pc.]

Associated University Presses
440 Forsgate Drive
Cranbury, NJ 08512

Associated University Presses
16 Barter Street
London WC1A 2AH, England

Associated University Presses
P.O. Box 338, Port Credit
Mississauga, Ontario
Canada L5G 4L8

The paper used in this publication meets the requirements of the American National Standard for Permanence of Paper for Printed Library Materials Z39.48-1984.

Library of Congress Cataloging-in-Publication Data

Folkart, Jessica A., 1969–
    Angles on otherness in post-Franco Spain : the fiction of Cristina Fernández Cubas / Jessica A. Folkart.
    p. cm.
Includes bibliographical references and index.
ISBN 0-8387-5486-4 (alk. paper)
1. Fernández Cubas, Cristina, 1945—Criticism and interpretation. 2. Difference (Psychology) in literature. I. Title.

PQ6656.E72138 Z66 2002
863'.64—dc21

2001049955

PRINTED IN THE UNITED STATES OF AMERICA

For Robert Spires

Contents

Acknowledgments	9
Introduction: Subjectivity and Difference in Post-Franco Spain	13
1. Looking Objectively at the Subject: The Spectacle of Power in *Mi hermana Elba*	29
"Lúnula y Violeta"	31
"La ventana del jardín"	45
"Mi hermana Elba"	56
"El provocador de imágenes"	60
2. Performing and Reforming Gender in *Los altillos de Brumal*	67
"El reloj de Bagdad"	68
"En el hemisferio sur"	76
"Los altillos de Brumal"	85
"La noche de Jezabel"	91
3. Re-Citing and Re-Siting the Story of the Subject in *El año de Gracia* and *El columpio*	101
El año de Gracia	101
El columpio	117
4. The Space of Oppositional Subjectivity in *Con Agatha en Estambul*	139
"Mundo"	140
"La mujer de verde"	149
"El lugar"	157
"Ausencia"	165
"Con Agatha en Estambul"	174

5. Plotting Desire: The Visual Construction of the Subject
   in *El ángulo del horror*   186
      "Helicón"   187
      "El legado del abuelo"   198
      "El ángulo del horror"   207
      "La Flor de España"   213
(In)conclusion   224

Notes   232
Works Cited   244
Index   250

Acknowledgments

THIS BOOK IS CREDITED TO ME AND, IN MANY WAYS, IT TELLS THE STORY of the evolution of my thinking over the years. Yet many people who have influenced my life have left their mark on these pages as well. First, I thank Cristina Fernández Cubas for meeting with me one summer afternoon in 1996 to talk about her work. Her stories have provided me with endless hours of entertainment and provoked me to interrogate my interpretations as well as those of others.

My love and thanks go to my entire family for their persistence in keeping me grounded as I worked through these readings. I especially thank my mother, Joyce Folkart, who kindled my love for language when I was small.

To all the friends who have shared my path over these last years, too numerous to name here but never forgotten in my mind: know how much I appreciate you, for the journey has been much brighter for your company. I am particularly grateful to Kirsten Adlung Kellogg (a.k.a. Cosme), Sheila Avellanet, Craig Brians, Francie Cate-Arries, Lisa Gaskill Nowak, Barry Nowak, Bob Hershberger, Lorena Llano, Mary O'Day, and Dan Rogers, indispensable colleagues and friends whose perspectives—so often different than my own—have galvanized and enriched my thinking about worlds both fictional and real. Special thanks go to Vicky Unruh, Andrew Debicki, John Brushwood, William R. Blue, and Jacqueline Bixler, who gave valuable feedback on various versions of this manuscript, and Elizabeth Calvera, who gave excellent advice on the translations of quotations. I am also grateful to my colleagues at Virginia Tech, a rare breed of intellectuals, for their enduring support and incorrigible mirth.

Finally, I especially want to thank Robert Spires: teacher, scholar, and friend. Unable to articulate my gratitude, I dedicate the efforts of this book to him.

A previous version of sections of chap. 2 appeared as "Interpretations of Gender: Performing Subjectivity in Cristina Fernández Cubas's *Los altillos de Brumal*," *Anales de la literatura española contemporánea* 25, no. 1–2 (2000): 101–27. A previous version of sections of chap. 5 appeared as "Desire, Doubling, and Difference in Cristina Fernández Cubas's *El ángulo del horror*," *Revista Canadiense de Estudios Hispánicos* 24.2 (Winter 2000): 343–62. A previous version of part of chap. 3 is to appear as "Almost the Same, but Not Quite: Re-Orienting the Story of the Subject in Cristina Fernández Cubas's *El año de Gracia*," *Studies in Twentieth Century Literature*, forthcoming. Excerpts from *Mi hermana Elba y Los altillos de Brumal*, *El año de Gracia*, *El ángulo del horror*, *Con Agatha en Estambul*, and *El columpio* (all published by Tusquets) are reprinted with the generous permission of Cristina Fernández Cubas and Mercedes Casanovas, her literary agent. Finally, I thank Jerry Bauer for allowing me to use his photograph of Fernández Cubas in this book.

Angles on Otherness in Post-Franco Spain

Introduction: Subjectivity and Difference in Post-Franco Spain

"La diferencia estaba en mí [. . .]"
[The difference was in me {. . .}][1]
—"Los altillos de Brumal"

As Cristina Fernández Cubas tells it, her days growing up in a beachfront town outside of Barcelona contained many literary elements. Her family included four sisters who shared the fantasies, terrors, and sicknesses of childhood, and a brother who embellished on the details of *The House of Usher* for his sisters, with the result that when Cristina read the Poe tale herself, she found humorous fault with it: "I thought he was an excellent writer. But in certain passages I discovered missing at least three chairs and one folding screen" (Fernández Cubas 1991, 114). She also had a mother who "wandered around the entire house at all hours" and a father who aspired to "create a dictionary in all the languages of the world" (115). The family was watched over by the ancient and seemingly eternal Antonia, a voracious storyteller who possessed "a complex arsenal of prodigious stories" (114). Hearing these tales, the children were delighted with the notion that the most astonishing events had certainly happened somewhere, and could possibly happen to them at any moment.

Yet Fernández Cubas was unable to mold these experiences into stories until she left Spain to live in Latin America for two years, starting in 1973. The return from this trip radically changed her perspective on the past and her vision of the present:

> The very day of my return, no sooner had I set foot in Barcelona than I realized the distance implied by an ocean and the deception, with regard to reckoning time, involved with changing countries but not languages. I felt like a foreigner in my own land, a completely uprooted being, but also, after a little while, I confirmed that during those two years on the other side of the ocean

things had gone about occupying their true place in my memory and my life. And so I could walk by the house of my birth without any hint of melancholy and, above all, I could invent myself a sister, whom I called Elba, and write a story. (116)

Distance, deception, time, crossing to the other side and then returning with a new perspective, feeling foreign within the realm of the familiar, sensing sameness in a land of difference, finding the place of things in memory and in life—all these motifs intertwine in the intriguing fictions that this author has imagined, beginning with the stories of *Mi hermana Elba* [My Sister Elba]. In exploring the fragments that have influenced her life and inspired her to tell her stories, Fernández Cubas also delves into multiple facets of subjectivity. How do we define who we are? How do we develop our identities in contention with or collusion with other people? What difference does being male or female make in who each individual is able to become and in what he or she is able to do? How does all we read influence our concepts of self and others? How might that vision change with time? How do the spaces that surround us contour the shape of what we see, the way we see it, and the way we see ourselves? These issues indelibly inform the study of the subject, which may be viewed as that never-yet-completed entity structured by forces such as the social, political, and cultural. At the risk of being reductive, subjectivity might be summed up as the always-changing identity that each individual takes on in the socialization process.

The concept of subjectivity has figured as the central thread of diverse theoretical tasks, winding its way through historical, political, social, cultural, psychoanalytical, and numerous other treatises, including literary works. Particularly in fields influenced by philosophical notions, the subject is generally viewed as the center of perception and power, in contrast to the object, which is what the subject perceives and considers to be "other" than itself. Traditional Western philosophical ideas consider the subject as a multifaceted yet cohesive entity that is the center of perception of everything around it: the subject perceives objects (Smith 1988, xxvii).[2] Following more recent, poststructural approaches that tend to undermine the validity of privileging the subject over the object, the fiction of Cristina Fernández Cubas enters into the debate by interrogating the very markers of difference that distinguish the subject from the object. Whereas phenomenal perception has traditionally informed the consideration of philosophical subjectivity, Fernández Cubas alters the angles of perception in her tales to depict a worldview that undermines the positing of any single center of subjectivity. In doing so she reveals that the effort to define an enclosed identity is, in essence, a construction that can be deconstructed. Her texts thus offer "angles on otherness," shifts in perception that destabilize absolute terms of difference and power between the subject and the object, in order to engage subjectivity as a dynamic process open to the influence of the other.

Fernández Cubas, born in Arenys de Mar, Barcelona, in 1945, has been acclaimed in Spain and the rest of Europe as one of the key writers who express the exploration of identity in post-totalitarian Spain.[3] While the concept of "generations" is a questionable construct at best, critics place Fernández Cubas in the generation of '68: authors born in the late 1930s–1940s who were inevitably influenced by the 1968 upheavals in France and around Europe and who came into their own "coinciding with the final agonizing moments of Francoism, the apogee of experimental narrative and the influence of structuralism, at the same time that, at the end of the indicated period, a recuperation of the classical elements of storytelling was beginning to be discernable" (Basanta 1990, 64–65). Other members of her group who share in the glory of the *nueva narrativa española* [Spanish New Novel] include Manuel Vázquez Montalbán, Alvaro Pombo, Lourdes Ortiz, Eduardo Mendoza, José María Guelbenzu, Juan José Millás, Ana María Moix, and Soledad Puértolas.

Although most of these writers began publishing around the early 1970s, Fernández Cubas first studied law and journalism, becoming a professional fiction writer relatively late in her career. She emerged in the Hispanic literary world in 1980 with her first collection of short stories, *Mi hermana Elba* [My Sister Elba], which critics and writers alike have hailed as the initiator of a renaissance in the short fiction genre in Spain.[4] A few years later she published another collection entitled *Los altillos de Brumal* [The Attics of Brumal] (1983). Her first novel, *El año de Gracia* [The Year of Grace] (1985), ensued shortly thereafter. She followed this work with two more collections of short stories, *El ángulo del horror* [The Angle of Horror] (1990a) and *Con Agatha en Estambul* [With Agatha in Istanbul] (1994), which truly established her as a master of the genre. Fernández Cubas released her second novel, *El columpio* [The Swing] in 1995, and a theatrical work, *Hermanas de sangre* [Blood Sisters], in 1998. Most recently, in 2001, she published *Cosas que ya no existen,* a collection of personal memoirs. Fernández Cubas's texts emerge from the context of contemporary Spanish culture and interrogate the issues that inform and define that culture. Whereas conventional history would tend to weave an orderly design from an often tangled mass of events, this author's stories tease out the contradictions and unravel the contrived order, revealing new possibilities for creation and interpretation.

Spain is Different. The Spanish Ministry of Tourism of the 1960s proliferated this slogan to cast Spain in an appealing light and to attract international tourism and favor to General Francisco Franco's fascist regime (1939–75). Yet, this claim has often been viewed negatively: "It seemed just a step away from saying that 'Spaniards are different,' which was one of the ways that Franco had justified his dictatorship—on the assertion that, unlike other Europeans, they could not be trusted to handle their own destiny" (Hooper 1995, 445). Alternatively, General Franco's insistence that Spain was different—i.e., better—than the rest of the world also served as an ex post facto justification and adulation of the country's political and economic isolation from and rejection by the rest of the West. Under Franco, the cultural construction of Spain reinscribed the traditional, univocal representation of the country, as was constantly intoned in his mantra of *"una* patria, *una* lengua, *una* religión" [*one* fatherland, *one* language, *one* religion]. Although the dictator occasionally changed the individual elements of the phrase to suit his rhetoric of the moment, the essential *oneness* of its discursive trinity remained constant in his message. Franco's slant on the situation posited Spain as the center that was superior to the other, the (marginal) rest of the world.

The nearly three decades that have passed since Franco's death in November 1975, however, have been marked on many levels by a shift away from emphasis on the center to a valorization of previously marginalized groups.[5] In this light, the post-totalitarian period in Spain may be characterized by the embracing of difference. The changing politics of the country were the most visible marker of the rejection of a unified, centralized power in recognition of the role of multiple centers of power.[6] After Franco's death the 1978 Spanish Constitution established the parliamentary monarchy as a union of seventeen autonomous communities and acknowledged four official languages of Spain: *castellano, catalán, gallego,* and *euskera.* Since 1978 the various regions have negotiated the intricacies of regional versus state authority that were sometimes only vaguely delineated in the constitution. Beneath this apparent embracing of difference and centrifugal dispersal of power, however, a centripetal tendency has come to the fore within each culture to define itself on the basis of its difference from the others and, consequently, to distance or denigrate other regional groups within the nation.

This drive toward micro-political identity and differentiation at the regional level is a reaction in part to the increasing homogenization imposed by globalization. Spain's entry into the European Economic Community (EC) in 1986 underscored its role in the European and international political realm—another opening of its borders to the difference of political forces. Paradoxically, though, this move also represented a union with other European powers into a centralized force. Gonzalo Navajas emphasizes the resistance to globalization as a prime motivator for the separate regions to traverse the past in an effort to trace out their individual identities: "In this temporal regression, I perceive an imperative angst to affirm difference, however miniscule or even provincial it may be, against the invasion of indifferentiation by global culture and technology. Solidly affirming ourselves in a specific idiosyncrasy is a guarantee against the superstructural uniformity in which we refuse to recognize ourselves" (Navajas 1997, 242).

The tension between sameness and difference in relation to the other, as the fundamental demarcation of identity, is an overarching issue that Fernández Cubas examines in her texts. It informs perceptions of national identity in "La Flor de España" ["The Flower of Spain"; *El ángulo del horror*], for example, as an arrogant Spanish woman living in northern Europe feels threatened by the transplantation of Spanish culture to the north in the form of a small Spanish shop that sells Spanish goods and that is run by a woman of both northern and southern heritage. In an effort to cope with her cross-cultural angst, the exiled protagonist criticizes the shop for its outrageous oversight of not stocking *turrón de coco*, even though it boasts a wide variety of other flavors of the Spanish candy. Moreover, she obsessively and obnoxiously harps on the bicultural shop owner, driving the poor woman to the brink of a nervous breakdown. The trope of doubling and the search for difference are treated on the level of individual identity with similarly humorous obsession in stories like "Helicón" ["Helicon"; *El ángulo del horror*]. Here a male narrator invents an insane twin upon whom he can blame his own bizarre and antisocial behavior, but his careful construction of a stable identity is unbalanced when he discovers that his girlfriend (whom he criticizes for being obsessed with doubles) is actually two people, twin sisters, and that the more passionate sister prefers the aberrant, fictional brother to the narrator himself. Fernández Cubas's depictions of subjectivity highlight how forces such as power and gender play into the dichotomies of those who duplicate us versus those who are different from us, those who are desirable versus those who are dismissible.

On the national level of identity in Spain, shifts of power in the posttotalitarian political scene have heralded the new democracy's ability to peacefully accept and integrate difference within its borders. For well over a decade Felipe González and the Partido Socialista Obrero Español (PSOE, the Spanish Socialist Party) dominated the government with a liberal agenda that witnessed tremendous economic and cultural success in the 1980s but wilted under charges of conspiracy and corruption in the 1990s. Consequently, the 1996 elections brought the marginal victory of José María Aznar's conservative Partido Popular (PP, the Popular Party). Whereas some Spaniards lament that this handover of power signaled a return to more reactionary politics, others are relieved at the smooth transition from one ruling party to another, which, together with King Juan Carlos's squelching of the attempted military coup in 1981, may be seen as evidence that democracy is solidly in place in Spain. As the country has moved from dictatorship to democracy, the oppositional forms of government have underscored their distinction from one another. Yet a consideration of the contradictory messages projected by political action on the regional, national, and multinational levels suggests that the dictatorial and democratic Spains share at least one similarity: they discursively define their identities by emphasizing their essential *difference* from other groups. Indeed, the cynical and nostalgic leftist mantra of the *desencanto* years, "Things were better *against* Franco," underscores this tendency (Labanyi 1995, 397; italics mine).

Although Fernández Cubas's stories do not overtly focus on issues of Francoism, subtle time markers in certain texts do reveal a reflective commentary on the age. For instance, as if to lay to rest the nostalgic wish of some Spaniards for a return to the perceived safety and structure of dictatorial control, in *El columpio* the author uncannily superimposes the Francoist past of the 1950s with the post-Franco present of the 1990s. In this novel a young woman travels for the first time to her deceased mother's childhood home. She finds the house preserved exactly as it was in her mother's youth and discovers that her adult uncles secretly play out rituals of acquiescence and reverence with the supernatural figure of her mother as a tyrannical child. Within a single, shared space then, Fernández Cubas juxtaposes two distinct moments in time and two radically deviant perspectives of history and identity. Like the movement of the metaphorical swing of its title, *El columpio* highlights the importance of the passage of time to the production of knowledge through change and difference.

As *El columpio* indicates, the status of women has markedly changed over the last three decades in Spain's increasingly liberal social environment. The five years before Franco's death saw a marked increase in women working outside the home, and in 1980 they constituted 27% of the workforce; by 1990 that figure had increased to 35% (Montero 1995, 382). The year of Franco's death also witnessed the abolition of the *permiso marital*, which had prohibited women from undertaking any activity outside the home without their husband's consent. Prior to this, husbands had extensive control over their wives' dealings in society—they even had rights over the women's salaries and could deny permission for them to open bank accounts or make large purchases such as a car. As of 1978, adultery and concubinage were no longer crimes (previously, adultery committed by women was a crime punishable by prison whereas concubinage—committed by men—met with much less severity), and the sale of contraceptives was legalized. By 1981, notwithstanding ecclesiastical opposition, divorce was officially permissible in Spain. After much dissension, abortion under limited circumstances was legalized in 1985, which has somewhat ameliorated the high numbers of abortions performed illegally or abroad on Spaniards. The advancement of women's status in society has been fomented by social organizations such as the Instituto de la Mujer, established by the Socialists in 1983. Women have increased their numbers in education, making up more than one-half of the graduates at all levels in 1990. Nonetheless, equality can hardly be said to reign on all levels. Eight out of ten men make no contribution to housework at all, the lowest figure of any country in the EC (Montero 1995, 382). As with politics, the "difference" in women's roles over time is a relative condition, evaluated in terms of the roles of men.

Although Fernández Cubas chooses not to ally herself as a writer with the feminist movement in Spain, her works do question the social formation and performance of men and women—exposing both to an equally critical and often humorous perspective.[7] In "En el hemisferio sur" ["In the Southern Hemisphere"; *Los altillos de Brumal*] the angst-ridden male narrator is a book editor who belittles his neurotic, best-selling author when she suffers a breakdown. She eventually dies, but he seems unperturbed. Then he discovers that his every word and deed have been pre-scripted in the writer's posthumously published novel, which playfully and vengefully wrests away any sovereignty he thought he had. Lest womanhood be read as a sort of utopian ideal that justly turns the tables on men, however, in other texts such as "Lúnula y Violeta" ["Lúnula and Violeta"; *Mi hermana Elba*] Fernández Cubas explores how women deploy manipulative power plays against one another. Fundamental to these depictions is the author's ongoing exploration of the nature of gender, power, and socially invested codes of behavior in relation to identity.

Whereas women's emergence in the extradomestic sphere has reflected and effected many changes in the Spanish sociocultural scene since the end of the dictatorship, the marked opening in the industry of media communication has revolutionized the way Spaniards see themselves and the rest of the world. The dominion of the state-run Televisión Española (TVE) was curtailed when a 1983 law passed by the PSOE authorized the introduction of regional television channels, reiterating the shift away from centralism. Then in 1989, Antena 3, Spain's first private television channel, went on the air. It was then followed by Tele 5 and private subscription channels. This relative openness of airtime—echoed in the print media by national, regional, and private newspapers and journals—has been a key step in the country's democratization.

A window to the world, television capitalizes on and intensifies the sensory emphasis on vision in postmodern culture; logically, then, the play of optical dynamics in the mediation of identity permeates Fernández Cubas's fiction. For instance, in "La ventana del jardín" ["The Garden Window"; *Mi hermana Elba*] a man spies on a young boy whom he believes to be developmentally stunted and cruelly restrained by his parents. Watching the boy in secret from outside the child's window, the protagonist believes that he can accurately observe and interpret the child's alarming situation. The adult eventually discovers, however, that the boy conversely watches *him* through the window as well, and that the knowledge that he thought he gleaned about the world that he watched through the window is skewed and incomplete. In this and other tales the knowledge imparted to each person by the reversible dynamics of vision is certainly partial and restrictive, but also unsettling and ultimately enlightening.

The economic success and the opening up of the media in the 1980s in Spain coincided with tremendous investment in and proliferation of the arts. Music festivals, new art galleries—such as the Reina Sofía, the Thyssen and the Instituto Valenciano de Arte Moderno—and the Compañía Nacional de Teatro Clásico—a repertory theater company dedicated to the classics—all promoted public interest in the arts. To undergird the floundering Spanish film industry, the PSOE appointed Pilar Miró, a film director herself, as the Director-General of Film in 1982. Although the late Miró was a polemical figure, the *Ley Miró* of 1983–84 did much to subsidize the production of quality Spanish films. Nonetheless, the Spanish movie industry has struggled against formidable foreign competition, particularly Hollywood. The democratic government instituted various quotas to advance Spanish cinema production with only limited success, which was aggravated even more when Spain's entry into the EC meant that European films counted toward the Spanish quota.

Spain's best-known director, Pedro Almodóvar, introduced the movie world to the *movida madrileña*, the quintessential expression of the cultural and economic prosperity and growing political cynicism of 1980s Madrid. The *movida* embodied society's successful boom as well as its *desencanto*, its disillusionment that democracy was hardly utopia:

The *Movida* was the social expression of this individualism that was both hedonistic and pessimistic.... [I]ts artistic and intellectual expression may be grouped into two clearly differentiated categories: on one hand, the controlled heroism of cultural events, summer university programs, national prizes or talk shows, in a word, *fiesta*; on the other hand, the expression of disillusionment, including the most apocalyptic pessimism, and hence of a certain protest. (Subirats 1995, 212)

A synthesis of the traditional and the new, the banal and the sophisticated, Almodóvar's films projected the anachronous irony that a country barely immersed in modernity should be swept up in the dizzying cynicism of postmodernism.

In much of her fiction, Fernández Cubas subtly reflects the juxtaposition of past/present, primitive/postmodern, and traditional/technological that typifies postmodern Spain. For example, *El año de Gracia* refigures the story of the Western civilizing mission and drive toward modernity in the tale of a shipwrecked Spaniard who is subjected to and enlightened by the "savage" on a seemingly distant island, which turns out to be lethally contaminated with chemical waste dumped by the continental center of "civilization" that is actually quite close by. As Fernández Cubas's fiction suggests, Spain embodies an uneven postmodernity full of contradictions, with the rejected reality of the past still penetrating the hyperreality of the present.[8]

Of course, "postmodernity" and "postmodern" are highly debated terms that have been defined, questioned, and undermined by many theoreticians; entire tomes could be—and have been—written on the subject. Because it is beyond the scope of this study to recount all the arguments in the debate, I shall highlight only the central ideas that directly inform my own analyses in this project.[9] Alejandro Herrero-Olaizola draws on Linda Hutcheon's *A Poetics of Postmodernism* in an effort to distill what might be called common characteristics in Spanish "postmodernist" fiction: "a discursive heterogeneity that points toward the questioning of the limits of the text itself [and] of genre, and that makes problematic the existence of an authority figure who might carry out an omniscient narration; a clear exhibition of marginality that defies the limits of the text, as well as a change of the dominant that consequently translates to an integration of 'Culture' into 'culture'" (Herrero-Olaizola 1995a, 124). The issue of difference is the thread that connects these diverse postmodern elements: instead of advancing univocalism, postmodern texts foreground discursive heterogeneity, question the limits of text and genre, and undermine the validity of authority/subjugation and centrality/marginality, all of which demotes any centralized "Culture" to the level of multiple "cultures."

This crisis of Culture/culture precisely characterizes concerns for identity in contemporary Spain. Jo Labanyi associates Spain's experience of postmodernity with the country's anxiety to assert its difference from the rest of the West: "If, as has been said, postmodernism is an expression of political impotence resulting from loss of belief in the master narratives of liberalism and marxism, and from the media's monopoly control of the images of reality available to us, then Spain is suffering from a bad attack: [. . .] Spain is no longer different" (Labanyi 1995, 397). Labanyi further connects democratic Spain's focus on internal cultural heterogeneity with its lost sense of difference on the international front:

> Postmodernist theory deconstructs the concept of unity—and by extension that of identity, in its sense of "sameness"—exposing it as a political manoeuvre designed to suppress recognition of difference within. It is because Spain has now recognized its cultural plurality that it is no longer possible to make clear-cut distinctions between what is and what is not Spanish: both because incompatible cultural forms may be equally Spanish, and because cultural forms found in Spain are found elsewhere. (Labanyi 1995, 397)

This is not to say that "Spanishness" does not exist. Postmodernism does not obliterate identity, but instead unveils it as a construct, examining the pieces and challenging the process of its composition. In this light, the reconstruction of identity in postmodern Spain is an open-ended task, always subject to alteration and contradiction by another difference.

Hence postmodernism blurs the demarcation lines that trace out the perceived difference and identity of any single force, voice, or point of view. In Hutcheon's words, "the contradictions that characterize postmodernism reject any neat binary opposition that might conceal a secret hierarchy of values. The elements of these contradictions are usually multiple; the focus is on differences, not single otherness . . ." (Hutcheon 1988, 42–43). In light of the contradictions produced by constant subversion, many have criticized postmodernism for what might be viewed as its inherent deconstruction of everything, including itself. If everything can be displaced from its former centrality, the argument generally goes, then all that remains is nihilism. Yet postmodernism rejects the absolutism manifest even in the total denial of any valid center. It does not invalidate the effort to establish priorities of order, but rather as Hutcheon points out, has quite the opposite effect: "What [postmodernism] does say is that there are all kinds of orders and systems in our world—*and* that we create them all. That is their justification and their limitation. They do not exist 'out there', fixed, given, universal, eternal; they are human constructs in history. This does not make them any the less necessary or desirable. It does, however, condition their 'truth' value" (Hutcheon 1988, 43). Postmodernism proposes that a multiplicity of perspectives is key to obtaining a broader vision of the world, by highlighting the constructed nature of discourse.

As the quintessential creation of language, literature uniquely projects the possibilities and limitations of discourse. Within the context of contemporary Spain, the experimental novels of writers such as Juan Goytisolo, Luis Goytisolo, and Juan Benet reveled in the way discourse constructs and is constructed almost to the exclusion of telling a story. Their language play posed a radical questioning that reflected the environment of increasing *apertura* [opening] in Spain and the influence of postmodernism and structuralism in the 1960s and 1970s. Out of this impulse emerges what Sobejano has termed "the poematic novel: that which aspires to be entirely, *par excellence*, an autonomous creative text" (Sobejano 1985, 1). In relation to the poematic novel, Sobejano registers various manifestations of discursively conscious texts: "The one closest to a poem, so much so as to become confused with it, would be metafiction. . . . The historical novel then appeared . . . ; as did the ludical novel (which cultivates entertainment by parodying or renovating the norms of detective, spy, science fiction, dark, and erotic novels); the novel of memory; and—finally—the testimonial novel, which would occupy the most distant point" (Sobejano 1985, 1). For Sobejano, Camilo José Cela's *Mazurca para dos muertos* (1983) embodies the poematic, Luis Goytisolo's collection *Antagonía* (1973–81) heralds the metafictional, Lourdes Ortiz's *Urraca* (1982) rewrites history, the detectivesque fictions of Manuel Vázquez Montalbán and Eduardo Mendoza foreground the ludic, Carmen Martín Gaite's *El cuarto de atrás* (1977) exemplifies the novel of memory, and Juan José Millás's *Visión del ahogado* (1977) represents the testimonial novel.

I would add that many of these works, as products of postmodernism, overflow the constructed borders of such categories to occupy more than one or to question the discursive nature of each. Indeed, the tendency of contemporary Spanish novels to destabilize notions of history, myth, memory, metafiction, high and popular culture, and of genres such as the *novela negra*, constitutes a literary demonstration of the constructive nature of discourse. Such works frequently turn back on themselves to destabilize the very tenets that define them, as seen in Schaefer-Rodríguez's observations about the new Spanish *novela negra*: "the *novela negra* calls into question the idea of 'crime' itself as well as the possibility of a solution" (Schaefer-Rodríguez 1990, 137). Whereas the novel has been a devouring genre since its inception, the postmodern novel proves to be deliberately self-conscious in its voracious questioning of the totalizing possibilities of all discourse in general, and its own discourse in particular.

Applying the degree of this overt consciousness of discourse as a litmus test, Spires hones Sobejano's paradigm by plotting post-Francoist fiction along a spectrum of "writerly" versus "readerly" texts. For Spires, the year of Franco's death constitutes an apex of the two extremes in Spanish narrative. Positing Juan Goytisolo's *Juan sin Tierra* (1975) as one pole that focuses solely on the discursive construction of narrative, and Eduardo Mendoza's *La verdad sobre el caso Savolta* (1975) as the opposite endpoint that emphasizes the story told, Spires views works of contemporary fiction as relative combinations of writing-centered and reading-centered approaches: "To a large degree Spanish fiction from 1975 to the present can be seen as an effort to reconcile the conflict between process and product, between discourse and story" (Spires 1996, 200). Their structural opposition notwithstanding, the novels of this period all display a questioning of absolutes and a consciousness of how stories come to be told; in doing so, they promote agency within the limits imposed by discourse.[10] For Spires, this is the "common legacy" of the distinct works of post-totalitarian fiction (87).[11]

In numerous articles, conference papers, and several book chapters, scholars have acclaimed the innovation and dynamism of Fernández Cubas's work in contemporary Spain. Spires examines how the author dismantles authority when she explores "the illogic of logic" in *El ángulo del horror* (Spires 1995, 234). Moreover, he features *El año de Gracia* as a key representation of the postmodern episteme in his *Post-Totalitarian Spanish Fiction* (Spires 1996). Margenot examines *El año de Gracia* as a parodic repetition of *Robinson Crusoe* (Margenot 1993), whereas Bellver concludes that the intertextual juxtaposition with Defoe's novel condemns the nihilistic social context of the postmodern novel (Bellver 1995, 115). On the other hand, I tend to view Fernández Cubas's first novel as regenerative and celebratory through its act of repeating foundational literary models with a difference.[12]

Many critics have signaled the subversive element of the fantastic in Fernández Cubas's stories, as seen in articles by Bretz (1988), Ortega (1992), Talbot (1989), and Zatlin (1987a). Alborg notes this quality as typical of fiction of the Spanish transition period (Alborg 1987). The fantastic is indeed one prominent mode of blurring the boundaries of absolute conceptions of reality in these texts. As Suñén observes, Fernández Cubas's works reveal "the other side of the real, of what could well be called the hidden side of people and objects" (Suñén 1984, 5). The Spanish author does not restrict her exploration of the other side of reality to the fantastic genre; she also has written marvelous, uncanny, and even realistic stories.

Apart from the fantastic, other studies of Fernández Cubas's work focus on her manipulation of language. Language figures prominently as one of the strategies in Pérez's analysis of narrative unreliability in the author's fiction (Pérez 1998). Similarly, Glenn shows how the writer highlights "the arbitrariness of boundaries" by stressing the indecipherability of language and the inability of language to communicate (Glenn 1992, 126). Scholars such as Rueda (1988) and Valls (1994a) emphasize a polarity between orality and the written word, or between irrational and rational language. Bellver treats *El año de Gracia* as a postmodern text in which both the oral and written word are finally displaced. She concludes that "since . . . words—both oral and written—are dis-placed, communication on a collective level ceases" (Bellver 1992, 232). Displacement of the meaning of language is certainly a key technique, yet I argue that communication does not cease in Fernández Cubas's texts. Instead, the author dislodges hierarchical, patriarchally privileged meanings to create new possibilities for communication.

By exploiting the multiple and often ambiguous meanings of language, the author reveals that the multiplicity of difference, incarnated in the displacement of a single, all-encompassing meaning, can enhance instead of impede one's understanding of the other. Because Fernández Cubas is one of those writers who reject extreme experimentalism (although she does play with metafiction) in favor of a *vuelta a la palabra*, her tales could be categorized as reading-centered. Yet her return to the word does not express ingenuous faith in its capacity to capture absolute meaning. In her fictional world, Fernández Cubas deconstructs any direct correlation between the signifier (the letters of the word) and the signified (the meaning of the word), which readers might assume to exist, in order to unleash the creativity and elusiveness of the sign (the word as mark and meaning). If language is the basis of how we conceive of ourselves and our world, as Saussure and Lacan have indicated, the poststructuralist awareness of the multiplicity of meaning inherent in every sign may be seen as the cornerstone to understanding Fernández Cubas's work. She wields the written word to question the worldview, based on binary oppositions, that society—or patriarchy—has conditioned us to accept.

Implicit in those patriarchal structures is a fear of difference, expressed in the identification of the self in opposition to and through the subjugation of the other. In Fernández Cubas's representation of the mediation of identity, she constantly destabilizes the limits of subjectivity by making problematic the issue of difference. Why do all subject positions depend on the status of difference? What do we leave out of our subjectivity in order to define who we are? Does not that excluded otherness reveal as much about the contours of our identity as what we profess to embrace as part of ourselves? The characters in this writer's stories experience quintessentially postmodern crises with their search for cohesion in the midst of disjunction; as such, they engage issues of identity pertinent both to Spain and to the broader realm of postmodern Western culture. Indeed, alongside considerations of *lo español* in these texts, one finds the specter of *lo no español*. Fernández Cubas engages these concepts in dialogue with one another to unveil the similarities and differences of both constructions.

This blurring of the borders between roles is appropriate, considering the shifting identities being negotiated in Spain today: gender, family, job, region, country, EC, global community, and so on. It may seem surprising at first, then, that this female writer from Barcelona refuses to engage specifically issues of Catalan nationalism or of feminism. I suspect that this may be because, rather than to accentuate and reify distinctions of cultural and sexual identity, Fernández Cubas prefers to interrogate the parameters by which such identities are constituted.[13] In this post-Franco period of flux, uncertainty, and redefinition, Fernández Cubas's texts play with alternative "angles"—opposing perspectives of any given situation—to show how alterity not only informs but can also expand and enrich the subject's vision of itself. Her works are also universal in that they explore the formation, erasure, and reconstruction of identity in the contemporary human subject and subvert basic binary structures of patriarchal thought. Finally, her often disquieting texts position themselves as oppositional "others" in relation to readers, serving as direct mediators in readers' own processes of subject formation. By shifting the angle of vision and making readers look from the outside, from the otherness of those structures, she challenges them to rethink the terms of *their* identities.

In this book I examine how Fernández Cubas explores the contemporary reconstruction of identity as negotiated through the differences implicit in power relations, gender roles, literary and historical depictions of the subject, space, and altered perspectives. Although these concerns emerge in almost every text Fernández Cubas has published, this study is organized so that each chapter foregrounds one theme as manifested in a collection of short fiction or in the two novels.[14] In chap. 1, "Looking Objectively at the Subject: The Spectacle of Power in *Mi hermana Elba*," Foucauldian concepts of power inform my exploration of how subjects and objects define their differences from one another in Fernández Cubas's debut work. In 1980, at a time when much fiction in Spain reveals a general preoccupation with a central authority figure that controls the balance of power in society, *Mi hermana Elba* is emblematic of a shift toward a theme of how relations of power and resistance pervade all types of human interaction.[15] This collection of stories exposes the discourses of power that position subjects and objects in relation to one another. Beyond merely revealing the strategies of power inherent in objectification, however, it explores how objects, too, wield power to manipulate, paradoxically, those who perceive themselves as subjects.

In chap. 2, "Performing and Re-forming Gender in *Los altillos de Brumal*," I draw on Judith Butler's theories of gender as performativity to show how the creation of narrative discourse can alter the prescript of gender. Many critics have argued that Fernández Cubas's work advocates the feminine in rejection of the masculine. I propose, however, that her tales contest the very power structure that governs oppositional hierarchies such as female/male or male/female. Highlighting how the characters strive to advance their personal power by making choices that perpetuate or, conversely, deconstruct the performance of the masculine and the feminine in their daily lives, these stories invite a questioning of which characters benefit from projecting such discourses of essentialized gender. *Los altillos de Brumal* seeks not to invert the hierarchy of masculine and feminine, but to dispute the viability of such constructions; Fernández Cubas explores what is excluded from these polarized identities in order to redefine the contours of the human subject.

The third chapter, "Re-Citing and Re-Siting the Story of the Subject in *El año de Gracia* and *El columpio*," shows how the concept of the excluded other, examined as a configuration of gender in chap. 2, also underlies historical and literary constructions of political power relations. Fernández Cubas's two novels destabilize the parameters of Western identity laid out in discourses of history and canonical Western literature, by repeating those texts with a fundamental difference. Within the theoretical frameworks elaborated by Homi Bhabha and Edward Said, I discuss *El año de Gracia* as a postcolonial revision of such texts as *Robinson Crusoe* and the Bible. Similarly, Gianni Vattimo's philosophy of postmodernity as a repetition, weakening, and hence revision of modernity sheds light on my study of *El columpio* as a re-interpretation of the Francoist depiction of the historical Spanish subject. Fernández Cubas's novels demonstrate that, although citing a given discourse may purportedly confirm it as an original, authoritative source, repetition can also undermine such claims to singularity by allowing for multiple duplication, distortion, and redefinition.

This discursive strategy of repositioning perspective brings into question the role of space in subject formation, which is the focus of my fourth chapter, "The Space of Oppositional Subjectivity in *Con Agatha en Estambul*." In these tales space is the fundamental delineator of subjectivity: some characters exiled from the familiar must construct a new self based on their surroundings, whereas other characters encased in a restricted space entice outsiders in to their peculiarly defined subjectivity. Key spatial images and ontological subversions are repeated throughout the collection so that the tales reflect one another and intertextually penetrate one another's borders. My analysis engages the work of Julia Kristeva, Brian McHale, and Ross Chambers to examine how the subject defines itself oppositionally against the space of its other. Ultimately Fernández Cubas's tales rupture the notion of space as enclosure, for by transgressing the boundaries that enclose individuals in predefined modes of identity, they represent the space of subjectivity as an arena open to the fluctuations of power and the productiveness of change.

The fifth and final chapter, "Plotting Desire: The Visual Construction of the Subject in *El ángulo del horror*," considers how Fernández Cubas treats the concept of duality, which underlies all her explorations of subjectivity. Why do all constructions of identity fundamentally hinge on some permutation of the self/other dichotomy, wherein the subject desires the object to both define and differentiate itself? I draw on Peter Brooks's theories on desire in narrative and Mikhail Bakhtin's concepts of dialogic perspective to explore how shifting angles of vision, motivated and mediated by desire, construct both the subject that sees and the object that is seen. With its overt emphasis on "angles" on otherness, *El ángulo del horror* serves as an overarching metaphor for Fernández Cubas's fictional project: by underscoring the limits inherent in the viewpoint afforded by any single, closed-off subject position, her works advocate difference as an indispensable force for pulverizing subjective stasis.

The dynamic of difference is fundamental to all constructs of identity, be they individual, national, global, or even textual, such as this book I have written. Hence I recognize the essentially open-ended nature of my own construction, which requires the interpretations of others to further identify the myriad angles in Fernández Cubas's fiction. Indeed, if the vice of the literary critic is her perennial desire to construct a cohesive argument, then the greatest virtue of Fernández Cubas's texts is their persistent and often playful positing of an alternate, ulterior message, which taunts and tantalizes readers to delve further into the unsettling illuminations of difference. With her initial work, *Mi hermana Elba*, the author offers a kind of *arte poético* on the reversibility of dialectical relationships through power, which I address in chap. 1.

1
Looking Objectively at the Subject: The Spectacle of Power in *Mi hermana Elba*

"Los ojos de Elba [. . .] me perseguían a donde quiera que fuese."

[Elba's eyes {. . .} pursued me wherever I went.]
—"Mi hermana Elba"

CRISTINA FERNÁNDEZ CUBAS EMERGED ON THE LITERARY SCENE IN SPAIN in 1980 with the release of her first collection of short stories, *Mi hermana Elba* [My Sister Elba]. In his anthology *Son cuentos: Antología del relato breve español, 1975–1993*, Fernando Valls credits the publication of this debut work as the inauguration of a renaissance in the short story genre in Spain (Valls 1993). Surprisingly, relatively few critical analyses have been published on this collection. Bretz (1988), Talbot (1989), Ortega (1992), and Zatlin (1996) have stressed elements of the fantastic and gothic in Fernández Cubas's narrative. The polarity between orality and the written word, or between irrational and rational language, is the focus of studies on this work by Rueda (1988) and Valls (1994a). Situating language as a manifestation of power fundamental to the negotiation of subjectivity, I analyze the stories of *Mi hermana Elba* as representations of the discursive practices that determine how people think, act, and view themselves and reality.

In all her works, Fernández Cubas investigates discursive constructs of the self imposed by society and explores ways in which the subject can exercise agency. Key to this endeavor is her examination of the struggle for power between individuals in their efforts to define themselves, as they play out their attractions and repulsions to difference in one another. Whereas power constitutes a significant motif in all her texts, the release of *Mi hermana Elba* in 1980 foregrounds the dynamic at a key point in Spain's political and cultural evolution. Critics have debated about exactly when the transition toward a post-Franco mode of thinking actually began—whether in the late '60s before the dictator's death in 1975, or in the late '70s after the change of government.[1] Overall, however, as Spires notes in *Post-Totalitarian Spanish Fiction*, the early narrative of this type reveals a common preoccupation with a central authority figure that governs the balance of power in society (Spires 1996, 106). *Mi hermana Elba* is emblematic of a shift in this paradigm, wherein the post-totalitarian portrayal of the dynamics of power in fictional worlds evolves toward an examination of how relations of dominance and struggle permeate all levels of human interaction.

Many of Michel Foucault's observations on power deal with the struggles of interpersonal relationships such as those that Fernández Cubas depicts in her fiction. The French philosopher analyzes the right to power not as something legitimately possessed, but as a phenomenon effected by a temporary condition of domination. Foucault's study centers on the tactics that realize subjugation: "Let us not, therefore, ask why certain people want to dominate. . . . Let us ask, instead, how things work at the level of on-going subjugation, at the level of those continuous and uninterrupted processes which subject our bodies, govern our gestures, dictate our behaviors etc." (Foucault 1980, 97). In effect, Foucault explores not just the way power circulates through people as its vehicles, but the way it functions at the level of the discourses that produce people as subjects.

Inherent in these power operations is the element of knowledge, for power and knowledge produce and feed off one another. This symbiotic relationship implies an ongoing struggle between the subject who knows and the object who is known:

> These "power-knowledge relations" are to be analysed, therefore, not on the basis of a subject of knowledge who is or is not free in relation to the power system, but, on the contrary, the subject who knows, the objects to be known and the modalities of knowledge must be regarded as so many effects of these fundamental implications of power-knowledge and their historical transformations. (Foucault 1979, 27–28)

Power relations establish an ever-present, though ever-changeable, dialectic between the dominated and the dominant. Those individuals are produced, according to Foucault, by a collaboration of power and knowledge that imposes patterns of discipline:

> The individual is no doubt the fictitious atom of an "ideological" representation of society; but he is also a reality fabricated by this specific technology of power that I have called "discipline." We must cease once and for all to describe the effects of power in negative terms. . . . In fact, power produces; it produces reality; it produces domains of objects and rituals of truth. The in-

dividual and the knowledge that may be gained of him belong to this production. (Foucault 1979, 194)

Thus technologies of power produce individuals, who in turn strive for power over one another in order to alter or affirm their own positions.

Struggles for power permeate the four stories of *Mi hermana Elba* as the characters observe, document, evaluate, and define one another in their efforts to evoke truth through rituals and thereby establish their own identities as dominant, normal, and right. The dynamics of watching and being watched emerge, therefore, as fundamental to the mediation of power. Often the characters, aware that they are being observed, perform their chosen roles in order to convince their spectators that their representation is truly reality. Images of the gaze and theatrical techniques highlight the concepts of life as performance and of identity as a changeable role. Moving from a theme of performance to one of the written page, the stories underscore the uncertainty of authorship and the alteration of written records, to emphasize the distance between representations of language and the "truth" of reality. In effect, this collection of stories unveils the discourses that position one character over another in the game of power. Furthermore, the characters themselves struggle to alter these discourses as they subvert the power of the gaze and the word by manipulating language and even rewriting one another. Ultimately, in *Mi hermana Elba*, identity is unveiled as a construct to be modified and dominance as a precarious balance to be undermined.

"Lúnula y Violeta"

"Lúnula y Violeta" ["Lúnula and Violeta"], the first and most complex story in *Mi hermana Elba*, underscores the unstable nature of power relations between individuals in the clash between the two eponymous characters. Violeta's initial position of superiority is established by her role as narrator. She gradually cedes her power to Lúnula in what might be compared, in Foucault's history of shifting power relations, to sovereign power yielding to a mechanics of discipline. Such a transition is represented by the combination of the spectacle of torture, which Foucault studies as the classic tool of control wielded by a central power figure, and the panoptic power of the gaze, emblematic of the ever-present, ever-penetrating dynamic of discipline. In this story Lúnula dominates the tactics of discipline and appropriates Violeta's power. Finally, even the power of Violeta's narrative discourse is undermined when other voices contest its validity and question the identity of Violeta herself. In this story, then, domination hinges on the power of the word and subjectification by the gaze. Yet, if power is never static, how is it transformed? How and why might the subject and object change places in a given relationship, as Violeta and Lúnula do? By exploring these dynamics, Fernández Cubas ventures beyond Foucault's paradigm to explore what happens when the object exploits the subject's position of strength in order to wrest control, and what happens when the subject surrenders its power because of its need to become the object of the gaze.

In this story Violeta incarnates the lost, lonely woman hoping to find herself reflected in the gaze of an "other," a motif expressed through numerous references to mirrors. In the beginning she is eager for Lúnula, still a stranger, to share her table in a café, because the chance encounter affords the protagonist a much longed-for conversation partner who can obviate "la necesidad, apenas disimulada, de repetir en alta voz los monólogos tantas veces ensayados frente al espejo" [the barely disguised need to repeat out loud the monologues rehearsed so many times in front of the mirror] (Fernández Cubas 1988, 13). Symbolically, after meeting Lúnula, Violeta shatters the glass of a mirror in the hope of obliterating the hated image it returns: "Al recoger mis cosas, mi última mirada fue para la luna desgastada de aquel espejo empeñado en devolverme día tras día mi aborrecida imagen. Sentí un fuerte impulso y lo seguí. Desde el suelo cientos de cristales de las más caprichosas formas se retorcieron durante un largo rato bajo el impacto de mi golpe" [Upon collecting my things, my last glance was toward the worn crystal of that mirror determined to return to me, day after day, my abhorred image. I felt a strong impulse and obeyed it. From the floor hundreds of shards of the most capricious shapes twisted about for a great while under the impact of my blow] (14). Although textual evidence, such as it is (considering the unreliability of the narration, which I will address later) suggests that Violeta is not unattractive physically, her self-image is odious until *Lúnula's* admiring gaze replaces the unappealing image returned by the "*luna* desgastada de aquel espejo" [the worn crystal of that mirror] (14; italics mine). The reflection of this live *luna* projects a relative view of Violeta in a more pleasing light, for Lúnula's ugliness—the narrator depicts her as a sexless bulk with bad teeth—enhances by contrast Violeta's attractiveness. Violeta imagines that Lúnula, whose name evokes the moon, is simply an object that will passively reflect a fine image of herself to replace her abhorrent one. Thus, the narrator initially establishes herself as the center, polarizing Lúnula as the "other" whose difference delineates Violeta as the superior one.

Violeta's superiority is duly esteemed by her new friend, whose position of subservience precludes her from having any power at all—or so Violeta believes. Initially, this state of affairs seems plausible indeed, for Lúnula invites Violeta to stay at her country house and gives the guest the spacious bedroom while she herself occupies a tiny, claustrophobic room. Violeta muses contentedly about Lúnula's eagerness to please in an excerpt from her notebook, which she intercalates into her narration: "Lúnula se mostraba preocupada porque yo me encontrara a gusto en todo momento. Cocinaba mis platos preferidos con una habilidad extraordinaria, escuchaba interesada mis confesiones en el zaguán y parecía disfrutar sinceramente de mi compañía" [Lúnula showed herself to be concerned that I felt at home at all times. She cooked my favorite dishes with extraordinary skill, she listened with interest to my confessions in the vestibule, and she seemed to enjoy my company sincerely] (20). These ingratiating efforts of the hostess confirm Violeta's improved sense of self.

Violeta's apparent supremacy over Lúnula is paradoxically upheld by a game of her subservience to her friend: the act of confession. Violeta is unaware, however, of the power she invests in this woman through her confessions; by giving away information about herself, she discloses ways in which Lúnula can invert the power equation. In fact, although Violeta glories in the pleasure of confiding her secrets to another, she simultaneously inscribes herself into a discourse that defines and controls her, as elaborated by Foucault:

> The confession is a ritual of discourse in which the speaking subject is also the subject of the statement; it is also a ritual that unfolds within a power relationship, for one does not confess without the presence (or virtual presence) of a partner who is not simply the interlocutor but the authority who requires the confession, prescribes and appreciates it, and intervenes in order to judge, punish, forgive, console, and reconcile; a ritual in which the truth is corroborated by the obstacles and resistances it has had to surmount in order to be formulated; and finally, a ritual in which the expression alone, independently of its external consequences, produces intrinsic modifications in the person who articulates it: it exonerates, redeems, and purifies him; it unburdens him of his wrongs, liberates him, and promises him salvation. (Foucault 1990, 61–62)

Hence the relationship of confession embodies multiple nuances of the word "subject." In confessing her secrets to Lúnula, Violeta is a speaking subject. Her active voice is only a mirage of power, however, because by inscribing herself as the subject of discourse, she also becomes in effect an object of a discourse (confession) with a long history of producing the "truth" about the self. Finally, by placing Lúnula in the position to judge, castigate, console, or pardon, Violeta subjects herself to her friend's power.

For Foucault, the "truth" of a confessant is ultimately determined by the one who hears the confession. In an inversion of subject/object dominance, the act of confession invests the receiver of the discourse with the power to interpret: "The truth did not reside solely in the subject who, by confessing, would reveal it wholly formed. . . . [I]t could only reach completion in the one who assimilated and recorded it. It was the latter's function to verify this obscure truth: the revelation of confession had to be coupled with the decipherment of what it said" (Foucault 1990, 66). Thus Lúnula not only receives knowledge through Violeta's confessions, but also constructs the truth of Violeta's identity by *interpreting* that knowledge. Confession gives Lúnula the power to constitute the truth of Violeta as a subject turned object.

Thanks to the women's intimate conversations, Lúnula discovers that her key weapon to invert the balance of power is her talent for telling stories. From the beginning Lúnula's talent shines in her oral dexterity: "El arte de la palabra, el dominio del tono, el conocimiento de la pausa y el silencio, eran terrenos en los que se movía con absoluta seguridad. Sentadas en el zaguán, a menudo me había parecido [. . .] una fabuladora capaz de diluir su figura en la atmósfera para resurgir, en cualquier momento, con los atributos de una Penélope sollozante, de una Pentesilea guerrera [. . .]" [The art of the word, the dominion over tone, the knowledge of the pause and silence, all were terrain through which she moved with absolute certainty. Seated in the vestibule, she often seemed to me a storyteller capable of dissolving her figure into the atmosphere to reappear, at any moment, with the attributes of a sobbing Penelope, a warlike Pentesilea {. . .}] (Fernández Cubas 1988, 21). Lúnula's role as storyteller could potentially subjugate her as an object whose truth is interpreted by her listener. Violeta foregoes this opportunity for power, however, when she willingly suspends her disbelief. She prefers to envision Lúnula as the embodiment of the characters that she orally impersonates in her tales. With its kaleidoscopic display of discursive artifice, fiction suggests that the truth is constructed by both the teller and the receiver of the tale; it is a contract that can be negotiated, betrayed, and revamped accordingly. Violeta is outwitted in this game, for she willingly suspends her disbelief instead of subversively interpreting the "truth" projected by the speaker.

Lúnula's verbal skill soon encroaches onto Violeta's domain of the written word. The storyteller closets herself away to read a manuscript that Violeta has painstakingly composed and, when Violeta stumbles upon

Lúnula interpreting the text, she paradoxically feels as if she has transgressed on some private sanctum. The would-be writer later discovers her manuscript pages strewn across the floor, and her indignation turns to angst with the realization that Lúnula has superimposed her own words over Violeta's:

> Lo que en algunas hojas no son más que simples indicaciones escritas a lápiz, correcciones personales que Lúnula, con mi aquiescencia, se tomó el trabajo de incluir, en otras se convierten en verdaderos textos superpuestos, con su propia identidad, sus propias llamadas y subanotaciones. A medida que avanzo en la lectura veo que el lápiz, tímido y respetuoso, ha sido sustituido por una agresiva tinta roja. En algunos puntos apenas puedo reconocer lo que yo había escrito. En otros tal operación es sencillamente imposible: mis párrafos han sido tachados y destruidos. (20)

> [What on some pages are no more than simple comments written in pencil, personal corrections that Lúnula, with my acquiescence, took the trouble to include, on others become veritable superimposed texts, with their own identity, their own reference marks and footnotes. As I advance in my reading I see that the pencil, timid and respectful, has been replaced by an aggressive red ink. In some parts I can scarcely recognize what I had written. In others, such an undertaking is simply impossible: my paragraphs have been crossed out and destroyed.]

Unlike Violeta, Lúnula does not suspend her disbelief but instead interprets and rewrites her companion's tale. Just as with the confessions, Lúnula has effectively taken control of Violeta's discourse, this time by replacing the manuscript's story with her own. In this case the power of the critic eclipses that of the writer. Readers, then, are uncertain whether the words they consume in this tale are the words of Violeta or those of Lúnula.

Beyond altering the power paradigm by undermining Violeta's literary prowess, Lúnula paradoxically solidifies her control over Violeta by falling ill, a helpless condition that she exploits to the fullest. In his analysis of the sick as categorized and subjugated, Foucault does not deal explicitly with the corresponding subjugation of the caretaker. Fernández Cubas underscores this side of the equation, however, as a technique of opposition and inversion of power. It seems more than mere coincidence that Lúnula's sickness should ensue immediately after she first reads the manuscript. In addition to forcing Violeta to prolong her stay in the isolated country house, the illness provides plausible cause for a switch in bedrooms: Violeta moves into the smaller one and Lúnula the larger one, "mucho más adecuado para su estado actual" [much more suitable for her current condition] (19). Hence Lúnula's physical decline paradoxically furthers her hierarchical ascent.

From the apparently invalidated position as the "invalid," Lúnula disciplines Violeta into obeying the vigilance of her gaze. As the household rapidly deteriorates under Violeta's inept control, the "healthy" woman is forced in desperation to kill a rooster for food, because the grocer has mysteriously neglected to make his delivery. The slaughter takes place under Lúnula's supervision, as she shouts orders from the window: "Remátalo con el hacha. Así. Otra vez. No, ahí no. Procura darle en el cuello. No te preocupe la sangre. Estos gallos son muy aparatosos. Aún no está muerto. ¿No ves cómo su cabeza se convulsiona, cómo se abren y cierran sus ojitos? Eso es. Hasta que no se mueva una sola pluma. Hasta que no sientas el más leve latido. Ahora sí. Murió" [Finish him off with the hatchet. That's the way. Again. No, not there. Try to get him in the neck. Don't worry about the blood. These roosters are very showy. He's not dead yet. Don't you see how his head is convulsing, how his little eyes are opening and shutting? That's it. Until not a single feather moves. Until you don't feel the slightest heartbeat. Now, now he's dead] (Fernández Cubas 1988, 23–24). Such a blood-and-gore confrontation, described in minute detail, recalls the famous depiction of the execution of Damiens in the opening pages of Foucault's *Discipline and Punish*, a scene emblematic of the rule of torture.[2] Indeed, both encounters reveal much about roles within the performance of power.

Under the rule of torture, which for Foucault lasted until the late eighteenth century, the people held the role of spectators. Spectatorship is a crucial component of the theatrical performance of power: "Not only must people know, they must see with their own eyes. Because they must be made to be afraid; but also because they must be the witnesses, the guarantors, of the punishment, and because they must to a certain extent take part in it" (Foucault 1979, 58). Violeta, incorporated under the surveillance rule of Lúnula, is called to extend her role of spectator and become the inflicter of torture and execution in this scene. She is still a kind of audience, nonetheless, for even as she participates directly, she also witnesses it via Lúnula's grotesque description presented under the guise of giving orders. One can imagine Violeta directly experiencing with her five senses the horrific torture and killing, while also enduring the verbal assault of Lúnula's explicit representation. Lúnula's direct discourse, cited in the text, vividly paints the scene for readers and interpellates them, too, as spectators. By directly transmitting Lúnula's words to the readers, Violeta momentarily positions them in her place as the object of Lúnula's discourse.

Yet, as Foucault chronicled, the spectacle of torture posed an intrinsic danger to the rule of the sovereign. There was always the risk that empathy might provoke the witnesses to revolt: "the people never felt closer to those who paid the penalty than in those rituals intended to show the horror of the crime and the invincibility of power; never did the people feel more threatened, like them, by a legal violence exercised without moderation or restraint" (Foucault 1979, 63). The execution of the rooster—who is killed here, significantly, not in punishment for a crime but in sacrifice to the needs of the greater power—reveals a shift from a dying power structure (the sovereign's display of absolute control) to an emerging disciplinary structure: Lúnula deters any revolt by imposing discipline with her vigilant gaze, which guarantees Violeta's obedience. Foucault uses Jeremy Bentham's panoptic prison as the quintessential image of the ideal disciplinary paradigm in which all prisoners are exposed to a potentially omnipresent gaze that they cannot see: "Full lighting and the eye of a supervisor capture better than darkness, which ultimately protected. Visibility is a trap" (200). Fernández Cubas translates the optical power play of this objectification into language. Lúnula's directly cited words underscore the status of the rooster as the object of torture and Violeta as the object of the gaze: the rooster is the direct object acted upon by her discourse, while Violeta is the indirect object inscribed as the receiver of her discourse. The juxtaposition of the two technologies of power emphasize, finally, the shared role of Violeta and the rooster—and readers— as objects of discursive power.

By giving Lúnula's words precedence in her text, Violeta (or Lúnula, who may be the controlling narrator by now) reveals how much her friend has come to dominate. Only after reporting Lúnula's direct discourse does Violeta translate her experience into her own words: "Y yo me he quedado un buen rato aún junto al charco de entrañas y sangre, de plumas teñidas de rojo, como mis manos, mi delantal, mis cabellos. Llorando también lágrimas rojas, sudando rojo, soñando más tarde sólo en rojo una vez acostada en mi dormitorio: un cuarto angosto sin ventilación alguna al que sólo llegan los suspiros de Lúnula debatiéndose con la fiebre" [And for a good while I remained next to the puddle of entrails and blood, of feathers stained red like my hands, my apron, my hair. Crying, too, tears of red, sweating red, dreaming only in red later when lying in bed in my room: a narrow room with no ventilation, penetrated only by the sighs of Lúnula battling her fever] (Fernández Cubas 1988, 24). The two accounts of the killing doubly subject the reader to the horrific experience of exerting power over an object, while simultaneously being objectified and observed by a more powerful subject. The protagonist's objectification beneath Lúnula's gaze during the butchery is all the more disturbing because of the implication that Violeta, too, could be suffocated and sacrificed—figuratively or literally—by one more powerful than she. The suffocation, at least, has already commenced, as she suffers in her room, imprisoned into acquiescence by the "helpless" groans of her sick friend.

Despite her illness, Lúnula soon displays a prowess at killing, quartering, and cooking a rabbit that offsets Violeta's botched massacre of the rooster. Beneath Violeta's focalizing gaze, the supposed invalid slaughters the creature in a chillingly efficient display of control:

> [E]scoge un conejo del corral y, con mano certera, lo mata en mi presencia de un solo golpe. Casi sin sangre, sonriendo, con una limpieza inaudita lo despelleja, le ha sacado los hígados, lo lava, le ha arrancado el corazón, lo adoba con hierbas aromáticas y vino tinto. Ahora parte los troncos de tres en tres, con golpes precisos, sin demostrar fatiga, tranquila como quien resuelve un simple pasatiempo infantil; los dispone sobre unas piedras, enciende un fuego, suspende la piel de unas ramas de higuera. (25)

> [S]he selects a rabbit from the corral and, with a sure hand, kills it in my presence with one blow. Almost without blood, smiling, with incredible cleanliness she skins it, she has removed its innards, she washes it, she has pulled out its heart, she seasons it with aromatic herbs and red wine. Now she divides the trunk into threes, with precise blows, showing no fatigue, as calm as if it were child's play; she arranges the pieces over some stones, lights a fire, hangs the skin from some fig tree branches.]

Lúnula's masterful dismemberment of the rabbit makes Violeta's clumsy butchery of the rooster seem, in contrast, all the more appalling and macabre for its incompetence. Thus Violeta's focalizing gaze in this passage does not just register Lúnula's skill, but also causes her to recognize her own ineptitude at performing rituals of power and subjection.

Immediately after the killing, Lúnula directs her efficient, examining gaze toward Violeta herself. Violeta has begun to feel ill and mentally befuddled, whereas Lúnula has been revitalized: "Ella en cambio parece renacida, pletórica de salud, llena de una vitalidad alarmante" [She, in contrast, seems reborn, brimming with health, full of an alarming vitality] (25). Now Lúnula describes Violeta in the same graphic terms she used to portray the spectacle of the rooster's suffering: "'Pero Violeta . . . Qué mal aspecto tienes. Deja que te mire. Tus ojos están desorbitados, tu cara ajada . . . ¿Qué te pasa Violeta?' Pienso también que es la primera vez que habla de ojos, de cara, que no vaya referido a un animal, a un cuadro" ["But Violeta . . . You look awful. Let me look at you. Your eyes are popping out, your face is crumpled. . . . What's wrong, Violeta?" I also think that this is the first time that she speaks of eyes, of a face, that are not in reference to an animal, a painting] (26). Lúnula verbally fragments Violeta—her eyes, her face—the way she neatly dismembered the rabbit's body. Hence her discourse inscribes Violeta as an object to be seen, to be punished, to be passive. This verbal juxtaposition of Violeta and the rabbit as objects under the control of a newly energized Lúnula signals the obsolescence of bloody, agonizing torture as spectacle, bungled by Violeta's catatonic horror, and the imposition of an efficient, dispassionate operation of discipline, executed under Lúnula's calculating gaze and controlling voice.

Lúnula not only objectifies her friend, but also categorizes her as abnormal. Beneath Lúnula's examining gaze, Violeta is branded as "deformed" and thus inferior: "'¡Y qué rara alimentación te has debido preparar en estos días! . . . Te noto deformada, extraña'" ["And what odd food you must have prepared for yourself these last few days! . . . You look disfigured, strange"] (26). With the normal/strange qualification, Lúnula wields the same binary oppositions to control her other that Violeta used earlier. Such labeling is a common tactic of power, according to Foucault:

> Generally speaking, all the authorities exercising individual control function according to a double mode; that of binary division and branding (mad/sane; dangerous/harmless; normal/abnormal); and that of coercive assignment, of differential distribution (who he is; where he must be; how he is to be characterized; how he is to be recognized; how a constant surveillance is to be exercised over him in an individual way, etc.). (Foucault 1979, 199)[3]

Through her submission to constant surveillance, Violeta endures a visual examination that designates and differentiates her as "other." As Foucault notes, the examining gaze is fundamental to the dynamic of discipline: "It is a normalizing gaze, a surveillance that makes it possible to qualify, to classify and to punish" (184). Finding her former dominator to be lacking, Lúnula's evaluative gaze effectively objectifies Violeta to convert her into the abnormal and subjugated other.

Lúnula's power becomes so pervasive that Violeta recognizes her own inability to control even language, in contrast to Lúnula's linguistic adroitness. As a result, the narrator considers abandoning her efforts to compose a manuscript: "Mi palabra no basta, como no bastan tampoco las escasas frases felices que he logrado acuñar a lo largo de este cuadernillo. Ella en cambio parece disfrutar en demostrarme cuán fácil es el dominio de la palabra. No deja de hablarme, de cantar, de provocar imágenes que yo nunca hubiese soñado siquiera sugerir. Lúnula despilfarra. Palabras, energía, imaginación, actividad" [My word is not sufficient, just like the scarce felicitous phrases that I have managed to coin throughout this notebook are not enough either. She, in contrast, seems to enjoy showing me how easy it is to dominate the word. She won't stop talking to me, singing, provoking images that I never would have even dreamed of suggesting. Lúnula squanders. Words, energy, imagination, activity] (Fernández Cubas 1988, 27–28).[4] While Violeta cannot even summon the bare minimum of words, her nemesis is so prolific that she is positively wasteful. Hence Violeta recognizes her defeat in the manipulation of discourse.

Now, in a rather bizarre quirk of victim psychology, Violeta ridicules and berates herself. Remembering her previous attempts to define how Lúnula dominated everything, Violeta mocks her own futile efforts at rational, adequate expression through language: "'Lúnula,' había escrito en una de esas hojas que ahora devora el fuego, 'es *excesiva.*' ¿Qué he pretendido expresar con *excesiva*?, me pregunto. ¡Y con qué tranquilidad intento definir la arrolladora personalidad de mi amiga en una sola palabra! Pienso excesiva, exceso, excedente, arrollo, arrolladora, arroyo y me pongo a reír a carcajadas" ["Lúnula," I had written on one of the pages that the fire now devours, "is *excessive.*" What was I trying to express with *excessive*?, I ask myself. And how serenely I try to define the overpowering personality of my friend in a single word! I think excessive, excess, surplus, roll, overbearing, brook and I burst out laughing] (28).[5] Having set up a grammatical pattern of adjective ("excesiva"), noun ("exceso"), adjective and noun in one ("excedente"), and then starting to repeat the pattern with the synonymous noun ("arrollo") and adjective ("arrolladora"), Violeta suddenly twists her constructed order by listing a homonym ("arroyo"). This shift in the logic of categorization evokes Foucault's fascination with Borges's alternative modes of classification, which the French philosopher cites in *The Order of Things*: "This passage quotes a 'certain Chinese encyclopaedia' in which it is written that 'animals are divided into: (a) belonging to the Emperor, (b) embalmed, (c) tame, (d) sucking pigs, (e) sirens, (f) fabulous. . . .'" (Foucault 1994, xv). Upon glimpsing a surrogate pattern, different from the established norm, Violeta is wildly amused. Indeed, her outburst of laughter at her own illogical digression makes her seem almost insane. Yet, as Foucault has demonstrated in *Madness and Civilization*, insanity itself is a marginalized category of the "other" that serves to reflect and define what it means to be normal. Violeta's move toward insanity—toward a skewed perception of life—cinches her submission to Lúnula, who is the subject that establishes the norm.

Significantly, Violeta feels impotent because she can approximate neither the power of Lúnula's gaze nor the skill of her narrative discourse. Moreover, she cannot begin to imitate her superior's captivation of an audience: "¿Cómo puedo atreverme a intentar siquiera transcribir cualquiera de sus habituales historias o fábulas si no sé suplir aquel brillo especial de su mirada, aquellas pausas con que mi amiga sabe cortar el aire, aquellas inflexiones que me pueden producir el calor más ardiente o el frío más aterrador?" [How can I even dare to try to transcribe any of her habitual stories or tales if I don't know how to compensate for that special glitter of her gaze, those pauses with which my friend knows how to cut the air, those inflections that can produce in me the most burning heat or the most terrifying cold?] (Fernández Cubas 1988, 28). As Violeta recognizes, the manipulation of the gaze, of language, and of others are three key tactics in the technology of power. Lúnula has effectively usurped them from Violeta, transforming herself from object to subject in the struggle for control.

At this point, Violeta would rather surrender to her friend than resist her domination. Her need for Lúnula is greater than her desire to defend the autonomy of her written work: "Ella seguramente quiso ayudarme, ¿para qué seguir, pues? Oigo ya sus pasos, pero intento releer algún párrafo más. No encuentro los míos. Están casi todos tachados, enmendados... ¿Dónde termino yo y dónde empieza ella?" [Surely she was trying to help me, so why continue? I already hear her footsteps, but I try to read one more paragraph. I don't find mine. Almost all of them are marked out, corrected.... Where do I end and where does she begin?] (29). Violeta's submission is now total: projecting her writing as the symbolic image of her self, she can no longer separate her identity from that of Lúnula. Thus, the victim sutures herself to her victimizer and loses all hope of resistance. The destructive outcome of this power play culminates when Violeta seeks to burn the rest of her manuscript, a final gesture that aims to obliterate any remaining vestiges of her own discursively represented identity. Like Violeta's text, her identity is already substantially erased and rewritten by Lúnula.

The inversion of power between the two women is complete by the end of the story, when Violeta portrays herself as a servant, willingly subjected and confined by Lúnula. Significantly, Violeta now describes Lúnula as beautiful instead of as a sexless lump: "Estaba hermosa. Antes, mientras le cepillaba y trenzaba el cabello, se lo he dicho. Cada día que pasa sus ojos son más luminosos y azules, su belleza más serena" [She was beautiful. I told her so earlier, while I brushed and braided her hair. With each day that passes her eyes are more luminous and blue, her beauty more serene] (29).

In the final pages of the story, we find that Violeta has devotedly groomed Lúnula before the latter's departure for town, and now she plans out the arduous tasks she will accomplish in order to win Lúnula's approval upon her return. Violeta has become a true product of discipline, as described by Foucault: "it defined how one may have a hold over others' bodies, not only so that they may do what one wishes, but so that they may operate as one wishes, with the techniques, speed and efficiency that one determines. Thus discipline produces subjected and practised bodies, 'docile' bodies" (Foucault 1979, 138). Completely disciplined by her master, Violeta positions herself to sleep on the floor in front of the door, "como un perro guardián" [like a watchdog] who occupies herself "vigilando constantemente por si algún zorro intenta devorar nuestras gallinas" [constantly keeping watch in case some fox tries to devour our chickens] (Fernández Cubas 1988, 30). In this debased state of objectification and animalization, the constant vigilance of the "panopticon" flourishes, as Violeta now watches for any stray predator who might seek to transgress the borders of Lúnula's prison.

Even as Violeta would now obediently slaughter other animals to protect her master's realm, she gladly sacrifices herself to Lúnula to the point of denying herself water. Moreover, she has accepted the practices that she earlier abhorred under Lúnula's domain, for she obsessively cures the pelts of the rabbits "que h[a] debido sacrificar en los últimos tiempos" [that {she has} had to sacrifice lately] (30). This tone of sacrificial rhetoric heightens the sense of ritualization that imbues Violeta's submission to Lúnula. In effect, Violeta now functions as a sort of intermediary—a priestess, one might say—who disciplines herself and sacrifices animals to appease the wrath of the omnipotent one. Lúnula, whose name evokes a celestial body, thus becomes a sort of goddess who is all-seeing, all-knowing, and all-powerful. She has created a cult of visibility that operates smoothly even in her absence, just as Foucault's panoptic paradigm creates self-regulating subjects who ensure obedience from everyone, based on the mere possibility of suddenly being observed: "He who is subjected to a field of visibility, and who knows it, assumes responsibility for the constraints of power; he makes them play spontaneously upon himself; he inscribes in himself the power relation in which he simultaneously plays both roles; he becomes the principle of his own subjection" (Foucault 1979, 202–3). By remaining subservient to Lúnula's gaze, whether absent or present, Violeta perpetuates her own imprisonment and ensures the automatic functioning of Lúnula's "panopticon."

With the conclusion of Violeta's story, any vestige of authority and power that readers might attribute to her narration is undermined completely by an editor's note. This addendum ruptures the illusion, normally created in stories, of a direct relationship between the narrator and the receiver of the tale. The editor's note reveals not only that the narrative control is different from what readers expected, but that the narrative sequence is quite possibly random or coincidental instead of planned and ordered. Before reading this final part, it is confusing to try to establish the temporal relationship between the textual sections narrated in the present tense and the segments from Violeta's notebook cited in the past tense. If the former are narrated in installments, much like a diary, at what point in this eternal present did Violeta record her notebooks in the past, and why? Not even Violeta can answer this question: "¿Por qué hablaré de Lúnula en pasado?, me pregunto ahora" [I wonder why I speak of Lúnula in the past tense?, I ask myself now] (Fernández Cubas 1988, 22). In this sentence alone, the inclusion of the future tense (which, in this case, expresses speculation about the present in Spanish), along with the present and past tenses underlines the problematic and contradictory nature of time in this story.

Readers might hope to solve the mystery and suture this lacerated chronology back together. Yet the editor of the text questions the viability of such an endeavor: "NOTA DEL EDITOR: Estos papeles, dispersos, deslavazados y ofrecidos hoy al lector en el mismo orden en que fueron hallados (si su disposición horizontal en el suelo de una granja aislada puede considerarse un orden), no llevaban firma visible [. . .]" [EDITOR'S NOTE: These papers, dispersed, barely legible, and offered today to the reader in the same order in which they were found {if their horizontal arrangement on the floor of an isolated farmhouse can be considered an order}, did not bear any visible signature {. . .}] (31). The indeterminate sequence of the papers precludes any effort to impose what might be considered a "normal, logical" order. Moreover, in the vein of Borges's Chinese encyclopaedia and Foucault's *The Order of Things*, this textual dishevelment serves to question the concept of order itself. Thus, by constantly undermining any conventional interpretation or categorization, the narrative presents itself as a bizarre mutation that might have been conjured directly from Borges's delightfully random construction of knowledge.

To enhance the emerging chaos, the true authorship of Violeta's papers is questioned as well. According to the editor, the cadaver found in the house was eclectically dressed in a flowered skirt and a sportshirt with the initials "V.L." hand-embroidered on it. This is the only clue to the woman's identity, because no other documentation of any kind was found. Some neighbors testified that the woman who lived at the farm was one señorita Victoria, while others asserted that she was called señora Luz. Still others thought that the name Victoria Luz sounded familiar, while none recognized the names Violeta or Lúnula. Such a dizzying array of possibilities and impossibilities regarding the identity of "la(s) posible(s) moradora(s) de la granja" [the possible inhabitant{s} of the farm] (31) cancels out any hope of certainty for readers.[6] Thus, the text itself engages readers in a sort of power play, the goal of which is to determine the dominant order. Although readers attempt to analyze the events according to conventional logic, the text imposes the "logic" of chaos and uncertainty.

Narrative unreliability is also generated by the ambiguous textual sources of the story, which are doubted, subverted, and sometimes destroyed—or so readers are told. Did Violeta really burn her writing, as she claimed? If at least some of her writing survived, does the story "Lúnula y Violeta" consist of the manuscript, the notebook, or a combination of both? If this tale is what remains of Violeta's text, how much of it originated, in fact, from Violeta, and how much of it comes from the "corrections" of Lúnula, who receives top billing in the title? If Violeta lied about burning her manuscript, is she a trustworthy narrator? Furthermore, if she was "crazy" enough to sacrifice herself completely to Lúnula, as the text describes, what reader would trust her as a narrator anyway? Finally, the very existence of Lúnula and Violeta is called into question by the testimonies of the neighbors, as reported by the editor. In order to prove his own credibility, the editor evokes the authority of a forensics expert who examined the body, and cites a known biologist who denies the existence of a jacaranda plant in that region. Readers are left with one testimony, subjected by another testimony, subjected by another testimony; in the end, the very construction of this text dramatizes the struggle for power. The tale draws readers in, inviting them to subject it to their analytical gaze, daring them to impose an order onto its chaos.

"Lúnula y Violeta" thus demonstrates how Fernández Cubas employs language to explore relations of power as a means of challenging traditionally established modes of thought and order. By positing methods for subverting existing power structures, Fernández Cubas's stories deepen and extend the ramifications, initially posed by Foucault, of the ways in which subjects—whether characters or readers—exercise agency in the midst of the mechanics of power. Dominated objects resist in Fernández Cubas's texts by using the very tactics of the powerful in order to gain agency. By exploring the nuances of attraction and repulsion to the gaze, as well as the imposition and evasion of the gaze, the author shows how the seen and controlled object becomes the seeing and controlling subject.

Key to that dominion is the ability to manipulate discourse, particularly the way the subject inscribes the other as its object of discourse. Simultaneously, the object inscribes the truth of the subject through its interpretation of that discourse. Fernández Cubas challenges readers' efforts to construct an absolute truth of subjectivity through this power relation. While the act of telling, like confession, inscribes the speaker into discourse and allows the listener to interpret the truth of the speaker, by constantly eroding the authenticity of origins this text denies readers the power to interpret with certainty or to construct any singular, all-embracing truth. In the end, fiction potentially empowers its "listeners" much more than confession; its very nature unveils truth as a simulacrum by flaunting the art of lies.

"La ventana del jardín"

Whereas Violeta lost the struggle for power with Lúnula because she could not manipulate language as well as her other, the narrator and protagonist of "La ventana del jardín" ["The Garden Window"] finds himself powerless and confused because, on a remote farm, he confronts a language and logic entirely different from his own. Given that discourse itself is an imposed order that reflects the way one is conditioned to see the world, as "Lúnula y Violeta" illustrated, it follows that the constant efforts of the narrator of "La ventana del jardín" to interpret the new language, actions, and gazes that he encounters are futile, because the lens of logic through which he perceives his new surroundings is always out of focus. In that sense, the entire narration constitutes his search for the correct prescription to adjust his sight so that he might understand the events that occur. Indeed, as with the author's later collection *El ángulo del horror* [The Angle of Horror], vision is a central motif in this rich and complex story, magnified by the narrator's frequent comparisons of the events to performance and spectacle. This entire tale foregrounds the theatricality of power, to which Foucault alludes in *Discipline and Punish*. While Foucault features the subject who gazes as the one with power, Fernández Cubas inverts the paradigm to show the object of the gaze as the manipulator of the spectator, in a trick similar to that of "Lúnula y Violeta." In the end, the narrator of "La ventana del jardín" discovers that the dynamics of power are not at all as he imagined, for the "order of things" in this fictional world follows a different logic altogether.

The first story Fernández Cubas wrote as an adult, "La ventana del jardín" is the first-person narration of an unnamed man who arrives, unannounced, to visit his old high school friends, José and Josefina Albert, and their only son, Tomás. He recalls that when he last saw Tomás, two years earlier, the boy had seemed developmentally delayed and had slipped a bizarre note into the visitor's bag. The Alberts are not overjoyed to see their uninvited guest, who becomes increasingly suspicious of the way they keep their child isolated from the world. The discovery that the child speaks a completely invented language, encouraged by his parents, induces the protagonist to fabricate an excuse to spend the night so as to study the situation more. A secret rendezvous with Tomás convinces him that the child needs to be rescued. The protagonist tries to help him escape in the morning, only to discover that the boy is extremely ill and unable to interact or function outside of the protective environment of his home. When he finally departs in a hired car, the protagonist is stunned that the driver seems to accept the family's situation as perfectly normal.

The rational view of life of the narrator/protagonist is epitomized by his detectivesque approach, wherein he notes a mystery afoot and seeks to uncover the secret and explain it analytically. Even as he attempts to pursue a logical outcome, however, nothing turns out to be the way he expects, such as when he anticipates examining the progress of his friends' avocados and chickens, only to discover that they now raise onions and rabbits. Later, he decides that Tomás must be dead because he has not yet seen the boy on this visit, then is surprised when Josefina takes him up to see the child playing in his room. The protagonist's epistemological attempts to find a rational resolution are constantly foiled, for the enigma is never what he imagines.

Tomás's special language incarnates the radically different logic of this place. Indeed, the narrator opens his story with the note written in concentric circles that the child had slipped into his bag two years before this visit:

> Cazuela airada,
> Tiznes o visones. Cruces o lagartos. La
> noche era acre aunque las cucarachas
> llorasen. Más
> Olla. (Fernández Cubas 1988, 33)

> [Huffy casserole,
> Stains or minks. Crosses or lizards. The
> night was acrid even though the cockroaches
> cried. More
> Stew.]

The concentric structure of this note evokes the dizzying vortex of a radically different logic that sucks the detective into its center. Compounding the puzzle of the note, the protagonist discovers suspicious evidence that convinces him that a mystery is brewing: the toothbrushes in the bathroom bear the names *Escoba* [Broom], *Cuchara* [Spoon], and *Olla* [Stew]. In this world where nothing appears to corroborate his reasoning, the protagonist determines to stay for the night so that he can unravel the clues and restore order.

In his suspicion that his friends are attempting to conceal the truth from him, the narrator views them as actors in a play. In particular, he notes, his questions about Tomás seem to prompt the theatrical performance:

> [R]esultaba evidente que la comedia o el drama iban destinados a mí, único espectador, y que ambos intérpretes se estaban cansando de mi presencia. De pronto Josefina estalló en sollozos.
> —Había puesto tantas ilusiones en este niño. Tantas . . .
>   Y aquí acabó el primer acto. Intuí en seguida que en este punto estaba prevista la intervención de un tercero con sus frases de alivio o su tribulación. Pero no me moví ni de mi boca salió palabra alguna. (37)

> [It was evident that the comedy or drama was intended for me, the only spectator, and that both performers were tiring of my presence. Suddenly Josefina burst into sobs.
> —I'd invested so many hopes in this child. So many . . .
>   And here the first act ended. I intuited right away that at this point the intervention of a third person, with his expressions of consolation or his tribulation, was anticipated. But I did not move nor did I utter a single word.]

Through the metaphor of representation, the protagonist views each of his friends as enacting a given role, while he himself refuses to interpret the script of commiseration that they assign to him. Instead, he subjects José and Josefina to the critical power of his gaze by casting himself as the spectator of their performance.

As the viewing public, the protagonist has the right to examine and judge the actors, much as Lúnula critiqued Violeta's performance in the rooster massacre. For Foucault, the examination is the supreme ritual of a disciplining gaze: "It establishes over individuals a visibility through which one differentiates them and judges them. That is why, in all the mechanisms of discipline, the examination is highly ritualized. In it are combined the ceremony of power and the form of the experiment, the deployment of force and the establishment of truth" (Foucault 1979, 184). The protagonist elevates himself to the status of examiner, a position that merges theatrically with spectatorship. As a spectator, furthermore, he is conceivably outside the actors' line of vision and thus beyond their control.

Whereas the gaze played an important role in the power shift in "Lúnula y Violeta," here Fernández Cubas explores the implications of vision in a more complex way by factoring the realm of the invisible into the equation. The dynamics of visibility and invisibility are central to the theatrical representation of power in this tale. For Foucault, the examination consecrated the union between visibility and power:

> Disciplinary power . . . is exercised through its invisibility; at the same time it imposes on those whom it subjects a principle of compulsory visibility. In discipline, it is the subjects who have to be seen. Their visibility assures the hold of the power that is exercised over them. It is the fact of being constantly seen, of being able always to be seen, that maintains the disciplined individual in his subjection. . . . In this space of domination, disciplinary power manifests its potency, essentially, by arranging objects. The examination is, as it were, the ceremony of this objectification. (Foucault 1979, 187)

The narrator's desire for power influences the way he interprets all his friends' lines, which he, like Violeta before him, categorizes as "excesivas y fuera de lugar" [excessive and out of place] (Fernández Cubas 1988, 37)—in essence, "abnormal." By subjecting José and Josefina to his examining gaze, he judges them to be aberrant criminals guilty of mistreating their son and covering up their crime with a farcical performance. His examination gives way, at least in his mind, to a judicial ceremony of condemnation.

When readers take up their role as examiners, however, they can see at least one other, alternative performance enacted in this text. What really bothers the protagonist is that, in the real-life drama of José, Josefina, and Tomás, he has no role. His friends have evaluated their son's situation and written a script that constructs a theatrical world tailored to his needs; they direct the scenes as well as act in them and view our protagonist as an intruder, not a spectator whose approbation they seek. Nonetheless, the protagonist, as Fernando Valls has noted, projects himself as the hero of his own fantasy (Valls 1994a, 19). Aspiring to pass judgment, the would-be hero imposes his own interpretation of the Alberts' representation—an evaluation that is ultimately proven to be incorrect. Imagining that they need him to perform in their play as a sympathizer, he exercises his "power" to reject that role. Instead he assumes the power of director and recasts himself as the spectator—theoretically exiting the stage of the visible.

This entire story unfolds as one representation inserted within another, with one play's actors becoming another play's spectators. The protagonist perceives the other characters' performance as manipulations of words, action, and light in order to control him, the spectator. For instance, from the ceiling of Tomás's room hangs a "luz conscientemente tenue" [consciously tenuous light] (Fernández Cubas 1988, 41). Despite his desire to abstain from performance, he himself becomes an actor when he steals Tomás's book of drawings the first time he goes to the child's room: "Fue un espectáculo bochornoso. El espejo me devolvió la imagen de un ladrón frente al producto de su robo: un cuaderno de adolescente" [It was a shameful spectacle. The mirror returned to me the image of a thief before the proceeds of his theft: an adolescent's notebook] (41–42). Now the protagonist has mounted his own little spectacle, casting himself in the starring role of "thief," within the farce that he imagines his friends to be enacting for him. With the reflection of the mirror in the above quote, the protagonist operates simultaneously as actor and audience, as subject and object of the gaze. This scene presents the first step in his role reversal.

A web of metatheatrical levels soon ensnares the sleuth. Having spun his own secret plot to solve the mystery, he must stage still another show for his friends in order to conceal his real intentions: "Iba a dormirme ya cuando Josefina irrumpió sin llamar en mi cuarto. Traía una toalla en la mano y miraba de un lado a otro como si quisiera cerciorarse de algo. El cuadernillo, entre mi pierna derecha y la sábana, crujió un poco. Josefina dejó la toalla junto al lavabo y me dio las buenas noches. Parecía cansada. Yo me sentí aliviado por no haber sido descubierto" [I was finally falling asleep when Josefina burst into my room without knocking. She brought a towel in her hand and she looked from one side to the other as if she were trying to make sure of something. The notebook, between my right leg and the sheet, rustled a little. Josefina left the towel by the sink and said good night. She seemed tired. I was relieved that I hadn't been discovered] (42). Now that he, too, is an actor, the protagonist is correspondingly the object of the gaze of himself and others. In this series of reversals subjects become objects, and one play is staged to counteract the effects of another. It is to be expected that the integrity of theatrical space and roles will be violated, for in this text all characters are ultimately actors in their own representations.

As highlighted by the title of the story, "La ventana del jardín," the consummate threshold between these theatrical worlds is the window between Tomás's room and the garden, through which the protagonist communicates with the child and views his illogical domain. The window is literally an opening in the theatrical "fourth wall" that entices the protagonist as "spectator" to leave the audience and interact with the characters on the stage:

> Me deslicé hasta la ventana de Tomás y me apoyé en el alféizar; los postigos no estaban cerrados y había luz en el interior. Tomás, sentado en la cama tal y como lo dejamos, parecía aguardar algo o a alguien. La idea de que era YO el aguardado me hizo golpear con fuerza el cristal que me separaba del niño, pero apenas emitió sonido alguno. [. . .] Tomás, súbitamente, reparó en mi presencia. Con una rapidez que me dejó perplejo, saltó de la cama, corrió hacia la ventana y la abrió. Ahora estábamos los dos frente a frente. Sin testigos. (Fernández Cubas 1988, 43)

> [I slipped toward Tomás's window and propped myself on the windowsill; the shutters weren't closed and the light was on inside. Tomás, seated on the bed just as we left him, seemed to wait for something or someone. The idea that I was the one he waited for made me pound on the glass that separated me from the boy, but it scarcely made a sound. {. . .} Suddenly, Tomás noticed my presence. With a quickness that bewildered me, he jumped from the bed, ran to the window, and opened it. Now the two of us were face to face. Without witnesses.]

The casting call that the protagonist perceives becomes irresistible, and he is recruited into the performance. Indeed, he literally clamors for attention until he gets a part in the play. His mistake, however, is believing his actions to be "sin testigos" [without witnesses], exempt from submission to the gaze. For in the spectacle of power, shadows and covert action eventually cede to visibility.

The protagonist quickly discovers that this is a part for which he is ill-equipped, because the play is written in a language and governed by a logic that he does not understand. He glimpsed this other language in Tomás's note from years before, and in the child's notebook stolen on this visit: "Frases absolutamente desprovistas de sentido se barajaban de forma insólita, saltándose todo tipo de reglas conocidas. En algún momento la sintaxis me pareció correcta pero el resultado era siempre el mismo: incomprensible" [Sentences totally devoid of meaning were jumbled in an unusual way, breaking every kind of known rule. At one point or another the syntax seemed correct, but the result was always the same: incomprehensible] (42). Despite this sneak preview, the protagonist is unprepared for his first scene in the play with Tomás:

> Tomás extendió su mano hacia la mía y dijo: "Luna, luna," con tal expresión de ansiedad en sus ojos que me quedé sobrecogido. [. . .] Después de un

titubeo me señalé a mí mismo y dije "Amigo." No dio muestras de haber comprendido y lo repetí dos veces más. Tomás me miraba sorprendido. "¿Amigo?," preguntó. "Sí, A-M-I-G-O," dije. Sus ojos se redondearon con una mezcla de asombro y diversión. Corrió hacia el vaso de noche y me lo mostró gritando "¡Amigo!". Luego, sonriendo—o quizás un poco asustado—, se encogió de hombros. Yo no sabía qué hacer y repetí la escena sin demasiada convicción. De pronto, Tomás se señaló a sí mismo y dijo: "Olla."[. . .] (43–44)

[Tomás extended his hand toward mine and said, "Moon, moon," with such an expression of anxiety in his eyes that I was taken by surprise. [. . .] After stammering I pointed to myself and said, "Friend." He gave no sign of having understood and I repeated it twice more. Tomás looked at me, surprised. "Friend?" he asked. "Yes, F-R-I-E-N-D," I said. His eyes widened with a mixture of astonishment and amusement. He ran to the chamberpot and showed it to me, shouting, "Friend!" Then smiling—or perhaps a bit frightened—he shrugged his shoulders. I didn't know what to do and I repeated the scene without much conviction. Suddenly, Tomás pointed to himself and said, "Stew." {. . .}]

The protagonist's confusion about the meaning of "luna" magnifies when the child reveals that "amigo" is not a friend but a chamberpot, and that his name is not Tomás but "Olla."[8] Bewildered by the language of this theatrical world, this neophyte cannot play his scene with conviction.

Tomás's or Olla's language does not relate in any apparently "logical" way to the protagonist's. Its radical alteration takes the discursive rupture of "arroyo," uttered by the possibly "insane" Violeta in the first story of this collection, to greater extremes of dissonance:

El lenguaje que había aprendido Tomás [. . .] era EL MIO sujeto a unas reglas que me eran ajenas. [. . .] Ni siquiera se trataba de una simple inversión de valores. Bueno no significaba Malo, sino Estornudo. Enfermedad no hacía referencia a Salud, sino a un estuche de lapiceros. Tomás no se llamaba Tomás, ni José era José, ni Josefina, Josefina. Olla, Cuchara y Escoba eran los tres habitantes de aquella lejana granja en la que yo, inesperadamente, había caído. (Fernández Cubas 1988, 44–45)

[The language Tomás had learned {. . .} was MINE, subject to rules that were foreign to me. {. . .} It wasn't even a matter of a simple inversion of values. Good did not mean Bad, but Sneeze. Sickness did not refer to Health, but to a pencil holder. Tomás was not called Tomás, nor was José José, nor Josefina, Josefina. Stew, Spoon and Broom were the three inhabitants of that distant farm where I had landed unexpectedly.]

Olla's language might well be classified in some alternative order straight from Borges's encyclopaedia; disturbingly, it is the narrator's own language subject to a different logical order. Considering Saussure's definition of the sign as an arbitrary relationship between the signifier (the symbol) and the signified (the meaning), Olla employs the same signifiers as the protagonist, but his signifieds are entirely disparate from the arbitrary relationship the protagonist—as well as the readers—understand. As a result, the frustrated hero is completely thrown off the track in his detectivesque search for meaning.

The protagonist rallies, however, when he believes that he finds a common means of communication that will enable him to draw conclusions and pass judgment on José and Josefina. Bypassing language altogether, he seeks the answer through images, noises, numbers, and gestures:

> Olla y yo hablamos todavía un largo rato a través de gestos, dibujos rápidos esbozados en un papel, sonidos que no incluyesen para nada algo semejante a las palabras. Descubrimos que la numeración, aunque con nombres diferentes, respondía a los mismos signos y sistemas. Así, Olla me explicó que el día anterior había cumplido catorce años y que, cuando hacía dos, me había visto a través de aquella misma ventana, me había lanzado ya una llamada de auxilio en forma de nota. Quiso ser más explícito y llenó de nuevo mi bolsillo de escritos y dibujos. Luego, llorando, terminó pidiendo que le alejara de allí para siempre, que lo llevara conmigo. (45)

> [Stew and I talked for a long while yet by means of gestures, drawings quickly sketched on paper, sounds that in no way resembled words. We discovered that numeration, although with different names, complied with the same signs and systems. In this way, Stew explained to me that the day before he had turned fourteen and that when, two years earlier, he had seen me through that same window, he had already sent me a call for help in the form of a note. He tried to be more explicit and filled my pocket with writings and drawings again. Then, crying, he ended by asking me to take him away from there forever, to take him with me.]

The obvious question here is how, on the basis of numbers, pictures, and nonsensical sounds, could the protagonist be sure that his complex interpretation of José and Josefina's actions and Tomás's intentions is the precise one. By the end of the story, in fact, he will realize that his interpretation is wrong. The protagonist errs because he does not understand that language is ruled by an arbitrary logic; even though he abandons his language in the exchange with Olla, he still uses his own logic to interpret the events. As a result, he does not really alter the perspective of his judgmental gaze. Moreover, he does not see that he cannot solve the mystery because the clues he is tracking are arranged differently than his experience dictates.

The protagonist is as yet unaware, however, that the trail he follows is merely his own fabrication; he continues to act out the drama in the hope of concealing his intention to kidnap the boy. After spending the night in "communication" with Olla, the protagonist pretends to awaken in his own room: "Regresé a mi cuarto y abrí la ventana como si acabara de despertarme. Me afeité e hice el mayor ruido posible. Mis manos derramaban frascos y mi garganta emitía marchas militares. Intenté que todos mis actos sugiriesen el despertar eufórico de un ciudadano de vacaciones en una granja" [I returned to my room and opened the window as if I had just woken up. I shaved and made as much noise as possible. My hands spilled bottles and my throat emitted military marches. I tried to make all my actions suggest the euphoric awakening of a man from the city on vacation on a farm] (46). As the climax of his play approaches, the protagonist becomes keenly aware of being watched: "Me sentía más y más nervioso: salí al jardín. [. . .] No sé por qué, pero no me atrevía a mirar en dirección a la ventana del chico. Sentía, sin embargo, sus ojos puestos en mí y cualquiera de mis actos reflejos cobraba una importancia inesperada" [I felt increasingly nervous: I went out to the garden. {. . .} I don't know why, but I dared not look in the direction of the boy's window. I felt his eyes on me, however, and each of my reflex actions took on an unforeseen importance] (48). Now the dynamics of spectatorship are reversed, for the window allows Olla to observe the protagonist. The sensation of being watched makes the latter recognize the import of his actions as performance and of himself as the object of another's gaze.

Finally, the detective discerns that his own judgmental gaze has been completely misdirected. In the morning, as he waits outside for Olla to join him in the great escape, he realizes that the child is not as he had perceived him to be:

> Sus brazos y sus piernas parecían obedecer a consignas opuestas; su rostro, a medida que iba avanzando, se me mostraba cada vez más desencajado. [. . .] Olla jadeaba. Se agarró a mis hombros y me dirigió una mirada difícil de definir. Me di cuenta entonces, por primera vez, de que estaba en presencia de un enfermo. [. . .] ¿Por qué el mismo muchacho que horas antes me pareció rebosante de salud respondía ahora a la descripción que durante todo el día de ayer me hicieran de él sus padres? (Fernández Cubas 1988, 48–50)

> [His arms and legs seemed to obey opposite instructions; his face, as he came closer, seemed more and more contorted. {. . .} Stew was panting. He

gripped my shoulders and gave me a look that was hard to define. I realized then, for the first time, that I was in the presence of an invalid. {...} Why was the same boy who hours before seemed brimming with health now fitting the description that his parents gave me all day yesterday?]

The foiled hero had not noticed Tomás's physical illness before because he desired or expected to see something else—for the perspective of the gaze determines how the object is seen. As in "Lúnula y Violeta," here the deceptive status of an "invalid" subverts the protagonist's expectations. Significantly, the child's gaze is now "difícil de definir" [difficult to define] for the visitor, who is finally aware that more than one interpretation of this "text" exists. Thus Tomás/Olla is suspended between two systems of vision, whose interpretations collide on the space of his deformed body.

Completely confused as to what his role or his lines should be in this unsettling play, the protagonist feebly grasps at the reigns of control by appropriating Olla's language: "Supliqué, gemí, grité con todas mis fuerzas. '¿POR QUE?' volvía a decir y, de repente, casi sin darme cuenta, mis labios pronunciaron una palabra. 'Luna,' dije, '¡LUNA!'" [I pleaded, I groaned, I shouted with all my strength. "WHY?" I was saying again and, suddenly, almost without realizing, my lips pronounced a word. "Moon," I said, "MOON!"] (50). *Luna* was Olla's initial plea to the outsider through the garden window, yet it is now devoid—for the visitor as well as readers—of the symbolic significance with which the moon is usually invested. Whatever meaning the word holds for the other characters is uncertain, but it is definitely not sufficient to elevate the protagonist to power in the eyes of José and Josefina: "Ambos, como una sola persona, parecieron despertar de un sueño. Se incorporaron a la vez y con gran cuidado entraron el cuerpo del pequeño Tomás en la casa. Luego, cuando cerraron la puerta, Josefina clavó en mis pupilas una mirada cruel. Corrí como enloquecido por el sendero" [Both of them, as one person, seemed to awaken from a dream. They got up at the same time and with great care brought the body of little Tomás into the house. Then, when they closed the door, Josefina pierced my pupils with a cruel gaze. I ran down the path like a man gone mad] (50). Objectified and tormented by this gaze, the protagonist realizes that he is the abnormal one, the insane one, the one who disrupted the established order. Consequently, the door to this other world is closed, and the transgressor is banished.

The protagonist's insanity and abnormality are stressed even more by their contrast to the town driver who picks him up from the road. Nonchalantly, the driver chats about the Alberts:

—Buena gente —dijo—. Magnífica gente —y miró el reloj—. Su autobús espera. Tranquilo.
   Me desabroché la camisa. Estaba sudando.
—¿Y el pequeño Tomás? ¿Se encuentra mejor?
Negué con la cabeza.
—Pobre Ollita —dijo.
Y se puso a silbar. (51)

["Good people, " he said. "Wonderful people," and he looked at his watch. "Your bus is waiting. Don't worry."
   I unbuttoned my shirt. I was sweating.
"And little Tomás? Is he any better?"
I shook my head.
"Poor little Stew," he said.
And he began to whistle.]

Whether or not the driver's use of the name "Ollita" suggests his acceptance of the different logical order that the word implies, his treatment of the situation as completely normal must surely be as unsettling for the protagonist as it is for readers. For readers, too, undoubtedly have been trying to "make sense" of the story, beginning with the boy's enigmatic note cited in the first paragraph and culminating with the ambiguous word *luna* that provokes the Alberts to enclose themselves in their space, hidden from the view of both the protagonist and us. By denying the protagonist—and readers—the right of spectatorship, the Alberts wield the final power of eclipsing the gaze.
   Yet what of the overarching perspective of the narrator of this text? At the level of narration it is possible to detect a change in the perspective of the "I": the narrator who recounts these events views them differently than the man who experienced them.[9] The narrator repeatedly emphasizes his efforts, as a protagonist, to document and trace the truth by his own reason—hence the proliferation of phrases such as "por esta razón" [for that reason]. At the same time, the narrator undermines and contradicts the motives of himself as a protagonist. For instance, he belies his declared intention of requesting a cab to leave immediately after his arrival at his friends' home: "Iba a hacer todo esto (sin duda iba a hacerlo) cuando reparé en un vasito con tres cepillos de dientes" [I was going to do all this {without doubt, I was going to} when I noticed a little glass with three toothbrushes] (Fernández Cubas 1988, 36). His parenthetical insistence makes readers doubt the veracity of his assertion. Elsewhere, he admits that, as protagonist, he deliberately misrepresented his intentions to his friends from the beginning, while supposedly telling the truth to his readers: "no

había coche. O sí lo había, pero, sin saber la razón una vez más, fingí un contratiempo" [there wasn't a car. Or, there was, but again, without knowing why, I feigned an excuse] (39). Of course, this makes readers question the narrator's reliability; like Lúnula in the preceding story, readers may interpret this confession as true or false. This very uncertainty communicates the possibility of multiple interpretations of any given text.[10] The understanding of such ambiguity pervades the narrator's perspective as he "re-presents" the plot on the page for readers' observation.

In essence, the temporal difference of this story—a narrator who tells of things that happened to him in the past—imposes a spatial alteration on the self: seeing things from a different point in time makes the narrator see from a different perspective.[11] He has learned that, as a subject who sees, he is also an object who is seen, and that it is precisely the angle of vision that establishes the boundaries of normality and of right. It is no wonder, then, that the protagonist—when in search of a logical explanation to his friends' aberrance in their past—found them to exhibit a "normalidad alarmante" [alarming normality] (46). He is alarmed because he begins to perceive that his notion of normality is a construct superimposed over what he considers to be abnormal, but what is Olla's, Cuchara's, and Escoba's conception of "normal."

With the close of the narration itself, then, the spectacle comes to an end. A replay of its scenes, in search of understanding, reveals a constant subversion of language, of logic, of the norm, and of the gaze. Everything visible through the window of this other world perpetuates and revels in the instability of power and knowledge. In a similar fashion, the next story in the collection presents an extraordinary young girl named Elba, who guides her sister and friend through another world of a markedly different order.

"Mi hermana Elba"

Fernández Cubas manipulates strategies of power and sources of knowledge in the title story "Mi hermana Elba" ["My Sister Elba"], which is in many ways the most straightforward—and also the most haunting—tale in the collection.[12] Essentially, in this text the first-person narrator peruses her girlhood diary and recalls the events of the final two years of her younger sister's life. The narrator/protagonist is unchanged in one key respect: she yearns for the affirmation of the gaze of another and strives to establish herself as the center and subject of power in her life and in her text. As the narrator recalls, the two young sisters are sent to a boarding school at a convent while, unbeknownst to them at the time, their parents are in the process of divorce. At school, the protagonist longs for the approval of a sophisticated older girl, Fátima, who breaks all the rules without getting caught. Fátima possesses the uncanny ability to find secret spaces where one is magically invisible to everyone on the outside. The protagonist finally attracts Fátima's attention and is allowed to tag along, largely because Fátima respects young Elba, who is highly skilled at making use of these spaces and discovering secret passages that even Fátima does not understand. Together, the girls explore the forbidden zones of the convent, taking refuge in their hiding places when they need to escape detection by the nuns.[13] Elba's particular powers impress her sister so that the two become quite close, exulting with Fátima in the freedom of their clandestine world.

When school ends and the sisters return home, the protagonist carefully records in her diary all the information that pours from Elba's ramblings, presumably to share it with Fátima in the coming fall. At the end of that summer, however, the parents explain that Elba "no es una niña normal" [is not a normal child] (Fernández Cubas 1988, 74), and they send her to a special school. The protagonist returns alone to school, only to find that Fátima has grown up and has no interest in her or in their old games. The forsaken girl cannot endure the resulting solitude, made more agonizing by her sister's haunting gaze and cries that eclipse her thoughts. Driven to desperation, she shouts for Elba to leave her in peace, whereupon the child's voice gradually fades from her mind.

Once Elba ceases to haunt her, the protagonist makes new friends and eagerly anticipates beach excursions and meeting one friend's handsome cousin, Damián, that coming summer. Elba, too, returns home that summer, but she is "distraída y ausente" [distracted and absentminded] (79), although her sad, piercing gaze follows her sister through the window. To the protagonist's surprise, she does not mind the sensation of losing a sister. One day, she is summoned home from the beach because Elba has fallen from the terrace and has died. Amidst the ensuing mourning that the narrator recounts, she often refers to her feeling of being watched, pitied, and indulged by everyone, including the handsome boy, Damián, who kisses her cheek in condolence. To end her story, the narrator cites her diary entry for the day of Elba's death, in which she did not even note the loss of her sister: "'Damián me ha besado por primera vez.' Y, más abajo, en tinta roja y gruesas mayúsculas: 'HOY ES EL DIA MAS FELIZ DE MI VIDA'" ["Damián kissed me for the first time.' And, below, in red ink and fat capital letters: "TODAY IS THE HAPPIEST DAY OF MY LIFE"] (81).

In essence, "Mi hermana Elba" reveals how a girl discovers, revels in, and then destroys the telekinetic powers of her little sister in order to bask in the approving gaze of others. With her opening sentence the narrator immediately discloses her childhood efforts to control her family: "Durante el largo verano de 1954 sometí a mis padres a la más estricta vigilancia" [During the long summer of 1954 I subjected my parents to the strictest vigilance] (55). Like the narrator of "La ventana del jardín," she seeks to control others with her watchful eye. Perceiving that something is amiss in her household although not yet understanding that her parents are getting a divorce, she refuses to speak and thereby coerces everyone into paying special attention to her. Aware that silence can be as mighty a tool as speech, she surrenders her voice in a move calculated to make her the focal point of everyone's vision. Once at school, Fátima becomes the protagonist's ideal "other," but at first this other does not deem the protagonist a worthy object of her gaze: "Tuve que aguardar, pues, al recreo del mediodía y seguirla discretamente en sus paseos solitarios por el jardín, esperando una mirada de complicidad que no llegaba o alguna indicación que me animara a conversar con tranquilidad" [So I had to wait for midday recess and follow her discretely on her solitary walks around the yard, hoping for a look of complicity that never came or some sign that would encourage me to chat with ease] (69). The narrator seeks affirmation of herself in Fátima's eyes, and, without it, she hesitates even to speak and express herself in discourse.

Needing to control others in order to gain more power for herself, the protagonist takes advantage of Elba's knowledge of "hiding places" to attract Fátima's attention. Little Elba is gratified at earning her sister's respect for her discoveries of secret places: "Elba solía unirse a nuestros juegos con un brillo especial en la mirada y una emoción incontenible al comprobar cómo yo, de pronto, había empezado a considerarla seriamente. También Fátima trataba a mi hermana con mucho respeto [. . .]" [Elba used to join our games with a special sparkle in her gaze and uncontainable emotion at verifying that I had suddenly begun to take her seriously. Fátima also treated my sister with a great deal of respect {. . .}] (72). In this setting where they can "observar sin ser vistas" [observe without being seen] (72), the girls can revel in the experience of transcendent space and escape the vigilant gaze of the nuns. At the same time, each sister can bask in the approval of her respective idol.

Once the cherished Fátima "grows up" and loses interest in Elba, however, the protagonist also rejects her young sister. Fátima no longer needs to defy the established social system because she now enjoys being part of it. The narrator is devastated by Fátima's renewed disinterest: "Fátima, la gran Fátima que todas—y yo con mayor razón—admirábamos, había dejado de pertenecerme" [Fátima, the great Fátima that everyone—and I especially—admired, had ceased to belong to me] (Fernández Cubas 1988, 77). Following Fátima's lead in immersing herself in typical teenage preoccupations like boys and clothes, the narrator becomes convinced that Elba's "abnormality" is a liability. Although she protests when her sister is institutionalized, she finds it more comfortable to reject the traumatized girl's telepathic communication rather than to console her:

> Siempre Elba, con su expresión de angustia y su brazo extendido, con una mirada cada vez más exigente, sonriéndome a veces, gimoteando otras, tomando nota de todos y cada uno de mis pensamientos. Hasta que su mismo recuerdo se me hizo odioso. "¡Basta!," terminé gritando un día. "Vete de una vez para siempre." Y progresivamente su voz fue debilitándose, haciéndose cada vez más lejana, fundiéndose con otros sonidos y, por fin, desapareciendo por completo. (78)

> [Always Elba, with her expression of anguish and her arm reaching out, with an increasingly demanding gaze, sometimes smiling at me, other times whimpering, taking note of each and every one of my thoughts. Until the very memory of her was abhorrent to me. "Enough!" I finally yelled one day. "Go, once and for all." And her voice became progressively weaker, more distant, blending with other sounds and, finally, disappearing completely.]

Elba's examining gaze and anguished groans upset her sister by positioning her in the predicament of being a judged object and a guilty subject at the same time. Like the narrator of "La ventana del jardín," this protagonist is disturbed by a power paradigm that imposes such a paradoxical subjectivity. Instead of exploring and appreciating the other knowledge and freedom that Elba provides, the girl rejects her sister because she is no longer a useful tool in the struggle for Fátima's approval. She prefers a more familiar, unidirectional and limited power relationship. Thus the protagonist acquiesces to the definition of her sister as "abnormal" and contributes to her banished isolation. In the end, being the recipient of Elba's cries for help puts her in a doubly powerless position: she cannot bear to be the object of her sister's telepathic vigilance, nor is she capable of taking action and changing her parents' decision about her sister's interment.

The narrator's egoism peaks when she relishes the concern focused on her after the unexplained death of her sister. The attention she receives gives her the gratification, at last, of being the object of everyone's gaze: "Siguieron las frases de condolencia y los apretones de mano. Me sentía observada. Pasaron una a una todas las familias del pueblo. Pasó Damián con los ojos enrojecidos y me besó en la mejilla" [The condolences and the hand squeezes continued. I felt observed. One by one all the families of the town filed by. Then came Damián, with his eyes red, and he kissed me on the cheek] (81). Whether accidental or suicidal, Elba's death becomes a commodity traded in her sister's pursuit of power. Yet the death may possibly have been caused by the protagonist herself, although she does not openly confess. The narrator does not disclose exactly what she was doing when Elba "había perdido el equilibrio en la terraza" [had lost her balance on the balcony] (80). Was she playing at the beach, as her account implies (but does not state), or was she pushing her sister off the balcony? In this light, Elba's death potentially takes on the hue of a bizarre sacrifice for the comfort of her sister.

The narrative text itself, then, can be seen as a sort of confession with the guise of producing truth. While the apparent purpose of this story might be to exorcise a woman of troubling memories of an abnormal sister, the confession as fiction depends on its recipients—its readers—to interpret its truth. Thus the narrator may condemn herself inadvertently by the implications of her words. The young protagonist manipulates everyone in her life, and, as an adult narrator, her words snake out to ensnare readers. However, even though they are the receiving objects of her discourse, readers have the power to extract knowledge from this confession and interpret their version of the truth. This is a daunting task due to the nature of narrative itself: an undertaking inherently subject to memory, to reconstruction, to fictionalization, to manipulation. As in other Fernández Cubas stories, the task of struggling with the other in order to determine the truth—as the tradition of confession has trained us to do—is proven to be a virtually impossible one, for truth is merely a construct of a particular mechanization of power.

"El provocador de imágenes"

Tracing the truth is similarly futile in "El provocador de imágenes" ["The Provoker of Images"], the last tale in this collection. In this story, the first-person narrator (who refers to himself only by the elliptical alphabetical initials H.J.K.) remembers his long friendship with José Eduardo Expedito (also known as J.E.E.). Eduardo possesses a cornucopia of knowledge of every type imaginable, is a meticulous observer of people, and prides himself on being a *provocador de imágenes*, whereby he provokes people to the limit of their tolerance. H.J.K. delights in being the object of Eduardo's gaze and gladly submits his confessions to his friend's direction.

Whereas for the protagonist of "Mi hermana Elba" the power of Fátima's gaze seemed absolute, H.J.K.'s pleasure as the object of his other's examining gaze blazes into fury when he discovers that Eduardo's prowess has been defeated by his insipid girlfriend, Ulla Goldberg. While living with Eduardo and purportedly enduring his sadomasochistic humiliations and tortures, Ulla was actually subjecting the great J.E.E. to careful observation and examination, the results of which she duplicitously recorded in her recipe book. Eduardo tearfully confesses all this during a drunken encounter with the protagonist in a bar. Stunned, H.J.K. meanders around several countries before returning to Strasbourg, where he intuits Ulla to be. Finding the unattractive blond one night in a seedy bar, he casually asks about Eduardo. He watches her normally vacant, inhuman gaze become "radiante, vencedora" [radiant, victorious] (Fernández Cubas 1988, 106) while she recounts tale after tale of Eduardo's spiraling alcoholism and self-destruction. Without hesitation, H.J.K. informs her that Eduardo's apparent alcoholism is merely a guise for his investigation into his latest passion, the brewing of beer. Intimidating Ulla with his extensive and exclusive knowledge of Eduardo's activities, and deflating her glory at having defeated the great manipulator, H.J.K. provokes the image he desires to see: "Las mejillas de Ulla Goldberg habían recobrado su habitual palidez enfermiza. Sonreí; el brillo de sus ojos estaba dejando paso a su acostumbrada transparencia inhumana" [Ulla Goldberg's cheeks had recovered their habitual sickly pallor. I smiled; the gleam in her eyes was giving way to their accustomed inhuman transparency] (109). Finally, the protagonist justifies the "vómito de falsedades e incongruencias" [vomit of falsehoods and incongruities] (109) that he has just spewed onto Ulla with the fact that José Eduardo E. has always been his best friend.

Of all the stories in *Mi hermana Elba*, "El provocador de imágenes" displays perhaps most prominently the struggle for power through the accumulation of knowledge and the manipulation of the gaze. In the beginning, the narrator briefly examines Eduardo, then delights in being the object of Eduardo's examination. José Eduardo Expedito extensively catalogs information on everything from the mating rituals of scorpions, to the correct preparation of innumerable culinary delights, to the theory that the proliferation of different languages stems from the biblical Tower of Babel. His propensity to "provoke images" enables him to observe the way others react to his astounding knowledge. As Foucault has noted, the effect of this examining gaze is to define people as objects of knowledge: "*The examination, surrounded by all its documentary techniques, makes each individual a 'case':* a case which at one and the same time constitutes an object for a branch of knowledge and a hold for a branch of power" (Foucault 1979, 191). Curiously, though, the protagonist basks in Eduardo's attention and goes to great lengths to assure his friend's dominance, much as Violeta finally submitted to Lúnula. This twist, one not emphasized by Foucault, frequently appears in Fernández Cubas's texts. The protagonist's desire to be the object of the other's gaze propels the enigma of the entire story and motivates his final confrontation with Ulla.

Ulla disturbs H.J.K. so violently because, to his mind, she distorts his system of power to monstrous proportions. From the moment he first meets her, the protagonist dismisses Ulla as an unsuitable object for his own gaze: "[N]o me interesaba en absoluto. Su duro acento sueco me resultaba grotesco y sus enfermizos cabellos pálidos, cortados al estilo de cualquier institutriz de pesadilla, me parecieron de una total falta de respeto a las posibles ideas estéticas del prójimo. Reparé en los enormes zapatones que ahora movía nerviosa y mi mirada cambió al instante de dirección" [She didn't interest me in the least. Her harsh Swedish accent seemed grotesque and her sickly pale hair, cut like that of some governess from a nightmare, seemed to show a total disregard for the possible aesthetic ideas of her fellow human beings. I noticed the huge ugly shoes that she was now moving nervously and immediately I looked away] (Fernández Cubas 1988, 91). "Grotesco," "enfermizos," "zapatones" (not to mention "sueco")—all indicate that Ulla Goldberg exceeds the normal and qualifies, therefore, as monstrous.[14] The protagonist meditates on the monstrosity of objects that overwhelm their parameters and take control of their creators: "Pensé entonces en el brillante doctor Victor Frankenstein y su terror incontenible ante el primer signo de vida de su criatura. Unos párpados que se abren, un suspiro. . . ¿No era eso lo deseado? Sí. . . pero demasiado grande. Una escala demasiado grande. Justo el punto que separa la hermosura de la monstruosidad. . . [. . .] Como Ulla Goldberg. Exactamente igual que Ulla Goldberg" [Then I thought of brilliant Doctor Victor Frankenstein and his uncontainable terror at the first sign of life from his creature. Eyelids that open, a sigh. . . Wasn't that what was desired? Yes. . . but too large. On a scale that was too large. Precisely the point that separates beauty from monstrosity. . . {. . .} Like Ulla Goldberg. Exactly the same as Ulla Goldberg] (96). To the narrator's calculating eye, Ulla is lacking as an object of desire precisely because she exceeds his standards of normality and, at the same time, falls short of his standards of femininity.

Ulla's most monstrous sedition, however, is that her appearance deviates completely from her true identity. From the beginning, the narrator complains about her "mirada transparente" [transparent gaze], suggesting that one reason he dislikes her is that she does not play the game of the gaze: her eyes do not reflect the evaluation, definition, and affirmation of him, which the narrator needs for his gratification as a seen object. Eventually, he discovers that Ulla's gaze is monstrous in its duplicity: "Pero aquella mirada de una transparencia inquietante con la que acogía cualquier capricho ajeno por extraño o contra natura que pudiera parecer, ocultaba una terrible falsedad. Ulla Goldberg estaba experimentando, ensayando o probando [. . .]" [But that gaze of disquieting transparency with which she met each and every whim of others, no matter how strange or unnatural it seemed, concealed a terrible falseness. Ulla Goldberg was experimenting, practicing or testing{. . .}] (99). Fooled by her apparent ingenuousness into thinking that her gaze lacked power, the narrator is stunned and incensed to discover that she is "la más grande provocadora de imágenes que ser alguno pudiera concebir" [the biggest provoker of images that anyone could imagine] (99).

That translucent gaze conceals a crafty woman who has inverted the play of disciplinary power in the sadomasochistic torture sessions with Eduardo, and has used her subterfuge of submission in order to subject Eduardo to extensive observation. Ulla has reversed the equation so that Eduardo becomes the object of her knowledge and power through the examination. Key to such objectification is its representation in writing, as Foucault notes: "The examination that places individuals in a field of surveillance also situates them in a network of writing; it engages them in a whole mass of documents that capture and fix them" (Foucault 1979, 189). Ulla transcribes Eduardo in her medical or psychoanalytical discourse as the "paciente J.E.E." [patient J.E.E.] (Fernández Cubas 1988, 100), not to glorify him but to reduce him, as Foucault would say, to "a document for possible use" (Foucault 1979, 191). This Swede, an inexcusably unattractive but apparently submissive woman, has manipulated her feminine status—thanks to the masquerade of her examination record as a cookbook—to take control of Eduardo and, by extension, of H.J.K. himself.

Sickened by this monstrous violation of subject/object relations, the narrator literally vomits on Ulla's "irritante flequillo" [annoying bangs] (Fernández Cubas 1988, 95) one night in a bar, and figuratively coats her with "aquel vómito de falsedades e incongruencias" [that vomit of falsehoods and incongruities] (109) the final night in another bar when he stuns her with his fabricated knowledge about Eduardo. Making Ulla the object of his verbal and gastric spew, he determines to gain control and restore his friend to glory by means of reducing the gleam of Ulla's gaze to its "acostumbrada transparencia inhumana" [accustomed inhuman transparency] (109). If Ulla's gaze is transparent, then H.J.K. can *see through* her and possess all the knowledge and power in their relationship. He strives to dominate her difference, for as long as her inhumanity—her monstrosity—wields no control, it benefits the disciplinary system by accentuating, through deficient contrast, the normality and right to rule of the powers that be.

Knowledge is the key to power, yet the narrator's authority in this story is totally limited by his questionable knowledge of exactly what occurs. His constant proclamations of control are undermined by his admissions of a temporarily faulty memory: "Aunque suelo presumir de una memoria excelente y algunos hechos de mi vida así lo atestiguan—no confío en mi secretaria y sólo uso la agenda en contadas ocasiones—, hay ciertos datos que escapan ahora a mis intentos de ordenación y emergen del pasado envueltos en una nube de sombras y murmullos" [Although I normally pride myself on having an excellent memory, to which some facts in my life attest—I don't trust my secretary and I use an agenda only on rare occasions—, there are certain details that now escape my efforts to create order and that emerge from the past enveloped in a cloud of shadows and whispers] (83). He also admits to being slow to comprehend certain situations: "Confieso, en detrimento de mi supuesta sagacidad, que tardé bastante en dar con la clave [. . .]" [I confess, in detriment to my supposed shrewdness, that it took me quite a while to hit the nail on the head {. . .}] (97). A comical antidote to the narrator's presumptuous and anal-retentive character, this doubt about his control subsumes any expectation of stability in power relations between narrator and reader at the textual level. One suspects, however, that perhaps these frequent admissions of aberration from his normal character are deliberate attempts to keep the readers' attention and gaze focused on him, just the way he did with Eduardo. Like the older sister of "Mi hermana Elba," he understands that temporary abnormality attracts the attention of the examining gaze, which watches in search of knowledge. Thus H.J.K.'s narrative unreliability is conceivably a narcissistic enticement of readers' voyeurism. Presuming that readers like to watch, he is only too happy to give them plenty to see and ponder.

Further evidence of unreliability in this narration is the inferiority of the narrator's knowledge of foreign languages and customs in comparison with Eduardo's. The latter delivers his confession of Ulla's dominance in numerous languages, which impedes the narrator's understanding: "No puedo precisar con certeza cómo Eduardo llegó a descubrirse objeto de estudio (esa parte del discurso fue pronunciada casi enteramente en bávaro), pero me pareció entender que la científica Ulla había recopilado la mayor parte de sus impresiones en una agenda en la que simulaba anotar recetas alsacianas [...]" [I can't pinpoint with certainty how Eduardo came to discover that he was the object of study {that part of the treatise was given almost entirely in Bavarian}, but I thought I understood that the scientific Ulla had compiled the majority of her impressions in a notebook in which she feigned to note down Alsatian recipes {...}] (Fernández Cubas 1988, 99). Linguistic mastery affords knowledge of the other and the potential to dominate the difference of the other, as Eduardo amply demonstrates. With the proliferation of languages, nationalities, cultural customs, and countries in this story, Fernández Cubas highlights the issue of difference and the way it disconcerts people. This undercurrent, which resurfaces in many of her texts, divulges the need to control others by cataloging the exact ways in which they are different, thereby defining them through discourse. In this story, however, the narrator cannot dominate because he pieces together imperfect knowledge from linguistic ramblings that he does not understand.

Subject/object relations through the examining gaze constitute the key method for establishing relations of dominance that constantly get overturned in "El provocador de imágenes." This story illustrates how knowledge generates power and power propagates knowledge; always intertwined, the two produce subjects of discourse and the gaze. However, as often happens in the Fernández Cubas fictional world, the tables are turned in this text when the "powerless" wields the very tactics of the powerful in order to wrest control. H.J.K. submits to J.E.E., who is subjugated by Ulla, who is then stymied by H.J.K. Throughout this tale, and indeed the entire collection, the author dramatizes the way power functions based on a dual pleasure principle: the pleasure of observing and the pleasure of being observed. When being watched ceases to titillate, objects of the gaze endeavor to look objectively at their subjects and shift the balance of power in their own favor.

Conclusion

In the stories of *Mi hermana Elba*, self/other power relations are mediated as one character strives to dominate the discourse imposed by another. Leaving behind the preoccupation with a single figure of power proliferated in Spanish fiction during the transition years after the dictatorship, the protagonists of these tales undergo a kind of apprenticeship of power: they are exposed to a paradigm in which power is reversible, in flux at all levels of society, and in which other modes of knowledge and logic distort what they presume to be right. Essentially, Fernández Cubas's paradigm of subjectivity imbues the object with the agency to look "objectively" at the subject, and to manipulate the subject's own discourse and invert the hierarchy of control. Thus she exposes and extends the potential for opposition that is inherent, but never fully explored, in Foucault's concept of power as a fluctuating process.

Finally, in each of these tales the narrative text itself enters into play with readers, provoking its own images in order to question the way they see and interpret reality. Without doubt, power depends on oppositionality, and Fernández Cubas underscores the importance of both sides of the boundary: not only do binaries such as subject/object, logic/illogic, and orality/writing define and deconstruct one another, but the tension between them is precisely the arena for her discursive creativity. If the technologies of power displayed in this narrative discourse ultimately cause any interpretation of the texts to be as ambiguous as the identities of Violeta/Lúnula/Victoria/Luz, or as cryptic as Olla's language, then at least the spectacle of power is sure to continue—ever changing and enticing. Key to this spectacle are expectations of gender and their subversion, as Ulla indicates in "El provocador de imágenes." In the next chapter, on *Los altillos de Brumal*, the performance of gender occupies the spotlight in the subjective play of power.

2
Performing and Reforming Gender in *Los altillos de Brumal*

"[. . .] y la imagen de la virtuosa veinteañera, a quien, hasta hacía muy poco, todos compadecían, fue cobrando con irremisible rapidez los rasgos de una bíblica adúltera, de una castiza malcasada, de una perversa devoradora de hombres a los que seducía con los encantos de su cuerpo para abandonarlos tras saciar sus inconfesables apetitos."

[{. . .} and the image of the virtuous twenty-year-old—with whom, until recently, everyone sympathized—began taking on with unpardonable speed the traits of a biblical adulteress, of a poorly married true-born, of a perverse devourer of men, whom she seduced with the delights of her body only to abandon them after sating her shameful appetites.]
—"La noche de Jezabel"

THE COVER OF THE TUSQUETS JOINT EDITION OF THE SHORT STORY collections *Mi hermana Elba* [My Sister Elba] and *Los altillos de Brumal* [The Attics of Brumal] by Fernández Cubas displays Norman Rockwell's "Girl at the Mirror." It portrays a young, barefoot girl in a petticoat, crouching on a bench in front of a looming mirror. Discarded on the floor are a pretty doll, a tube of red lipstick, a comb, a brush. On the girl's lap, a magazine is opened to a full-page spread of Jayne Mansfield's haughty, flawlessly sculpted and made-up face. The girl's curled fingers timidly approach her own naked face, seeking in her reflection, perhaps, some promising germination of Jayne Mansfield. This picture illustrates not only the representation of gender, in the photograph of the great Hollywood movie star, but also what Judith Butler calls the re-presentation or performativity of gender—that is to say, the process of fashioning the self according to socially created codes of sexuality. As such, "Girl at the Mirror" aptly illustrates the way identity is formed, performed, and re-formed through constructions of gender.

While in chap. 1 I analyzed *Mi hermana Elba* as an exploration of the politics of power—the way individuals define themselves through power relations with others—in this chapter the politics of gender take central stage in the performance of identity. By foregrounding the issue of gender formation, the work of Fernández Cubas highlights a central concern of feminist theory in general, as well as the field of feminism within Spain in particular. To date, numerous critical studies have read Fernández Cubas's work as privileging the feminine over the masculine as a paradigm for agency.[1] Nonetheless, the author herself has emphatically rejected the idea that her work privileges the feminine and has insisted that she strives to explore idiosyncrasies and problems in characters of both sexes (Glenn 1993, 361). Moreover, she has proclaimed that "literature and feminism have nothing to do with each other" (Carmona, et al. 1991, 158). The reputation in Spain of feminism as simplistic, on the one hand, and extremist, on the other, may explain her adamant stance. I would argue that Fernández Cubas's fiction manipulates language as artifice in order to underscore the similarity of gender-based notions of both feminism and patriarchy. *Los altillos de Brumal* (1983), the author's second collection of stories, evokes images of the feminine as sources of inspiration, creativity, and agency, but which characters benefit from projecting such a discourse of essentialized femininity? How does the apparent binary opposition of masculine/feminine (or its inverse) dictate the actions of individuals as gendered beings? If gender is an ongoing representation and performance, as Butler proposes, what choices are made in these texts that perpetuate or, conversely, that deconstruct the masquerade of masculine and feminine? The answers to these questions suggest that, instead of inverting the binomial hierarchy in an elevation of the feminine, the stories of *Los altillos de Brumal* blend certainty with forgetfulness, "masculine" order with "feminine" fluidity, in an alteration of the stakes of power. She explores what is left out of such polarized identities, at the very limits of discursive construction, as the foundational borderland of the subject.[2]

"El reloj de Bagdad"

"El reloj de Bagdad" ["The Clock from Baghdad"], the first story of *Los altillos de Brumal*, foregrounds issues of gender through its marked contrast between feminine and masculine qualities and spaces. The female narrator recalls her childhood, much of which she spent in the kitchen listening to the fabulous tales of the maid, Olvido [Forgetfulness or Oblivion], and enjoying the company of the spirits who infused even inanimate objects with a creative voice. This idyllic existence is interrupted when the young girl's father brings home a looming clock from Baghdad, and installs it on the central landing of the staircase so that it will be visible from the main areas of the house. Soon after, all the household members seem to be mysteriously plagued by mishaps. Fearful and sensitive, the young girl perceives the entire house to be submerged in ominous silence. The calamities culminate with the death of Olvido and, shortly thereafter, the destruction of the house in a nighttime fire, from which the family barely escapes with a few random possessions. The clock is rescued, however, and to the child's ears its chimes are transformed into insidious laughter as the house burns to the ground. The girl's last reported memory is of her family's departure from that town, on the night of the Feast of Saint John. Amid the ritualistic bonfires, the child spies the dancing figure of her beloved Olvido, accompanied by the sprites of inspiration. This was, she recounts, her last vision of the spirits.

The feminine imagery of this story centers on the kitchen and its ruler, Olvido, in direct opposition to the phallic clock and the father who purchased it. Bretz has observed that "the world of the kitchen is clearly the pre-Oedipal, timeless world of the semiotic" (Bretz 1988, 183), in contrast to the patriarchal structure of the symbolic. The binary relation that she draws is based on Julia Kristeva's *Revolution in Poetic Language* (1984) and *Desire in Language* (1980). In these works, Kristeva develops her concept of the semiotic in an elaboration of Jacques Lacan's psychoanalytic model of subject development, which hinges on the Symbolic Order of patriarchy. For Kristeva, the symbolic is characterized by the subject's perception of complete castration and submission to phallic language:

> [T]he discovery of castration . . . detaches the subject from his dependence on the mother, and the perception of this lack makes the phallic function a symbolic function—*the* symbolic function. The subject, finding his identity in the symbolic, *separates* from his fusion with the mother [characteristic of the semiotic], *confines* his jouissance to the genitals, and transfers semiotic motility onto the symbolic order. (Kristeva 1984, 47)

Kristeva theorizes that the rigidity imposed by the Symbolic Order, which is entered through initiation into language and ruled by phallic law, can be penetrated by drives of the "semiotic chora"—the rhythmic, prelinguistic, nurturing, ungendered space in the unconscious where the drives that affect the subject are originally ordered. Kristeva associates the semiotic with the feminine, in contrast to the masculine, patriarchal structure of the symbolic. This feminine association is intensified as she develops her theory in *Desire in Language*, wherein the mother is emphasized as the origin of the semiotic drives. For Kristeva, those (feminine) semiotic drives that penetrate the symbolic structure have an effect that "pulverizes unity" in the phallocentric order (Kristeva 1984, 208). As a result, they allow the subject the possibility of altering absolute patriarchal formation in language. Finally, this dynamic enables the subject to continue in process.

In Bretz's view, Olvido epitomizes the eternal mother figure, as ruler of the uninhibited space of the kitchen—where all talk flows freely and even the hearth has a voice (Bretz 1988). Significantly, in the story Olvido is associated with the fluid communication of oral narration: "Y entonces Olvido tomaba la palabra. Pausada, segura, sabedora de que a partir de aquel momento nos hacía suyos, que [. . .] sus arrugas de anciana dejarían paso a la tez sonrosada de una niña, a la temible faz de un sepulturero atormentado por sus recuerdos, a un fraile visionario [. . .]" [And then Olvido would start to talk. Slow, sure, knowing that from that moment on she was making us hers, that {. . .} her old woman's wrinkles would yield to the rosy complexion of a little girl, to the fearsome face of a grave digger tormented by his memories, to a visionary friar{. . .}] (Fernández Cubas 1988, 116–17). Like Lúnula in "Lúnula y Violeta" (*Mi hermana Elba*), Olvido is a mesmerizing storyteller, adept at transforming herself into the characters of her tales.[3] Yet, in "El reloj de Bagdad," Olvido's communicative vitality contrasts not with another aspiring narrator, but with the imposing, rigid silence represented by the clock: "El Reloj de Bagdad estaba ahí. Arrogante, majestuoso, midiendo con su sordo tictac cualquiera de nuestros juegos infantiles. Parecía como si se hallara en el mismo lugar desde tiempos inmemoriales [. . .]" [The Clock from Baghdad was there. Arrogant, majestic, measuring with its mute ticktock each of our childish games. It seemed as if it had been in the same place since time immemorial {. . .}] (120). Even the seemingly eternal nature of the clock competes with Olvido's apparent agelessness.[4]

Together with the clock, the image of the father certainly evokes the patriarchal control of the symbolic. The father has a small but significant function in the story: he brings the clock into the home, he is "[f]iel a la ley del silencio" [faithful to the law of silence] (129), and—in an echo of the biblical Lot—he prohibits the young girl from looking back when they finally drive away from the town on the Night of Saint John. He and the upright clock, representatives of the phallic order, seem to be in direct opposition to Olvido and the feminine. Significantly, the father—like Olvido—is dead by the time the narrator tells her tale.

Despite its seemingly phallic alliance, the clock has qualities that undermine absolute gender associations. As the narrator recalls, time seems to have erased signs of gender from the dancing figures painted on the face of the clock: "[. . .] los cuerpos festivos de un grupo de seres humanos. ¿Danzarines? ¿Invitados a un banquete? Los años habían desdibujado sus facciones, los pliegues de sus vestidos [. . .]" [{. . .} the festive bodies of a group of human beings. Dancers? Guests at a banquet? The years had faded their features, the folds of their clothing {. . .}] (119). These ungendered bodies of uncertain identity deviate from the paradigm of the feminine that Olvido imposes, as well as the ideal of the masculine that the father enforces. The clock, then, is a paradoxical, ambivalent blend of phallocentric order, on the one hand, and the transcendence of sexually marked difference, on the other. Moreover, as the children of the house gaze at it, the sand in its weights inspires vivid imaginings of playtime on the beach. This fertile silence rivals the power of Olvido's oral storytelling to ignite the young ones' imaginations. In effect, the figure of the clock attenuates the negative polarity of the masculine with positive qualities, which disturbs the absolute control that Olvido formerly had wielded from her position in the feminine.

In addition to representing nongendered beings and stimulating creativity that transcends limitations of space, the clock from Baghdad also makes hierarchical concepts of subjectivity problematic. By virtue of its origin, the timepiece symbolizes the crossing of the border between East and West. This penetration of the West by the East is highly unsettling for Olvido, who insists on rejecting the Iraqis for their difference: "Ni siquiera deben de ser cristianos" [They're probably not even Christians] (122). Olvido attempts to duplicate her superiority in the Europe/Iraq paradigm through masculine/feminine relationships, by inverting the hierarchy of gender and wresting household control from the phallic realm of the father.[5]

Olvido's fear of the other and of losing control are prime motivators for her to cooperate in subjugation in order to invert its terms; nonetheless, her collusion still propagates domains of oppositional difference. Teresa de Lauretis has observed in *Technologies of Gender* that this polarity of thought, typical of some strands of feminism, is characteristic of patriarchy since the differences it pursues "ends up being in the last instance a difference (of woman) from man—or better, the very instance of difference *in* man. To continue to pose the question of gender in either of these terms, once the critique of patriarchy has been fully outlined, keeps feminist thinking bound to the terms of Western patriarchy itself. . . ." (de Lauretis 1987, 1). Any definition of woman based on her difference from man reproduces the oppositional relationship that binds woman to man. This polarity is precisely the basis for one of Judith Butler's criticisms of Kristeva's opposition between the semiotic and the symbolic: "Despite her critique of Lacan, however, Kristeva's strategy of subversion proves doubtful. Her theory appears to depend upon the stability and reproduction of precisely the paternal law that she seeks to displace. . . . If the semiotic promotes the possibility of the subversion, displacement, or disruption of the paternal law, what meanings can those terms have if the Symbolic always reasserts its hegemony?" (Butler 1990a, 80). Olvido's elevation of the feminine over the masculine similarly proliferates the patriarchal mode of thought.

By causing the qualities of the masculine/feminine binary to interpenetrate one another in "El reloj de Bagdad," Fernández Cubas undermines the viability of such absolute divisions, in order to point to a different way of envisioning the subject. Butler embarks on a similar deconstruction in *Gender Trouble*, in which she analyzes gender as an ongoing re-presentation of the self and probes into which powers stand to gain by depicting gender roles according to a binary opposition: "How are the sex/gender and nature/culture dualisms constructed and naturalized in and through one another? What gender hierarchies do they serve, and what relations of subordination do they reify?" (Butler 1990a, 37). She criticizes Kristeva for undertaking a utopian quest for gender-related origins in the semiotic without questioning who defined the origin as such: "The law that is said to repress the semiotic may well be the governing principle of the semiotic itself, with the result that what passes as 'maternal instinct' may well be a culturally constructed desire which is interpreted through a naturalistic vocabulary" (91). Privileging the feminine as the origin and as necessarily opposed to the masculine, Kristeva's schema of the semiotic does not consider which powers benefit by inventing gendered subjects and then positing them as *prior* to the existence of the law. Butler agrees with Foucault that such a temporal sleight of hand is precisely what institutes the patriarchal power structure (7). In essence, then, in Fernández Cubas's story the border-crossing symbolism of the clock projects power binaries such as male/female and West/East as constructs that can be manipulated, questioned, and deconstructed. Even if subjectivity is indelibly influenced by discourse, the very idea that gender is not innate but a construction allows for the potential to restructure the discourses that form the subject.

Who, then, in "El reloj de Bagdad," profits from the institution of gender oppositions? The father does, obviously, to some extent. Nonetheless, in the dynamics of the household, Olvido clearly gains power over the children by stressing the attractive qualities of her feminine realm in contrast to the patriarchal "law of silence" imposed by the father. When the clock arrives, however, it rivals Olvido's skill at awakening the children's powers of imagination. Moreover, the suggestive erasure of gender on the face of the clock threatens Olvido's control, which is predicated on the essential difference of her gender. Thus the clock unsettles the balance of power in the home. Indeed, Olvido's final words to her young charge, before dying, are an admonishment to be on guard against the invasion of the other into their world: "Y luego, como presa de un pavor invencible, asiéndose de mis trenzas, intentando escupir algo que desde hacía tiempo ardía en su boca y empezaba ya a quemar mis oídos: 'Guárdate. Protégete... ¡No te descuides ni un instante!'" [And then, as if prisoner of an invincible terror, seizing my braids, trying to spit something that had blazed in her mouth for a long time and that was already beginning to burn my ears: "Beware. Protect yourself.... Don't let down your guard for even an instant!] (Fernández Cubas 1988, 126). The gender opposition of masculine and feminine foments Olvido's power; thus, whether aware of it or not, she has a vested interest in protecting and perpetuating that representation of gender.

If Olvido's power ultimately rests on a discursive construct of gender, it is a representation that the narrating protagonist, even as a child, sometimes accepts and other times rejects in order to accommodate better the self-image she desires. When Olvido asserts her intention of living with her charge even after the child grows up and marries, the girl ponders this representation of her feminine obligations:

> [No] veía motivo suficiente para separarme de mi familia o abandonar, algún día, la casa junto a la playa. Pero Olvido decidía siempre por mí. "El piso será soleado y pequeño, sin escaleras, sótano ni azotea." Y no me quedaba otro remedio que ensoñarlo así, con una amplia cocina en la que Olvido trajinara a gusto y una gran mesa de madera con tres sillas, tres vasos y tres platos de porcelana... O, mejor, dos. La compañía del extraño que las previsiones de Olvido me adjudicaban no acababa de encajar en mi nueva cocina. "El cenará más tarde," pensé. Y le saqué la silla a un hipotético comedor que mi fantasía no tenía interés alguno en representarse. (117)

> [I didn't see sufficient reason to separate myself from my family or abandon, one day, the house by the beach. But Olvido always decided for me. "The apartment will be sunny and small, without stairs, basement or terrace roof." And I had no choice but to dream it that way, with an ample kitchen in which Olvido would bustle about at her pleasure and a large wooden table with three chairs, three glasses and three porcelain plates.... Or, better yet, two. The company of the stranger that Olvido's farsightedness awarded me did not manage to fit in my new kitchen. "He'll eat later," I thought. And I took away the chair from the hypothetical diner that my fantasy had no interest in representing.]

This passage provides a key illustration of the way gender is represented for the girl, who subsequently re-presents the image the way she desires it to be. Although she claims to be completely interpellated into Olvido's domain—"Olvido always decided for me"—the child does not hesitate to change the picture and humorously erase that hypothetical husband whom she has no interest in representing in her personal space. This juxtaposition of acquiescence and agency underscores the fact that, since the gender roles that Olvido projects are *constituted* by discourse, they can be *changed* by discourse.

Long after the deaths of her father and Olvido, the adult narrator draws on discursive elements of both gender poles when she textually re-presents a self-styled subjectivity. In her narration, she consciously blends forgetfulness with the "certainty" of memory, in a creative discourse that combines both sides of the gender opposition. Throughout this narration, as in many Fernández Cubas texts, there abound references to the uncertainty of recollection, such as: "No sé si la extraña desazón que iba a adueñarse pronto de la casa irrumpió de súbito, como me lo presenta ahora la memoria, o si se trata, quizá, de la deformación que entraña el recuerdo. Pero lo cierto es que [. . .]" [I don't know if the strange trouble that would soon take over the house invaded suddenly, as memory now presents it to me, or if, perhaps, it's a question of the distortion that memory entails] (121). At the textual level, the narrator's continual speculation about the potential certainty or uncertainty of memory incorporates the feasibility of *olvido* into her creative project, together with the possibility of accurate remembrance.

In addition to the amalgam of certainty and doubt, the story exploits multiple meanings and contexts of *olvido* to destabilize any purely "feminine" or liberating interpretation of fluid forgetfulness. Thus, the seemingly feminine, creative, positive symbolism of the maid Olvido (which, in itself, is problematic) is offset by the numerous, destructive *olvidos* that culminate with the burning down of the house: "Eran tantos los *olvidos*, tan numerosos los descuidos, tan increíbles las torpezas que cometíamos de continuo, que ahora, con la distancia de los años, contemplo la tragedia que marcó nuestras vidas como un hecho lógico e inevitable. Nunca supe si aquella noche *olvidamos* retirar los braseros, o si lo hicimos de forma apresurada [. . .]" [So abundant were the instances of *forgetfulness*, so numerous the acts of carelessness, so incredible the clumsy things we continually did, that now, with the distance of years, I ponder the tragedy that marked our lives as a logical and inevitable event. I never found out if that night we *forgot* to put away the braziers, or if we did it in a rush {. . .}] (Fernández Cubas 1988, 127; italics mine). In addition to emphasizing the destructive nature of these *olvidos*, the narrator allies them with the side of logic—the latter a prime characteristic of the symbolic. As a result, qualities that initially seem to be associated with one gender polarity or the other cross the border between the two and confuse the issue of difference.

With the further deconstruction of the notion of forgetfulness as an exclusively feminine quality, the very existence of the clock—and the truth of the story—is cast into doubt. The narrator traces the erasure of certainty and memory to the morning when the house burned down: "Aquella misma madrugada se urdió la ingenua conspiración de la desmemoria" [That very dawn the ingenuous conspiracy of forgetfulness was contrived] (128). Soon thereafter, the antique dealer from whom the father purchased the clock in the first place rejects the timepiece because of its deterioration, denying that he ever possessed an ungainly object of such poor taste. The "forgetfulness" of the "olvidadizo comerciante" [absentminded merchant] (129) infects the girl's family: "[mi familia] adquirió su pasmosa tranquilidad para negar evidencias" [{my family} acquired his amazingly calm ability to deny evidence] (129). Now forgetfulness is depicted as a deliberate denial of truth, exercised first by a man and then adopted by an entire family. With this contagion, the motif of *olvido* can no longer be seen as sacred to the realm of the feminine.

Similar to the increasing ambivalence of the gendered associations of forgetfulness is the symbolism of fire. While in the beginning, the hearth is part of the feminine space of the kitchen, linked to Olvido and the spirits, fire is also the instrument—associated with the clock—that destroys the house. Then, at the end of the story, the bonfires on the Night of Saint John seem to harbor both the clock and Olvido with her spirit friends: "[El reloj] Parecía más pequeño, desamparado, lloroso. Las llamas ocultaban las figuras de los danzarines [. . .]. Recordando antiguas aficiones, entorné los ojos. Ella estaba allí. Riendo, danzando, revoloteando en torno a las llamas junto a sus viejas amigas" [{The clock} seemed smaller, forsaken, weepy. The flames concealed the figures of the dancers{. . .}. Remembering old pleasures, I half-closed my eyes. She was there. Laughing, dancing, flying about the flames together with her old friends] (129). Associated now with both sides of the masculine/feminine opposition—embodied in the clock and Olvido—and recalling the degendered dancing figures on the face of the clock, the fire consumes the boundary between the two opposing forces. Similarly, the flames signal the capriciousness of power relations: whereas, at the end of her life, Olvido surrenders her power to the domination of the clock, in death she gleefully dances while the clock mourns. Bretz has interpreted this "victory" of

Olvido as the triumph of the feminine (Bretz 1988). In the context of gender unmasked as representation, however, I interpret this final scene as a triumph of the inspirational power of telling tales that Olvido and the spirits represent—a gift made all the richer by the provocative ambiguity of the messages it imparts.

In "El reloj de Bagdad," telling tales and (re)constructing discourse become fundamental tools of power. This story suggests that understanding constructs of gender presents a fundamental tactic for change. The greatest value of conceiving of gender as a *discursive* representation lies in the play that language allows—that is to say, representation as a noun, an already constituted absolute, can be deconstructed to unveil a verb, an action: to re-present. Similarly, the discourses that construct representations of gender need not be accepted as predetermined formulations, but instead can be manipulated as tools of agency, as Teresa de Lauretis underscores: "To assert that the social representation of gender affects its subjective construction and that, vice versa, the subjective representation of gender—or self-representation—affects its social construction, leaves open a possibility of agency and self-determination at the subjective and even individual level of micropolitical and everyday practices. . . ." (de Lauretis 1987, 9). In this same vein, Butler conceives of gender as performativity, a continually repeated practice: "Gender is what is put on, invariably, under constraint, daily and incessantly, with anxiety and pleasure, but if this continuous act is mistaken for a natural or linguistic given, power is relinquished to expand the cultural field bodily though subversive performances of various kinds" (Butler 1990b, 282). Thus the subject who plays with gender assignments appropriates power to recreate herself, under the constraint of the discourses available to her. In "El reloj de Bagdad," the artistic performance as a mediation of gender roles culminates with the narrator's creation of her text. The creatively defiant young girl-cum-self-styled woman exercises agency in the act of narrating her past, as she combines elements of the "masculine" and the "feminine" in a pastiche of discourses that expresses the subjectivity she desires. In doing so, she rewrites the prescript of gender in order to reconstruct herself as the subject of her own discourse.

"En el hemisferio sur"

If "El reloj de Bagdad" questions the mutually exclusive nature of masculine versus feminine constructs, the next story of the collection, "En el hemisferio sur" ["In the Southern Hemisphere"] explores exactly how gendered conceptions, inscribed in discourse, produce—or fail to produce—subjects. Because the masculine itself is just another discursive construct, its supremacy as the origin and locus of authority can be, and is, displaced and deconstructed in this tale. The account of a male narrator who finds himself acting out in his life what his friend Clara (aka Sonia Kraskowa) already wrote about him in her novel, this tale humorously illustrates what Butler would call making "gender trouble." The woman controls the male narrator of "En el hemisferio sur" with the discourse of her novel, thereby trespassing the border between the traditional gender functions of female passivity and male authorship, as well as challenging orthodox concepts of narrative authority.[6] Having lost the power of the pen—the power of the phallus—and finding himself inscribed by narrative language into a position of inferiority, the narrator plunges into a crisis of subjectivity. The very possibility that his entire identity is constituted by the already written raises the question of whether subject construction is predetermined, such as Althusser might argue, or whether there is room for agency.[7] With the allegory of finding oneself to be a character in another's text—a text that prescribes one's every move— this story examines how discourse shapes the subject, inscribing her or him into a gendered position that finally determines, in Butler's terms, "what counts as a valued and valuable body" (Butler 1993, 22). Then, by questioning the very discursive terms by which those bodies come to matter, the text reveals how subjugated bodies manipulate existing discourses to alter their own construction.

The nameless narrator and protagonist begins his tale describing how Clara Galván, an old college friend and a successful novelist, comes to see him in his cramped office, where he works as an editor for a publishing house. While Clara, greatly distressed and disheveled, recounts how she is hounded by a Voice that forces her to write without ceasing, the narrator muses about how he envies her current plight in comparison to his own angst-ridden inability to write. Clara further tells how her exhaustion from overwork turned to horror one day when she realized that the Voice had a foreign accent, and how soon after she discovered a novel written by one Sonia Kraskowa, whose photograph bears a disturbing resemblance to Clara. The narrator's friend is alarmed to find that the excerpts of Sonia's first-person novel describe her (Clara's) trauma with the Voice in detail, and anticipate her words and actions almost exactly: "'No puede ser,' dije ahogando un chillido. El dependiente me tendió un ejemplar: NO PUEDE SER, Sonia Kraskowa. Tuve que apoyarme en una estantería para no desplomarme. 'Creo que me estoy volviendo loca,' musité en un tono apenas perceptible. 'No exactamente,' intervino el hombre y, ajustándose las gafas, puntualizó: EL DIA QUE CREI VOLVERME LOCA. . ." ["It can't be," I said, holding back a scream. The clerk handed me a book: IT CAN'T BE, Sonia Kraskowa. I had to lean on the bookshelves in order not to collapse. "I think I'm going crazy," I mumbled in a barely perceptible tone. "Not exactly," the man intervened, and, adjusting his glasses, clarified, THE DAY I THOUGHT I WAS GOING CRAZY. . .].[8] Horrified at being predicted this way, Clara begs the narrator to help her. Although he conceals the condescension he feels toward her, the editor is unable to empathize when Clara laments being nothing more than a replica of the already written. Clara goes to the bathroom to wash the streaks of makeup and tears off her face, and she reflects that, in the Southern Hemisphere, the water disappears down the drain in the opposite direction from in the Northern Hemisphere. She considers going South to unwind.

Later Clara calls the protagonist, sobbing that someone mysteriously put a copy of Sonia Kraskowa's novel on her night table, and that when she glanced at one of its pages, it said that she had moved to a hotel. In fact, at that moment she is at a hotel, where she is hiding from her mysterious stalker. After meeting Clara for dinner that Friday evening, the editor gives her a file full of clippings about Kraskowa. He then spends that weekend at the home of his Aunt Alicia, a homemaker and gardener whose old-fashioned ways comfort him after his difficult week. He returns to the city the following Monday to learn from his secretary that his writer-friend has died. He sends a card inscribed "A Clara Sonia Galván Kraskowa. Los que te quieren no te olvidan" (Fernández Cubas 1988, 148) [To Clara Sonia Galvan Kraskowa. Those who love you do not forget you] (Fernández Cubas 1992, 90). Along with the card he sends flowers from the north and south, in tribute to the dual parental heritage of his friend. He remembers the identity crisis that Clara had suffered in college, and how she took her mother's maiden name as her pen name. Bitterly he recalls how, when they both submitted stories to a college competition, Clara and not he had won the prize (a defeat from which his wounded ego never recovered). Then the narrator reminisces about his decision the previous Friday to force Clara to confront her identity by giving her the file of newspaper clippings about her career. Inspired by Clara's trauma, he plans to transcribe it as the perfect plot for the novel that he will finally write in defiance of the taunting blank page.

Considering himself to be caught up in a "hurricane" of creative ideas for his novel, the narrator is surprised when his secretary interrupts him to deliver Sonia's recently submitted manuscript entitled, not *Huracán*, but *Tornado*. As he reads it, the narrator feels dizzy at the awful discovery that *her* novel transcribes *his* life, the story we have been reading, told from the sarcastic perspective of a female narrator. The novel predicts the man's disdain for Clara's suffering at the mercy of the Voice. Moreover, it reveals that she dreamed the whole encounter in advance, and enacted the scene with him as a challenge for life to imitate the discursive construct of her dream. The narrator is further unsettled that the book's dedication to him suggests that Clara herself had fixed the college contest so that he lost. He rushes to the bathroom to wash his face and stares at the water disappearing down the drain, in the same direction as in the Southern Hemisphere. That very afternoon, he takes refuge once again in the home of his Aunt Alicia.

The rivalry between the narrator and Clara sets up a clear dichotomy between the masculine and the feminine. On one level the story may appear to invert the sexual hierarchy so that the woman exercises control.[9] What happens, though, if one analyzes the discourses that establish the polarity between "masculine" and "feminine"? Considering that the subject comes into existence only with its emergence into a sexed identity, Butler delves beneath the idea of predetermined construction in *Bodies That Matter* to interrogate the normative process by which subjects come to have value at all: "What I would propose in place of these conceptions of construction is a return to the notion of matter, not as a site or surface, but as *a process of materialization that stabilizes over time to produce the effect of boundary, fixity, and surface we call matter*" (Butler 1993, 9).[10] Matter, she holds, is more than the mere physical substance of the body. Hence it cannot be posited as prior to, privileged over, or exempt from construction. Instead, bodies are perceived by virtue of certain norms that define who matters and is viable as a subject; that is, in order to *become* "matter," to figure as a subject, the body is materialized. Yet what of those bodies that do not materialize "properly," that do not "matter"? For Butler, such unviable subjects emerge as the rejected outside that delineates and constructs the valid subject. In this light, "En el hemisferio sur" explores both the center and the constitutive outside of discourses of gender, not to reaffirm but to destabilize the system.

In the characters of Clara/Sonia and her nemesis, the male narrator of "En el hemisferio sur," Fernández Cubas questions the materiality of sex as a given and proposes ways of repeating the norms differently in order to broaden the field of bodies that matter. Traditional discursive constructs of the feminine—such as madwoman, whore, and young innocent—dominate the male narrator's attempts to define his identity in relation to women. Even Clara's snakeskin shoes—which are missing one heel the day she shows up distraught in his office—associate her metonymically with the ideal biblical helpmate, Eve, and the serpent, who precipitated the downfall of the mighty, righteous Adam. The narrator's feelings toward Clara are tangled in the ambivalence of these contradictory constructs of the feminine, against which he perceives himself only oppositionally, as a man in control or a man who is controlled.

Constructs of sex define far more than individuals in this story, however, for the narrator draws an indelible parallel between sex and writing. The inspiration for narrative creation wells from a feminine and implacable Voice. Much to his frustration, though, the writer impelled by "la imperiosa Voz" (Fernández Cubas 1988, 133) [the imperious Voice] (Fernández Cubas 1992, 84) is not he but Clara. Moreover, the narrator is obsessed by the feminine defiance of the blank page: "Pero el papel en blanco seguía ahí. Impertérrito, amenazante, lanzándome su perpetuo desafío, feminizándose por momentos y espetándome con voz saltarina: 'Anda, atrévete. Estoy aquí. Hunde en mi cuerpo esas maravillosas palabras que me harán daño'" (134–35) [But the blank page was still there. Unperturbed, menacing, launching its perpetual challenge, growing more feminine by the moment, and piercing me with a taunting voice: "Go ahead, be daring. Here I am. Sink into my body those marvelous words that will hurt me"] (84). Such an image personifies the blank page as the feminine receptacle, as the lack, to be filled by the masculine "instrument."

Drawing from Irigaray, Butler discusses the trope of the feminine lack as one that excludes the "true" feminine by setting up "the feminine" as a mere specular reflection of "the masculine":

> Disavowed, the remnant of the feminine survives as the *inscriptional space* of that phallogocentrism, the specular surface which receives the marks of a masculine signifying act only to give back a (false) reflection and guarantee of phallogocentric self-sufficiency, without making any contribution of its own. As a topos of the metaphysical tradition, this inscriptional space makes its appearance in Plato's *Timaeus* as the receptacle. . . . (Butler 1993, 39)

Butler recounts Irigaray's demonstration that the receptacle image in *Timaeus* usurps even the function of reproduction from the "true" feminine by positing her as passive: "In the place of a femininity that makes a contribution to reproduction, we have a phallic Form that reproduces only and always further versions of itself, and does this through the feminine, but with no assistance from her" (42). Of course, any concept of the "true" feminine must also be a construct. The point is to interrogate the function and power (or lack thereof) attributed to the feminine by the discourses that construct it. Interestingly, in "En el hemisferio sur," the blank page does not originate as feminine, but becomes increasingly feminine by the minute, "feminizándose por momentos" (Fernández Cubas 1988, 134). The gerund here suggests that feminization is a process or, to use Butler's term, a materialization. Through the image of the feminine blank page, the narrator reifies the classical affiliation of men with writing and productivity, and attempts to transpose the pen onto the phallus. Yet he cannot live up to this grandiose discourse of the masculine, and this feminine "lack" taunts him for his inability to do so.

This description of the vacant page closely follows the narrator's meditation on the way his frustrated efforts to inseminate his own creative production drain what little vitality his already less-than-desirable physique can muster. Aging, balding, and professionally mediocre at best, this man cannot comply with the ideal construct of masculinity. Pondering his performance anxiety, the narrator muses, "A mi manera, yo también había oído voces" (135) [In my own way, I, too, had heard voices] (85). If the Voice that controls Clara is a discourse that dictates her activities and even her identity, the male narrator, too, is subject to voices, discourses that construct and determine the way he should be as a man. Instead of merely exalting the feminine in order to subjugate the masculine, then, this story demonstrates how suffocating constructed limitations can be for any "body" who is subjugated by discourse without any hope of agency.

If the subject is shaped by discourse, does that formation indelibly, fatally determine the subject, or is it possible to modify its construction? This question may be seen as the implicit springboard of *Bodies That Matter*, as well as of Fernández Cubas's texts. For Butler, subject formation implies "a process of iterability, a regularized and constrained repetition of norms. And this repetition is not performed *by* a subject; this repetition is what enables a subject and constitutes the temporal condition for the subject" (Butler 1993, 95). A subject comes to be through its submission to already existing norms. It does not exist apart from or outside of those norms: "bodies only appear, only endure, only live within the productive constraints of certain highly gendered regulatory schemas" (xi). In that sense, there is no such entity as a voluntary subject who can get outside of discourse in order to reconstruct its subjectivity completely apart from discourse. Nonetheless, Butler points out that the reiterative nature of a subject's materialization through discourse implies an uncertainty that destabilizes the notion of absolute determinism: "That this reiteration is necessary is a sign that materialization is never quite complete, that bodies never quite comply with the norms by which their materialization is impelled. Indeed, it is the instabilities, the possibilities for rematerialization, opened up by this process that mark one domain in which the force of the regulatory law can be turned against itself. . . ." (2). Within the constraints of the norms that materialize them, subjects can alter their constitution by repeating those norms differently than the pattern that the regulations themselves impose.

In "En el hemisferio sur," Clara/Sonia as an author manipulates the norms of gendered discourse even as she necessarily reiterates them. Aware that the very language she uses to express herself is conditioned by sex, she manages to find slippage within its gendered limitations. This maneuverability comes into play in Sonia Kraskowa's dedication of her final novel, *Tornado*, to the narrator: "En aquel concurso de nombre lejano, tu cuento era el mejor. Alguien (lamentablemente no existe el femenino para ciertos pronombres personales) se encargó de ocultarlo a los ojos del jurado. ¿Sabremos olvidarlo?" (Fernández Cubas 1988, 152) [In the contest of distant name, your story was the best. Someone {unfortunately, there is no feminine form for certain personal pronouns} took charge of hiding it from the judges' eyes. Will we be able to forget?] (Fernández Cubas 1992, 92). In traditional Western discourse, the subject, the "I," comes into being always already marked by a gendered matrix, one that presupposes the masculine as the center and the feminine as a reflection and, by extension, as an exclusion and erasure. Here in Fernández Cubas's text, the excluded feminine comes back to haunt the masculine identity implicitly attached to the "I," to question its authority and to decenter it from power.[11]

If the phallus, associated with the pen, is the emblem of this masculine power, Clara appropriates both tools for herself by being a powerful and prolific writer.[12] Rejecting discursive constructions of the feminine as passivity, lack, receptacle, or a blank page, Clara is active and productive: she wields the pen to express herself on the page. Significantly, her creation is not autonomous, nor totally voluntary—she is not exempt from the Voice nor from the rule of language. Nonetheless, she manages to manipulate discourse to question the mutually exclusive nature of the gendered regulations that define both herself and the narrator. Displacing the masculine as the origin of discourse and power, she transfers the power of the phallus/pen to herself by anticipating the narrator's actions and thoughts in her text. If this story is about the anxiety of being entirely predetermined by discursive constructs, Clara learns to modify them by manipulating established discourses for her own constructive ends: "Fue entonces cuando decidí poner en práctica mi sueño. Hasta aquel momento no había hecho otra cosa que escribir la vida; ahora, iba a ser la vida quien se encargara de contradecir, destruir o confirmar mis sueños. . ." (152) [It was then that I decided to put my dream into practice. Up until that moment I had only written life; now, it was life that would take charge of contradicting, destroying or confirming my dreams. . .] (92). Instead of writing in imitation of life, she alters life to repeat her dreams, which themselves can be seen as constructs of her mind.

If Clara gains so much agency, however, then how does one interpret her death in the story? If readers believe that Clara killed herself because she could not resolve the opposing terms of her mixed Northern and Southern parentage, then it would seem that her expression of agency was short-lived and—from a fatalistic point of view—perhaps even futile. On the other hand, this conclusion can only be surmised by interpreting a lack in the text, because the narrator never describes exactly how she died. Furthermore, he is markedly silent—and seemingly unsurprised—when the secretary informs him of the writer's death:

—¿Sabe ya la noticia?
Me limité a colocar el libro sobre los otros.
—Aquí tiene el diario. Dicen que, en los últimos tiempos, se encontraba muy deprimida. . . Usted la conoció mucho, ¿verdad?
Mi cabeza asintió. La mujer permanecía a mi lado, esperando pacientemente una opinión personal que no tenía la menor intención de proporcionarle. (Fernández Cubas 1988, 147)

["Have you heard the news yet?"
I merely put the book back on top of the others.
"Here's the paper. They say that lately she had been very depressed. . . . You knew her well, didn't you?"
I nodded my head. The woman remained at my side, patiently waiting for a personal opinion that I had no intention of giving her.] (Fernández Cubas 1992, 90)

One could conjecture that the narrator killed Clara/Sonia in order to steal her story. After all, whereas initially he plans to tell Clara to write it, after her death he plots to tell the tale himself. In any case this story dramatizes the suffocation of the subject—whether male or female—that believes itself to be entirely determined by discourse.

The two subjects in this story relate discourse, and relate *to* discourse, differently. Whereas Clara appears to recognize and redeploy discourse, the narrator blindly accepts its effects. Taking refuge in the hackneyed images with which he represents both Clara (whore, young innocent, madwoman) and his Aunt Alicia (patient, delicate, long-suffering mother figure), the narrator never learns to critique, evaluate, and manipulate the discourses that determine his world. He needs the comfort of phallogocentrism, where he perceives himself as the center of matronly care and where his word is the authority in the narrative text. Yet who is really the author, the originator of the work? Although the text of "En el hemisferio sur" would seem to consist of the narrator's words, we never know if those words were already written or not in *Tornado* because he, and thus readers, never peruses Clara's entire novel.

Ultimately, any attempt to trace the origin of this text becomes a dizzying array of possible placements and displacements of authority. If Clara dreamed the opening scene of this story, then woke up and decided to enact the story to replicate the scene constructed in her dream (the scene on the first page of "En el hemisferio sur"), then lived out the rest of the events and wrote them in her novel, which the narrator opens midway and reads—only to find his own actions transcribed in it—at what point does he narrate "En el hemisferio sur"? Does he become the narrator after he reads *Tornado*, thus placing his narration at a level superior to Clara/Sonia's and making his the "definitive" version? Otherwise, is it possible that Sonia's novel dictates his narration—and perhaps even intercalates his narration within itself? One might even wildly speculate that the narrator dreamed up the whole plot on his own. In the end, the spiraling sites of narrative control hardly seem to matter at all because the text obliterates any notion of inviolate authority.

The woman writer's novel calls into question the power of masculine origination within the very discourse—narrative—that the phallus/pen has used to establish itself as the first and only authority. Hence the language Clara/Sonia uses to condemn herself as a mere replica, "una farsante. Una vil y repugnante farsante" (138) [a fake. A vile and repugnant fake] (86), is ultimately aimed also at the narrator who, once displaced from being the origin to being the output of discourse, recognizes himself constructed in those words. In the end, both sexes propagate discourse even as they are produced through it. The whole discursive dichotomy of man versus woman hinges on a foundational tactic that creates the boundaries of one subject by excluding others. In an echo of the unsettling "otherness" of the clock from Baghdad, Clara is most terrified when she realizes that the Voice possesses a foreign accent—which suggests that the very discourse that shapes her is "other" than herself. This difference of the other as the constitutive element of the self is expressed metaphorically by the dichotomy of the Northern versus the Southern Hemisphere, the opposing heritages of Clara/Sonia's parents.

Hence North is defined by South, man by woman, the familiar by the foreign, each excluding the other to form itself.

"Los altillos de Brumal"

As the title story of the collection, "Los altillos de Brumal" ["The Attics of Brumal"] may be seen to epitomize the focus on discursive subjectivity that dominates the other stories. "El reloj de Bagdad" makes the privileging of one gender over another problematic and undermines the traditional view of genders as mutually exclusive constructs. "En el hemisferio sur" shows that discursive constructs, despite their tendency to elevate one gender while marginalizing another, determine subjects but also enable them to manipulate, to some extent, their own construction. "Los altillos de Brumal" continues the dialogue on discursive constructs of gender by foregrounding the relationship between subjects that matter and those bodies that do not matter in and of themselves, but that serve the vital function of defining, by contrast, the ones that do. If the first two stories of the collection deal with the construction of intelligible bodies, conventionally conceived of as masculine or feminine, then "Los altillos de Brumal" explores how gender constraints also produce unintelligible bodies that haunt the nether regions of acceptability. This story questions such exclusions to investigate how the "outside" constitutes the center and thus forms an essential part of identity.

Those "unthinkable" bodies that occupy the outside of normality are a fundamental preoccupation of Judith Butler's *Bodies That Matter*. Butler wrote this text partially in response to criticism that her previous work, *Gender Trouble*, ignored the concrete materiality of the body and portrayed gender as a completely voluntary and changeable condition. *Bodies That Matter* clarifies the fact that, although the body is indeed "real" and material, it operates within gendered constructions that determine the way it is perceived. Butler points to the fundamental link between the process of "assuming" a sex and the concept of identification. Furthermore, she highlights the discursive means by which the gendered matrix permits some sexed identifications while foreclosing others: "This exclusionary matrix by which subjects are formed thus requires the simultaneous production of a domain of abject beings, those who are not yet 'subjects,' but who form the constitutive outside to the domain of the subject...." (Butler 1993, 3). It is precisely this domain of the "abject," the "foreclosed," or the "excluded" that precludes gender constructions from being absolutely deterministic, for the existence of the outside ordains the possibility of questioning the right and supremacy of the center. Drawing from Derrida and Irigaray, Butler builds her case on the idea that a binary opposition spawns its own destruction—or de*construction*—by producing an exclusion that questions the inviolate authority of that binary: "A constitutive or relative outside is, of course, composed of a set of exclusions that are nevertheless *internal* to that system as its own nonthematizable necessity. It emerges within the system as incoherence, disruption, a threat to its own systematicity" (39). In other words, if the beings outside the system should penetrate the borders that exclude them, they could call into question the viability of the system itself.

Through the depiction of the narrator's home village of Brumal as an unrepresentable place that is rendered unworthy by those at the center, this story emphasizes the discourses that construct the subject, the narrator/protagonist, Adriana. Key to that formation are the influences that shape her as a woman. Although on the surface Brumal appears to have archetypally feminine qualities, it blurs the borders between the feminine and masculine and thus questions the validity of their differences. The protagonist's exploration of Brumal unmasks those discourses as constructs that can be manipulated and invested with different meanings. In the process, she confronts what lurks at the limits of the practices of gender and propriety that shape her.

In this tale Adriana recalls how, at a young age, she and her family moved away from her father's hometown of Brumal and how she had to learn to make her way in the world under her mother's urgent admonishments to forget all about Brumal after the father dies. Yet her past reclaims her attention one day when she receives some succulent strawberry jam to taste for her magazine cooking column. Not only does she detect that the amazing jam contains no strawberries, but she is able to discern that the faded label reads "Brumal." This mysterious item leads her on a search of her past and her abandoned childhood, as she returns to Brumal and discovers that things there are not necessarily as they appear to be. Ultimately, the ambiguous confrontation with a part of herself that her mother always urged her to deny leads the narrator to view her life quite differently.

As Adriana recalls her post-Brumal childhood, everything about her father's town contrasts sharply with the image of acceptability fashioned by her mother and the school for girls that the child attends after her father's death. The young Adriana's attempt to connect her identity with Brumal holds no weight in the realm of her new school: symbolically, Brumal is not even represented—or representable—on the school's map. Marginalized as the different and undesirable outsider in her new town, the young girl quickly learns the ways of these strange environs, wherein "[l]a diferencia estaba en mí y, si quería librarme de futuras y terribles afrentas, debería esforzarme por aprender el código de aquel mundo [. . .]" [The difference was in me, and if I wished to free myself from future, terrible affronts, I would have to force myself into learning the code of that world {. . .}].[13] The code of behavior the child must learn at school is mirrored at home by her mother, who can only communicate with her daughter by performing traditional womanly tasks. The mother constantly tries to erase Brumal from their past by admonishing, *"Huimos de la miseria, hija. . . Recordarla es sumergirse en ella"* (Fernández Cubas 1988, 157) [*We are fleeing from misery, my child. . . To remember it is to become submerged in it*] (Fernández Cubas 1990b, 55). Butler notes that, in the play between the inside/outside of the realm of right, those in the center cannot afford to recognize the outside that marks off the contours of their identity: "the subject is constituted through the force of exclusion and abjection, one which produces a constitutive outside to the subject, an abjected outside, which is, after all, 'inside' the subject as its own founding repudiation" (Butler 1993, 3). The mother's erasure of the unacceptable outside, Brumal, in order to affirm her own sense of power heralds her imprisonment in a place of imbalance and unrest, "ese extraño universo que le negaba el reposo" (Fernández Cubas 1988, 159) [that strange universe that denied her rest] (Fernández Cubas 1990b, 56).

On another level, nonetheless, the figure of the *Madre*—whose capitalized name indicates her importance—seems to be a laudable force of change in the story, for she strives to alter the parameters that repress women. Associating Brumal and her marriage with imprisoning power, she attempts to give her daughter a more autonomous future that would preclude her dependence on a man who might diminish her status and her freedom. The mother's lifelong devotion to her daughter and her nonchalance toward her twin sons culminates in an inversion of their gender roles. When she manages to sell the last bit of land her family owned, the mother sends Adriana to college and gives the boys the house. Upon the mother's death, however, Adriana abandons her career in order to write a cooking column, thus reincorporating into her identity the realm of the feminine that her mother urged her to reject on a professional level. Whereas Madre seems conventional, on the one hand, and liberal on the other, both of her approaches depend upon a binary structure that sets up genders as mutually exclusive domains of power in contention with each other. When the mother leaves Brumal, she wears her coat inside out, as if to symbolically exorcise herself of its power. In a parallel manner, she inverts the sides in the gender game to appropriate more power for woman.

However, like Olvido in "El reloj de Bagdad," she does not question the viability of the boundary that separates woman from man.

Enticed by the nebulous memories evoked by the Brumalian jam that she receives because of her cooking column, the adult Adriana embarks on a journey to Brumal to recover her excluded past. Finding this place is a challenge, for not only is Brumal nonexistent in the official ecclesiastic and civic records she searches, but it scarcely survives in her mother's town even in the memory of one resident, who implies that "Brumal" is a less-than-acceptable name for a place of unremarkable importance. Once Adriana finally arrives in Brumal, she discovers that its discourse is radically different than that of the center, her mother's chosen world.[14] Whereas the schoolteacher in that realm refused to refer to Adriana's paternal surname because she considered it to be foreign and hence insignificant, that name figures prominently in the book of records of the Brumalian church. There the protagonist meets a priest, who invites her into his home, serves her intoxicating strawberry liquor, and leads her into an attic, which is a virtual laboratory of strawberry jam.

About to lose herself in the written texts and culinary delights (which are the most alluring texts of all) the woman pauses at the sound of voices, echoes of her playmates in Brumal. The little girls' secret language that the narrator remembers expresses their exultation and epitomizes the different nature of Brumal:

> Sí; no tenía más que pegar los ojos al cristal para verlas y oírlas:
> > *Otnas Sen reiv se yo-h*
> > *Sotreum sol ed a-íd*
>
> Y yo, de pronto conocía la respuesta. Sin ningún esfuerzo podía replicar:
> > *Sabmut sal neib arre-ic*
> > *Ort ned nedeuq es e-uq*
>
> No necesitaba implorar *¿raguj siajed em? ¿raguj siajed em?. . .* porque formaba parte de sus juegos. Me estaban esperando y me llamaban: *Anairda. . . Anairda. . . Anairda. . .* (Fernández Cubas 1988, 178–79)

> [Yes; I only had to press my face against the glass to see and hear them:
> > *Yadirf Doog si yad-ot*
> > *Dae deht fo yad eh-t*
>
> And I suddenly knew the answer. Without any effort I could reply:
> > *Sevarg ehtl lew es-olc*
> > *Nih tiw yats yeh t-os*
>
> I did not need to plead *yalp em tel, yalp em tel. . .* because I was part of their games. They were waiting for me and calling me: *Anairda. . . Anairda. . . Anairda. . .*] (Fernández Cubas 1990b, 69–70)

When read in the traditional Western manner, from left to right, this language looks exotic and mysterious, its meaning unbounded. However, the code turns out to be Castilian written in reverse, with modifications in the division of syllables and in the capitalization, rendering a common poem about Good Friday. Much like Olla's language in "La ventana del jardín" (*Mi hermana Elba*), this defamiliarization suggests that, as an expression of a given logic and view of the world, any language is an arbitrary construct. In breaking the accepted rules, the girls' secret code explores the possibilities that abound in what standard Castilian leaves out, and heralds the fact that discourse is ultimately a creation that can be metamorphosed into something vastly "other."

Similarly, the attic of Brumal transmutes to something "other," from a delightful haven to a dreadful prison. When the protagonist tries to leave, she overhears the priest telling someone that the new housekeeper arrived that morning, as a key locks Adriana in the attic. The narrator does not remember what happens next, except that she evokes the memory of her mother as she fights against her imprisonment in Brumal. Somehow, she eventually finds herself running through the cold night, and is picked up, bleeding, incoherent, and reeking of alcohol. Returning to the familiar disorder of her apartment after spending a month in a psychiatric hospital, Adriana cancels all her obligations and spends weeks feverishly writing down her experiences in Brumal.[15] Then, feeling watched by the accusing eyes of her mother's photograph as she packs for a postponed trip with her editor, Adriana finally realizes how her mother always manipulated her and forced her to reject Brumal out of her fear of difference. Embracing Brumal as an integral part of herself, she heads to the train station at the end of the story and loses herself in dreams of Brumal, the haven of her past and the locus of her future.

It is possible that the text of "Los altillos de Brumal" is the narrative that Adriana constructs once she returns to her apartment. In this light, one can see her understanding and acceptance of Brumal and herself deepen as the narrative progresses, from an initial fixation on trying to "ordenar los principales acontecimientos de mi vida" (155) [set forth the principal events of my life] (53), to an increasing acceptance of the memory lapses, the inconsistencies and the unexplainable events that pervade her narrative, culminating with her total lack of explanation of how she escaped from Brumal. Finally, Adriana realizes that "reason" will only impede her process of reconstructing her past, of reconstructing herself: "tenía que seguir escribiendo, anotando todo cuanto se me ocurriese, dejando volar la pluma a su placer, silenciando las voces de la razón; esa rémora, censura, obstáculo, que se interponía de continuo entre mi vida y la verdad. . ."

(184) [I had to keep writing, noting down everything that occurred to me, letting my pen fly as it pleased, silencing the voices of reason: that obstruction, that censor, that obstacle interposing itself continually between my life and truth. . .] (73). The narrator has come to question the supremacy, the centrality, of the discourse that designates what is realistic and what is logical. Not only does she embrace the liberating possibilities of uncertainty and forgetfulness in her narrative, but she writes it deliriously unaware of the constraints of time, just as when she was in the attic of Brumal.

If the discursive borders that define the center become blurred, then those that delineate the abject zone of Brumal are no less imprecise. As one book in its attic suggests, Brumalian logic is not simply a reversal of standard order: "en el libro no hallé sones infantiles, ni canciones de rueda, ni me bastó, para captar el sentido, invertir el orden de los párrafos o leer, como en nuestros juegos, de derecha a izquierda" (Fernández Cubas 1988, 179–80) [in the book I found no childish sounds, nor songs sung in the round, nor was it enough to capture the sense, to invert the order of the paragraphs or to read, as in our games, from right to left] (Fernández Cubas 1990b, 70). In many ways, Brumal is a contradictory and uncertain place, appropriate for a town whose name evokes "fog." It would seem to defy the law of gravity and conventional norms of propriety. Nothing happens when Adriana tries to blow the dust off the book of records in the church; moreover, the priest seems oblivious to his filthy home but apologizes for the disorder in the impeccably kept attic. Does dirt, then, not respond in direct opposition to cleanliness in this realm? Also unexplained is how the totally barren land of Brumal can be used for the production of extraordinarily succulent strawberry jam, which seems to contain no strawberries.

Brumal is a place of paradox. It appears to be a site of discovery and liberation, yet Adriana is literally imprisoned in the attic there, just as her mother felt metaphorically trapped there. The question arises, then, of whether enclosure is a purely negative phenomenon, for while Adriana is within the closed attic walls, she discovers infinite passageways of knowledge and entertainment within the covers of the books and within the mysterious vials and vases.[16] To label Brumal as a site of "the feminine" is also problematic, for it is the hometown of Adriana's father, whereas it is despised by Adriana's mother and ridiculed by Adriana's female schoolteacher and female classmates. Highlighted in the title of a collection of stories that foreground the complexities of sexual roles, Brumal notably eludes definitive associations with sex in order to destabilize and undermine the exclusions by which genders are forged. It is neither "masculine" nor "feminine," neither completely open nor fully enclosed, neither order incarnate nor chaos unleashed, neither run solely by scientific laws nor ruled purely by instinct. Brumal is a combination of all these forces, and, as a result, it is precisely none of them. Instead, it may be seen as a place that is excluded from discursive categories because it defies the logic that defines those divisions. More aptly still, it is a construction of a logic, or illogic, that reaches beyond simple binary definitions. This may be why Adriana's mother associated it with misery: it prohibited her from wielding power according to the only rules—binary rules—that she knew.

Above all, "Los altillos de Brumal" illustrates that the borders of identity are never completely defined, but always drawn and redrawn, including and excluding, constructing the subject only in relation to what she or he cannot—or will not—comprehend. This zone of the foreclosed and forbidden must be explored as a space of empowerment, for it is as vital to preserve the outside as a challenge to discursive constructs as it is to question what unjust exclusions are banished there and what possibilities are harbored there. A story about coming to understand the exclusions that constitute one's own identity, "Los altillos de Brumal" makes evident that, although the abject may well be the subject's undoing, without it the subject could not exist at all.[17]

"La noche de Jezabel"

As the final story of *Los altillos de Brumal*, "La noche de Jezabel" ["Jezabel's Night"] culminates the collection's exploration of the formation and mediation of gender through discursive practices. In "El reloj de Bagdad," "En el hemisferio sur," and "Los altillos de Brumal," the characters who alter the limitations of their gendered subjectivity do so by interpreting the discourse of their gender differently than what regulatory norms would impose. "La noche de Jezabel" accentuates that the interpretation of discourse, with a play on the dual meaning of "interpretation" as *reading* and as *performance*, is key to the project of agency.[18] This final story underscores the way discourse, specifically narrative discourse, is constructed and repeated, and thus consolidated as true and right. Centering on a stormy winter evening when a group of people gathers to tell scary stories around the fire, the tale highlights the narrative webs spun to encircle various characters in their discursive limits, particularly the limits that define gender. All the narrations are subsumed into the discourse of the main narrator, a nameless woman who repeats other characters' tales along with her own interpretation of their stories. Finally, although her narrative discourse—the text we read—follows the tenets of a ghost story, it interprets and enacts the script slightly differently, complying with and yet defying the discourses of gender and genre.

The discourse of gender emerges in the opening tale as the narrator reiterates the true story that her best friend and lover, an older doctor named Arganza, loves to tell, while she comments on the deletions that Arganza has made from the tale over the years. When Arganza had just graduated, after carousing his way through medical school, he was called by a guard in the middle of the night. Hoping that the case would prove to be nothing, or that the patient would have already died, the poorly trained doctor goes to the scene and finds a young man lifeless on the ground. After checking his pulse and eyes, the neophyte pronounces the man dead and goes for a walk. Ten minutes later, the doctor returns to find that the body has disappeared and that the trembling guards, who also had briefly left the scene, do not know what happened. They discover a trail of blood, however, which leads them to the closed door of the mayor's house. The cadaver lies on the threshold, exactly as before, except that now it wears an expensive jacket and smells of an intense, sweet perfume. This corpse is literally a body excluded from the center (the mayor's house), a dead body that the guards and the doctor do not know how to explain. Unable to interpret what lies on the outside and eager to conceal their delinquency from their assigned duty that evening, the men report the second death outside the mayor's house as the original one. The youth's status as a reject is further inscribed when, because of his sin of suicide, he is buried outside the holy cemetery of the church—the zone of the abject that defines, by contrast, the periphery of Christianity. Scattered rose petals mysteriously appear on his grave and, although many of the graves are adorned with rose petals, the townspeople decide that these tokens are from the old mayor's lovely young wife, whom they believe to be the lover of the youth.

As the townspeople comment on what happened, basing their interpretation on a version of events that was radically altered in the first place by the doctor and the guards, they magnify the story into the discourse of the fallen woman who tries to corrupt man. The narrating voice takes a sarcastic view of the people's eagerness to impose such a paradigm even in defiance of other logical explanations such as the wind blowing the flowers astray:

> Pero los ánimos se hallaban demasiado enardecidos para rendirse ante una explicación tan simple, y la imagen de la virtuosa veinteañera, a quien, hasta hacía muy poco, todos compadecían, fue cobrando con irremisible rapidez los rasgos de una bíblica adúltera, de una castiza malcasada, de una perversa devoradora de hombres a los que seducía con los encantos de su

cuerpo para abandonarlos tras saciar sus inconfesables apetitos. (Fernández Cubas 1988, 194)

[But the spirits were too inflamed to surrender before such a simple explanation, and the image of the virtuous twenty-year-old—with whom, until recently, everyone sympathized—began taking on with unpardonable speed the traits of a biblical adulteress, of a poorly married trueborn, of a perverse devourer of men, whom she seduced with the delights of her body only to abandon them after sating her shameful appetites.]

The woman herself, who is never seen nor heard directly in the story, receives her characterization from the discursive construction of others in the tale. That characterization expands as the town reconstructs her as the violator of several discursive codes: as a *bíblica adúltera*, she sins against the mores of Christian fidelity; as a *castiza malcasada*, she breaches structures of social class; and as a *perversa devoradora de hombres*, she violates the proprieties of gender.

Such multiple identities cannot be completely separated. On the contrary, as Butler notes, they intermingle with and inform one another: "these identifications are invariably imbricated in one another, the vehicle for one another: a gender identification can be made in order to repudiate or participate in a race identification; what counts as 'ethnicity' frames and eroticizes sexuality, or can itself be a sexual marking" (Butler 1993, 116). Of course, the danger of the *perversa devoradora de hombres* is that, by violating the gender construction of the passive woman, she implicitly threatens every category of identity that is based on binary opposition, whether it be race, class, religion, or innumerable others. That is to say, by violating the power hierarchy of masculine/feminine, the devourer menaces the sanctity of all binary oppositions. Whereas the feminine permeates the woman's identities of *adúltera* and *castiza*, as seen in the feminine endings of the Spanish words, the peril of the feminine in the Fernández Cubas passage is precisely that it refuses to obey any boundary it encounters. The fearsome specter of the perverse devourer of men, long held to be a catalyst for the construction of borders that confine and control women, instead may be a figment contrived after the fact to justify those borders that were drawn long ago.

It is unclear whether the critical commentary in the passage on the mayor's wife comes from Arganza's voice or the main narrator's that overlays it, although one suspects that it is the latter because it is she who is critical of all she observes. Here the narrating voice condemns the people's eagerness to construct the young woman as the evil seductress, a ghostly Sucubus figure who takes what she wants from men. The evidence that confirmed the "truth" of the woman's malevolence for the townspeople humorously underlines that the creation and propagation of this discursive subject position is a blind act:

> El día, en fin, en que una vieja, parapetada tras sus gruesas gafas de carey, aseguró haber distinguido, en la noche sin luna, la figura de una mujer envuelta en una capa negra merodeando por las cercanías del camposanto, todos, hasta los más prudentes, identificaron aquella loca fantasía con los remordimientos de la malmaridada, negaron a los vientos la capacidad de manifestarse por ráfagas y, con el plácet del párroco, sufragaron una serie de misas por el alma del desdichado, con la firme convicción de que, en el umbral de la muerte, la fe había retornado a su espíritu afligido consiguiendo pronunciar—aunque sólo fuera con el corazón—el Dulce Nombre de Jesús. (Fernández Cubas 1988, 194)

> [In short, the day when an elderly woman, protected behind her thick Carey glasses, affirmed that she distinguished, in the moonless night, the figure of a woman wrapped in a black cape prowling around the vicinity of the cemetery, everyone, even the most prudent ones, identified that daft fantasy with the remorse of the ill-married one, denied the winds the capacity to manifest themselves in gusts and, with the approval of the parish priest, they paid for a series of masses for the unfortunate's soul, with the firm conviction that, on the threshold of death, faith had returned to his afflicted spirit managing to utter—even if it were only with his heart—the Sweet Name of Jesus.]

This passage is an entertaining example of what Bakhtin calls the effect of "double-voicing" from indirect discourse. By recounting indirectly the people's words and Arganza's words, but subjugating their voices to her own sarcastic perspective, the main narrator gives a humorous and yet caustic rendition of the people's point of view. Moreover, the Catholic litany, *el Dulce Nombre de Jesús*, evokes the ironic intonation of the chorus of women at the end of García Lorca's *Bodas de sangre* [Blood Wedding] ("Dulces clavos, dulce cruz, dulce nombre de Jesús" [Sweet nails, sweet cross, sweet name of Jesus] {García Lorca 1985, 122}), which criticizes the glorification of suffering and death in society. The main narrator's irony in the Fernández Cubas passage also accentuates the possibility that the people embrace the dead youth into the zone of Christian acceptability only as a ploy in their expulsion of the mayor's wife to the outside. Eventually, their archetypal gender construction persecutes the mayor's wife so much that she flees the town.

The narrator's criticism of Arganza becomes direct when she includes in her version the details that her friend chooses to leave out of his. She adds that the doctor, too, left the town on the same train as the mayor's wife, but was snubbed disdainfully by that lady when he tried to kiss her hand. Reeling from this rejection, all Arganza could think of was his erroneous and ill-fated pronouncement of death when he first saw the young man's body. Arganza no longer recounts his guilt-ridden encounter on the train, however, for he renders his discourse to serve his own ends: "Y así, la figura de aquel joven, inexperto y asustado médico iba adquiriendo, día a día, mayor juventud, inexperiencia y miedo [. . .]; y la desgraciada e indefensa alcaldesa, cuya hermosura se acrecentaba por momentos, terminaba erigiéndose en la víctima-protagonista de odios ancestrales, envidias soterradas y latentes anhelos de pasionales y escandalosos acontecimientos" [And so the figure of that young, inexpert and frightened doctor acquired, day by day, greater youth, inexperience and fear {. . .}; and the unfortunate and defenseless mayor's wife, whose beauty was growing by the moment, ended up being set up as the victim-protagonist of ancestral hatreds, buried envies and latent longing for passionate and scandalous events] (Fernández Cubas 1988, 196). Needing to project himself as the guileless witness of a scandal instead of revealing himself as a bumbler and the object of a persecuted woman's disdain, the man ends up earning the disdain of the narrator herself: "Arganza había conseguido arrinconar lo inexplicable en favor de un simple, común y cotidiano drama rural" [Arganza had managed to push aside the inexplicable in favor of a simple, common and daily country drama] (196). Arganza converts a fascinating story about the prohibited outside into a boring repetition of an old discursive code of literature that denigrates woman and, consequently, man. The main narrator's account of this tale shows the process by which a discourse is constructed and reified as true and original. Moreover, by relegating Arganza's story to her own interpreting voice, the narrator illustrates the power of repeating a discourse in order to alter the ends for which it was originally intended.

   The power of "interpreting" by performing a part as well as by analyzing a script comes into play as other characters' stories are introduced into the overall narrative text. When the narrator and Arganza bump into Jezabel, a high school friend of the main narrator's, Jezabel presumptuously invites herself and her cousin to the narrator's dilapidated beach house to tell stories. The designated evening turns out to be violently rainy, and as the guests arrive the narrator is forced to find them dry clothes to wear. This changing of costumes invites the metaphor of a performance, an idea that occurs to the narrator herself: "Constaté que existía más de un pequeño error en la precipitada elección de vestuario" [I observed that there was more than one small error in the hasty choice of wardrobe] (202). The "unsuitable" attire of the cast accentuates that these characters are not quite what the narrator expects.

As the personality of each guest unfolds, the narrator increasingly questions her own role in the performance. Although the narrator is the hostess, the evening's events seem to be dominated by the others: Arganza starts the narrative chain with his story of forbidden seduction, and during the rest of the night he becomes an admirer of Jezabel's wiles. Mortimer, a fastidious Englishman invited by Arganza, tells the story of how, when he was a small boy, his mother told him how to recognize ghosts on first sight. The pale young man invited by Jezabel bores them all with a pedantic explanation of seemingly inexplicable phenomena. Finally, Laura, whom the narrator assumes to be Jezabel's cousin, ruptures the somber mood by greeting Arganza's and every other tragic or ghostly tale with boisterous laughter. Because the storm has knocked out the telephone lines and the lights, and the stove has suddenly broken, the narrator feels that she cannot perform her expected role of hostess: "Me pregunté por mi verdadero papel en aquella cena sin cena en la que los invitados se permitían prescindir olímpicamente de la figura del anfitrión" [I wondered about my real role at that dinner without dinner in which the guests allowed themselves to disregard olympically the figure of the hostess] (203–4). Indeed, the narrator feels that she has no role at all in this play and that, to all appearances, Jezabel is running the show.

As indicated by the story's title, Jezabel attempts to establish herself as the center of attention on this night; to do so, she slips into the role of seductress. She thus corresponds to the legend of her biblical namesake, the Israeli queen of Phoenician origin who was associated with seducing the Israelis away from their God with witchcraft; in essence, Queen Jezabel was the "other" who menaced man and God. While Fernández Cubas's Jezabel plots to seduce Arganza, who seems to fall easily to her charms, she also performs as Scheherezade, seducing the rest of the audience with her storytelling powers. Jezabel's story—the only tale that truly captivates everyone—concerns her great-grandfather, a painter who revels in the ecstasy of capturing his wife's stunning beauty on canvas. In the supreme moment when he finishes the painting and pronounces it to be life itself, he turns to his beloved wife and finds that she is dead. Only the main narrator recognizes Jezabel's performance as mere mimesis: "Una bonita historia. Edgar Allan Poe la tituló, hace más de cien años, 'El retrato oval'" [A nice story. Over a hundred years ago Edgar Allen Poe called it "The Oval Portrait"] (Fernández Cubas 1988, 204). In her co-optation and masquerade of Poe's story as her own original creation, Jezabel highlights the fact that discursive repetition is never completely original. Butler holds that discourse derives its authority from the concealment of itself as the reproduction of a discursive norm. Indeed, far from being inceptive, performativity cites, repeats, and refers to a discourse in order to set up its viability.[19] At best, then, Jezabel only functions as a palimpsest, superimposing her rendition over the discursive model whose lines direct her performance.

Jezabel's story highlights the fact that "originality," if it exists at all, occurs only to the extent that one reiterates discursive norms differently. The stories of all the characters are just variations on a theme, or on a discourse—an Edgar Allan Poe story (Jezabel's appropriation), a country drama (Arganza's tale), a metaphysical treatise (the pale young man's lecture), or a ghost story (Mortimer's account). Mortimer's tale might be seen as an example of the marvelous, wherein supernatural beings are accepted as playing a role. The pale young man's discourse might be conceived of as the uncanny, for he explains how seemingly mysterious happenings such as the broken stove and telephone are simply natural, logical occurrences. "La noche de Jezabel" itself includes all the elements of a good ghost story: a dark and stormy night; the ominous setting of a remote, run-down house; mysterious events (the blackout could be "explained" by the storm, but the broken stove that spontaneously starts working again at the end of the evening is certainly enigmatic); and, most importantly, the ghost itself—not the pale young man, as the narrator supposes at one point, but Laura. As several critics have noted, "La noche de Jezabel" embraces the genre of the fantastic, for readers cannot really be sure whether the occurrences were supernatural or not.[20] By replicating the genre of the fantastic, then, "La noche de Jezabel," too, cites a discursive norm for its authority. In contrast to the other discourses cited in this text, however, "La noche de Jezabel" questions the very norms it repeats.

Although Fernández Cubas's tale reiterates the discourse of a ghost story, Laura hardly complies with Mortimer's or any other conventional constructions of a ghost. Interestingly, Mortimer's story is the only one that the narrator directly quotes at length; one might say that she "cites" his discourse directly in order to "re-cite" it, or repeat it, differently. Mortimer's constructs of ghosts are divided between masculine and feminine genders, which incarnate archetypal characterizations: "Una palidez excesiva" [An excessive paleness]; "tristeza *infinita*" [*infinite* sadness]; "una preferencia excluyente por dos colores, el blanco y el negro" [an exclusive preference for two colors, black and white]; and female ghosts typically wear "un traje vaporoso, un tejido liviano de color blanco, que se agite con el viento y deje entrever, discretamente, los encantos de un cuerpo del que ya no queda constancia" [a vaporous outfit, a light web the color white that flutters in the wind and discreetly allows a glimpse of the delights of a body of which there is no longer any evidence] (Fernández Cubas 1988, 210–11). Fernández Cubas's ghost is indeed an unknown figure. It turns out that Laura holds no relation to Jezabel, who later says sarcastically that she had assumed that Laura was the cleaning lady. Yet this stranger breaks Mortimer's model of a ghost, for she is chubby instead of sensual, rosy-pink instead of pallid-white, rambunctious instead of mournful, ordinary-looking instead of ethereal. She even breaches the dress code: rather than enveloping her in vaporous and revealing billows of black or white, Laura's choice of a colorful kimono precludes associations with binary oppositions of white/black, even as its layers evoke depth and mystery rather than transparency.

Just as Jezabel used both physical and narrative powers to spin her seductive web, Laura, too, may be seen on both levels as a would-be seductress. Essentially, Laura is the physically nonseductive woman who then seduces everyone into living and believing a ghost story, if only for a while. In doing so, she transforms each character into his or her own opposite—if only momentarily. At the end of the story, Laura disappears, leaving behind only the kimono and an inscription on the ground: "GRACIAS POR TAN MAGNIFICA NOCHE. NUNCA LA OLVIDARE" [THANK YOU FOR SUCH A MAGNIFICENT NIGHT. I WILL NEVER FORGET IT] (220). After seeing the inscription on the porch disappear in the wind, the dry, aged Mortimer, whom the narrator earlier could not imagine as a child who saw a ghost, "temblaba como una hoja y había adquirido el aspecto de un niño asustado" [trembled like a leaf and had taken on the look of a frightened child] (220). The pasty-white young man, too, seems more human: "Un saludable rubor campesino había teñido de púrpura las lívidas mejillas del joven de mirada profunda" [A healthy country flush had tinted purple the livid cheeks of the young man of the deep gaze] (220). The ravishing Jezabel, intent on vanquishing the narrator in any way possible, suddenly loses some of her strength and beauty: "Jezabel, súbitamente demacrada, se apoyó en mi hombro" [Jezabel, suddenly wasted away, supported herself on my shoulder] (220–21). The narrator herself, who had earlier been spooked by the shadows on the wall, now perceives in them a friendlier apparition: "Me fijé en las sombras oscilantes de la pared y, por un extraño efecto que no me detuve en analizar, me pareció como si mi amiga y yo peináramos trenzas y ambas nos halláramos inclinadas sobre un pupitre en una de las largas y lejanas tardes de estudio" [I noticed the oscillating shadows on the wall and, through some strange effect that I didn't stop to analyze, it seemed to me as if my friend and I were in braids and both of us were bent over a desk during one of the long and distant afternoons of study] (221). The seductive anomaly of Laura as a ghost has lulled them all and tempered the boundaries that characterize them.

In function, then, if not in appearance, Laura complies with the discourse of the seductress. Indeed, her physique and her manner of performing her role are the very elements that undermine the validity of this discourse of woman, even as she iterates it. Laura's performance as a different kind of seductress, and as a different kind of ghost, radically alters the script and encourages a distinct interpretation of enticement. Thus she serves as a foil for the discourse of seduction represented by Jezabel and described in stories by other guests. She envelops herself in that discourse, much as she dons the narrator's kimono; the ways in which both coverings fit poorly serve to question their suitability. Ultimately, the inscription of Laura's discourse disappears with the wind. Hence the very force that heightened the mystery of the dead youth's relationship to the mayor's wife in Arganza's story now intensifies the enigma of Laura's ghostly presence by sweeping her words into the domain of erasure, of nonexistence. In the end the narrator decides to convince herself that these events never happened at all, but one can not help but suspect that they leave their mark on her, just as they seduce readers—as acting subjects—into interpreting discourse differently.

Conclusions/Exclusions

In each of these stories narration itself, as discourse, proves to be a crucial battleground for the alteration of construction and for the confrontation with what any discourse attempts to erase: its own constitutive outside. In *Los altillos de Brumal*, narrators who manipulate language abound, but some manipulate discourse—and discursive constructions of gender—in order to change their subjectivity. In all her stories, Fernández Cubas demonstrates an awareness that, as Foucault points out, one can never escape the discursive power structures that condition our identities. However, her tales suggest that one can manipulate the codes advanced by those power structures, as well as what those norms ostracize, to create agency for the self.

As I ponder my analyses of Fernández Cubas's tales, I cannot help but wonder about the exclusions I have made, knowingly or not, in order to construct my conclusions. Part of me questions, for instance, whether Clara's death at the end of "En el hemisferio sur" might be interpreted instead as a suicidal renunciation of her efforts to defy the narrator and others who define woman as an inferior reflection of man. Moreover, in "Los altillos de Brumal," does Adriana simply chooses to embrace the outside (Brumal) and reject the center completely? In that case, she would not be interrogating borders that separate and denigrate people, but simply reifying those borders, albeit redefining Brumal as the center in her new paradigm. Even if this were so, I would argue that the lessons of discursive formation and exclusion are the same. If Fernández Cubas's texts teach us anything, it is to question the terms of the borders that define our construction; for only by performing our subjectivity—in the sense of interpreting it while repeating it—can we hope to reform the roles that inscribe who we are to be.

3
Re-Citing and Re-Siting the Story of the Subject in *El año de Gracia* and *El columpio*

> "Pero en la segunda mitad del siglo veinte, en Europa, no quedaba espacio para tierras ignotas, islas misteriosas o anacrónicas aventuras robinsonianas."
>
> [But in the second half of the twentieth century, in Europe, there was no room for unknown lands, mysterious islands or anachronous Robinsonian adventures.]
>
> —*El año de Gracia*

THE CONCEPT OF THE ABJECT OR EXCLUDED OTHER, WHICH I EXAMINED as the masquerade of the construct of gender in chap. 2, also underlies historical and literary constructions of political power relations. Fernández Cubas's two novels, *El año de Gracia* [The Year of Grace] (1985) and *El columpio* [The Swing] (1995), repeat discourses of history and canonical Western literature to question their representation of the power relations of self/other and center/periphery. Reciting a discourse ostensibly serves to reify it as authoritative and original. Yet, as Judith Butler argues, repetition also haunts such claims to unique difference with multiple manifestations of the same. In her repetition with a difference, Fernández Cubas foregrounds the notion that history and literature are constructed according to a given perspective, the perspective of the powerful. As she re-cites a given history—a mother's account of her life in *El columpio*—and a given story—the tale of *Robinson Crusoe* in *El año de Gracia*—Fernández Cubas re-sites the perspective from which those stories are told in order to unveil them as constructs that are erected for the propagation of power.

El año de Gracia

The political dialectics of self/other found in the European's discovery and conquest of an unknown island in this novel evoke *Robinson Crusoe*, a fundamental literary expression of Western imperialism, and echo the chronicles of the *conquistadores* of the "New World." Moreover, with this intertextuality *El año de Gracia* presents a postcolonial theme in its story of a Spaniard shipwrecked on an island off the British coast. Whereas *El año de Gracia* clearly foregrounds *Robinson Crusoe* as its model text, it also destabilizes the binary relationships of power and polarization that underlie the foundational texts of Western subjectivity. The author's first novel examines the ramifications of power in a context different from *Mi hermana Elba*, which features power as constantly mediated between individuals in their negotiation of identity, or from *Los altillos de Brumal*, which posits gender as the performance of a discourse invested with power. Combining the personal with the political, *El año de Gracia* underlines the way master texts discursively inscribe the powerful as the center of subjectivity in the cultural consciousness.

In Fernández Cubas's literary depiction of the European subject, she situates him—and he is male, like his canonical predecessor—on the margins of power in order to view the dynamic from a different angle. As such, this novel may be seen as a Spanish revision of what Edward Said has called "Orientalism." Observing that "European culture gained in strength and identity by setting itself off against the Orient as a sort of surrogate and even underground self" (Said 1995, 89), Said asserts that Europe has traditionally dominated the other in order to aggrandize itself: "The relationship between Occident and Orient is a relationship of power, of domination, of varying degrees of a complex hegemony" (89). Here the "Orient" may be extended to encompass the various empires of Western nations. If in "Orientalism" the West designates the other as a mirror of the self—a technique that has arguably shaped the novelistic Subject of the West since *Robinson Crusoe*—then Fernández Cubas's first novel subverts this paradigm of the Western novel. Her European castaway is at first overpowered by the other, and then, in his struggle for control, he comes to appreciate and learn from the qualities of the other instead of subsuming them beneath his personal dominance. Hence, whereas *El año de Gracia* clearly foregrounds *Robinson Crusoe* as its model text, it also reorients the once supreme subject in the site of exclusion. Moreover, he tells his story from a newly formed, hybrid perspective of the oppressor and the oppressed melded into one. In the process, the novel makes problematic the binary relationships of power and polarization that underlie the foundational texts of Western subjectivity.

El año de Gracia is the first-person account of Daniel, a Spaniard who, at the age of twenty-four, abandons seminary life and his study of dead languages when his father's death seems to dissolve the target of his pious opposition. Then Daniel's older sister, Gracia, grants him a year of finan-

3 / RE-CITING AND RE-SITTING THE STORY OF THE SUBJECT

cial freedom—a year of "grace"—to travel and explore life as he sees fit. The protagonist embarks on his adventures in Paris, where he has a love affair with a woman named Yasmine, but then, afraid that he is missing out on life, Daniel abandons Yasmine to go to Saint-Malo. There he sets sail on a boat called *Providence* with "tío Jean," a captain he meets at the wharf, and Naguib, tío Jean's surly and sinister boat hand. Eventually Daniel suspects that the two men accepted him not for his questionable skills as a mariner but as a hostage to blackmail Gracia for money. During a frightful storm, Daniel's two captors argue, and Naguib "falls overboard," according to tío Jean.

Soon the ship wrecks, and Daniel finds himself washed up on a barbed wire–enclosed island that is deserted except for the presence of a primitive old shepherd, Grock, and some extremely violent sheep, all of whom are mysteriously covered with infected pustules. Because Grock nurses him through a raging fever and teaches him how to survive on the island, Daniel, in a position of submission, must learn the shepherd's language and obey his orders. One evening, the protagonist spies a Bible in the man's hovel and begins to read it out loud. Enthralled by Daniel's power of language, Grock acquiesces to his demands for more freedom on the island in exchange for weekly sessions when Daniel intones the Scriptures for him. Thus Daniel finds ways to regain a little power for himself.

One day, a plane arrives with scientists, who drop off liquor for the shepherd, take Daniel's picture, and interrogate him as to his presence there. Leaving behind medicine to prevent Daniel's contamination and warning him to steer clear of the old shepherd, the scientists promise to return in a week to rescue him after the medicine has taken effect. The protagonist marks his gratitude to Grock on their last evening together by giving the old man tío Jean's red sheepskin jacket, which Daniel had rescued from the sinking ship and had worn ever since. On the appointed day, Grock tries to prevent his only friend's departure by hitting him with the huge Bible and then running onto the beach to divert the plane. Seeing the figure in the red coat, the men shoot and kill him. Then, descending from the plane, they search for the shepherd. When Daniel finally reveals himself, dressed in Grock's sheepskins, they believe him to be the shepherd and, assured that the subject of their study of the effects of chemical waste on humans remains intact, they abandon him again. Later, a group of ecologists arrives in secret to document the chemical waste and they return Daniel to civilization as proof of the island's contamination.[1] Because they believe Daniel's manuscript about his experiences to be tainted as well, they burn it but supply him with a photocopy of the document. Eventually, Daniel meets a woman named Gruda McEnrich, who bothers him because she laughs at everything, but he marries her anyway. However, in order to fall into peaceful sleep at night, Daniel often ponders his experiences on the island, which he is loath to share with anyone.

Of all Fernández Cubas's texts, *El año de Gracia* has elicited the most response from literary critics thus far. Margenot draws on intertextuality as a fundamental technique of parody and self-consciousness in *El año de Gracia* (Margenot 1993). Bellver studies Fernández Cubas's rewriting of the travel account as a rite of initiation (Bellver 1993–94) and as a questioning and displacement of the privileged word (Bellver 1992). In addition, she examines the literary intertexts that the author uses as metafictional targets of parody (Bellver 1992 and 1995). Alborg also points to the importance of the metafictional elements, and sees this novel as a return to the typical happy ending of the nineteenth-century sentimental novel (Alborg 1987). Casting the metafictional elements in a different light, Zatlin studies the novel as part of the genre of the fantastic (Zatlin 1987a). In another article, Zatlin notes the work's contribution to Spanish literature by women in its defamiliarization of the intertext of the male quest (Zatlin 1987b). Gleue also points to the various literary models that *El año de Gracia* draws on and subverts, while studying the tension of the epistemological and ontological perspectives in the novel (Gleue 1992). In his turn, Spires views the work as a process of *desaprendizaje* [disapprenticeship] that unravels the way Western logic shapes identity, and, in a separate study, he examines Fernández Cubas's depiction of gender as a discursive construct in this novel (Spires 1992a and 1997). Moreover, in his *Post-Totalitarian Spanish Fiction*, Spires situates the work as a fundamental text of post-Franco literature for its exploration of the impact of knowledge on the formation of the gendered human subject (Spires 1996). These critics highlight key techniques that Fernández Cubas employs—particularly those of intertextuality and metafiction—in order to subvert the literary tradition that has shaped the Western subject. I take their analyses a step farther by examining Fernández Cubas's use of these and other tactics in her representation of colonial power as a cornerstone of Spanish subjectivity.

A postcolonial reading of this novel sheds light on the complexity of Fernández Cubas's subversion of unidirectional power dynamics as traditionally depicted in Western literature. The postcolonial approach considers how the imperial center has marginalized the other and how that other appropriates the center's language and culture in order to cultivate its own identity and interests under the guise of colonial domination. Homi K. Bhabha has studied this process in terms of "hybridization," which "reveals the ambivalence at the source of traditional discourses on authority and enables a form of subversion, founded on that uncertainty, that turns the discursive conditions of dominance into the grounds of intervention" (Bhabha 1985, 154). Hybridization hinges on the ambivalence of colonial power that establishes itself as original, and yet is only "confirmed" as original when it is viewed retrospectively from the margins of empire, where the image of the central subject has been repeated and proliferated. Such repetition is the only means of securing colonial power, yet at the same time it discloses the arbitrary nature of that power as origin.

Bhabha holds that the power of colonial discourse disavows the ambivalent character of its own foundation. As the center's discourse reproduces itself in different (colonial) contexts, it transmutes into something that is the same yet is denigrated for being notably other: "Produced through the strategy of disavowal, the *reference* of discrimination is always to a process of splitting as the condition of subjection: a discrimination between the mother culture and its bastards, the self and its doubles, where the trace of what is disavowed is not repressed but repeated as something *different*—a mutation, a hybrid" (Bhabha 1985, 153). The hybrid, then, is the re-citing of the colonizing discourse at the site of the colonized, which necessarily imposes a new perspective and an "other" interpretation of that discourse. As Bhabha stresses, hybridity "is not a third term that resolves the tension between two cultures" (156), but it instead intensifies and propagates their tension.

Hybridization permeates *El año de Gracia*, for the entire novel can be seen as the repetition of colonial discourse that is so necessary to the institution of colonial authority and power. Part of Bhabha's postcolonial theorization poses colonial mimicry as "the desire for a reformed, recognizable Other, *as a subject of a difference that is almost the same, but not quite*" (Bhabha 1994, 86). Thus, while mimicry applies to the colonized who repeats the image of the colonizer almost completely, it also encompasses the never total resemblance to that origin that can harbor a mockery of the origin's constructed and imposed norms. Mimicry as mockery questions the authority of colonial discourse by stressing the *difference* which that discourse prohibits: "Mimicry does not merely destroy narcissistic authority through the repetitious slippage of difference and desire. It is the process of the *fixation* of the colonial as a form of cross-classificatory, discriminatory knowledge within an interdictory discourse, and therefore necessarily raises the question of the *authorization* of colonial representations" (90). By manipulating colonial language and repeating the image of the colonial origin from the contextualized perspective of the dominated other, Fernández Cubas's text supersedes the boundaries of colonial discourse and challenges the validity of the borders themselves, as well as the hierarchies they impose.

The motif of the repetition and subversion of an authoritative origin emerges most prominently in *El año de Gracia* with the referent of *Robinson Crusoe*, an intertext whose pattern Fernández Cubas reverses.[2] As Catherine Bellver observes, "To subvert the validity of literary models, the author patterns her novel on the underlying structure of the very stories and archetypes she is trying to debunk" (Bellver 1995, 106). Whereas the Spanish protagonist is shipwrecked on a virtually deserted island, instead of the founder and ruler of his domain, he figures as the subservient "Friday," attending Grock's every whim: "Aquel viejo simple no se parecía en nada al fiel Viernes de la única novela que, ironías de la vida, me había olvidado de evocar ante la visión del 'Providence' en aquel día, en Saint-Malo [. . .]" [That simple old man in no way resembled the faithful Friday of the only novel that—ironies of life—I had forgotten to evoke on seeing the *Providence* on that day in Saint-Malo {. . .}] (Fernández Cubas 1985, 124). For Fernández Cubas's Crusoe, *Providence* is not the force that delivers him from the island, but the ship that carries him to it. The oxymoronic name of the port from which the boat sets sail, Saint-Malo, only increases this irony. The ex-seminary student who has spent most of his life mired in books expects his life to mirror the fanciful tales he has read and he resists the idea that this experience could be a macabre version of the classic story: "Pero en la segunda mitad del siglo veinte, en Europa, no quedaba espacio para tierras ignotas, islas misteriosas o anacrónicas aventuras robinsonianas" [But in the second half of the twentieth century, in Europe, there was no room for unknown lands, mysterious islands or anachronous Robinsonian adventures] (72–73). Not only does Daniel fail miserably to live up to the standards of those literary constructs, but his own adventures digress markedly from their tidy prototypes, for Fernández Cubas seeks to undermine them.

Similar enough to the power paradigm of Robinson Crusoe/Friday to mimic it, the dialectical relationship between Daniel and Grock mocks the original text with an inversion of power. Daniel's attempts to master his domain and rule his other are repeatedly stymied. He must depend on Grock's physical knowledge of the island, as fog submerges the entire place for much of the novel and distorts Daniel's sense of perspective. With his vision—the dominant sensory mode for the "rational man" in traditional Western literature—so inhibited, the protagonist comes to depend, like an animal, on his remarkably heightened sense of smell. Nonetheless, whereas Robinson Crusoe had a good sense of direction, Daniel's is quite poor. He would be hard put to find food without the shepherd to subdue the violent sheep and to teach him to make cheese. Moreover, the castaway is unable to cultivate corn or any other crop as the agriculturally adept Crusoe did, for the island is rocky and infertile except for a forest that ominously forebodes death and destruction. Far from being the resourceful power that enslaves the ingenuous and acquiescent Friday, Daniel is dominated by and dependent upon Grock for his own education and survival.

The manipulation of language figures prominently in the opposition of power between Daniel and Grock, a repetition of the historical colonial preoccupation with language as a tool of control (Ashcroft, Griffiths, and Tiffin 1989, 7). Indeed, this is a key strategy of power in virtually every Fernández Cubas tale. Instead of imposing his language on the other, the castaway of *El año de Gracia* must master Grock's verbal signs. Daniel's erudite knowledge of dead languages ill serves him with Grock, who speaks a combination of English and Gaelic. This allusion to the English imperial domination of Ireland evokes the dialectic of colonial power, and Grock's use of "abundantes expresiones en gaélico" [abundant expressions in Gaelic] (Fernández Cubas 1985, 107) indicates that the "dominated" is not defeated. In his turn, Daniel tries to belittle Grock's language by calling it primitive and childlike—a classic tactic of the West toward its others. The two men eventually manage to communicate by reducing language to the essential act of naming. In fact, the first word Daniel hears Grock speak is "Grock," an act that establishes the Name of the Father and the law of patriarchy on the island. Founding himself as the origin, which must be reiterated in order to be verified, Grock repeats his name to encompass his property: for him the island, though officially called the Island of Gruinard, is the Island of Grock, and his beloved deceased dog is Grock. Of course, Daniel comes to contest Grock's status as the original power on the island. Gradually, the two become duplicate links within a chain of repetition, when their identities are finally confused by the scientists and Daniel, too, becomes Grock.

Besides establishing a hierarchy of power, Defoe's *Robinson Crusoe* foregrounds a faith in instinct and technological innovation as fundamental to civilization, which Fernández Cubas's text mockingly repeats. Like Crusoe, Daniel believes that his technological acumen will save him from the repetitious cycle that seems to damn his fate. In contrast to Defoe's hero, who constructed boats with great skill, Daniel's numerous attempts to build a simple raft culminate in comical disaster, as he is capsized into the sea and dashed against the rocks, just like his original, calamitous arrival on the beach: "terminé [. . .] en una posición curiosamente idéntica a la que recordaba del día de mi despertar en la isla. El círculo, que tan ingenuamente creía cerrar, estaba dejando paso a un remolino" [I ended up

{...} in a position curiously identical to the one I remembered from the day I awoke on the island. The circle, which I so ingenuously believed to be closing, was giving way to a whirlwind] (145). The repetition of the motif of the shipwreck introduces an intratextual irony that mocks Daniel's belief in his own intuition and ingenuity, just as it presents an intertextual parody of his literary forebear.

Two other targets of mimicry and mockery in *El año de Gracia* are the measurement of time and faith in God, fundamental constructions by which humans guide their existence. Whereas Robinson Crusoe modulated his life on the island with an almost exact record of the passing of time, Daniel loses all temporal bearing, which for him becomes "esa presencia inaprehensible que me sentía incapaz de medir" [that inapprehensible presence that I felt incapable of measuring] (87). Ironically, after his worldview and even his identity have been radically altered, he returns home to find that all these transformations happened in the mere span of exactly one year, "el año de Gracia."[3] Similarly, Daniel's experiences as a castaway—culminating with his discovery of a sign floating nearby indicating that the island is contaminated—defy his faith in God:

> Alcé la vista al cielo para descargar mi ira en el Todopoderoso y, a la vez, suplicar desesperadamente un milagro. Por un instante los ojos se me nublaron y el deseo me hizo creer que alguien muy semejante a Dios Padre se había compadecido de mi suerte y hacía acto de presencia en el mismo infierno. Pero, cuando me enjugué las lágrimas, la ilusión se desvaneció. Ahí estábamos sólo él y yo. Yo, con el puño alzado contra el cielo, y Grock, en lo alto del acantilado, saltando y riendo como un niño. (147–48)

> [I looked up to the sky to unload my wrath on the Almighty and, at the same time, to beg desperately for a miracle. For a moment my eyes clouded and desire made me think that someone very similar to Father God had taken pity on my luck and was putting in an appearance in hell itself. But when I dried my tears the illusion vanished. Only he and I were there. I, with my fist raised against heaven, and Grock, high atop the cliff, leaping and laughing like a child.]

The moment when Daniel lifts his gaze in search of God but sees only his master Grock, cackling and cavorting like a child, ironically repeats, re-sites and redefines the discourse of the "Supreme Being." The God/man dichotomy, which is both a justification for and a parallel to the power relation of colonizer/colonized, is undermined here by Daniel's gaze directed from a position of inferiority to Grock. This asymmetry exemplifies what Bhabha terms "this area between mimicry and mockery, where the reforming, civilizing mission is threatened by the displacing gaze of its disciplinary double" (Bhabha 1994, 86). Albeit unwittingly, Daniel's gaze deconstructs any faith he might have had in a Superior Being. Both God and time are unveiled as useless or irrelevant constructs, when seen from the colonized perspective on the Island of Grock.

Fundamental to mockery is its mimicry of discourse with the consciousness of its own *otherness*, its own *difference* from that discourse. In one highly amusing difference from the original discourse of *Robinson Crusoe*, Daniel's confrontation with the *sanguinarias ovejas* [bloodthirsty sheep] on the island before he ever meets Grock mimics Crusoe's masterful dominion of his island's placid goats. Finding a ewe caught between some rocks near her lamb, Daniel follows his instinct of pursuit instead of being daunted by the eczema and oozing sores bared in the patches on his prey's astonishingly hirsute coat: "Pero no era yo el que decidía, sino el instinto. Y fue él, sin consultarme, el que con maravillosa pericia logró sujetarlas, reducir la furia de la madre herida y convencerlas, a golpes de soga o a pedradas, de que ahora se encontraban bajo mi dominio y no les quedaba otra opción que dejarse conducir dócilmente a mi cabaña" [Yet it was not I who decided, but instinct. And it was instinct that, without consulting me, managed to subdue them with marvelous skill, reduce the fury of the wounded mother and convince them, with blows from a rope or stones, that now they were under my dominion and they had no choice but to allow themselves to be driven docilely to my hut] (Fernández Cubas 1985, 90). Then the supposedly rational man launches into an insane fit of bloodthirsty revenge when the mother resists Daniel's efforts to milk her: "Despellejé el cordero con la saña de un loco; lancé la cabeza a los ojos de su madre, sorbí la sangre aún caliente con ardorosa fruición y, con más rapidez que conocimiento, descuarticé una de sus piernas y ensarté los pedazos en el asador" [I skinned the lamb with the rage of a crazed man; I flung the head at the eyes of its mother, I sucked up the still warm blood with ardent and malicious pleasure and, with more speed than know-how, I cut up one of its legs and rammed the pieces onto the spit] (91).

Daniel is immediately distracted from his sacrifice by the clamoring of other ewes outside as they watch a violent and bloody battle for power between two of their rams. This scene, humorously juxtaposed with the scene of Daniel's own power play with the sheep, increases the would-be *conquistador's* consternation at the ovine thirst for power:

> las ovejas, hasta entonces inquietas espectadoras, comenzaron a bregar entre sí, a lanzar gemidos estremecedores, a revolcarse a su vez por entre las piedras. Parecían presas de una agitación incontenible. Las más audaces

lograron hacerse camino entre aquel hediondo rebaño y aproximarse al carnero herido. Nunca pude haber imaginado que las pezuñas de un cordero fueran capaces de rasgar la piel de un moribundo, arrancarle los ojos o despojarle en poco tiempo de sus entrañas [. . .]. (93)

[the sheep, until then quiet spectators, began to fight amongst themselves, to utter alarming groans, to flounder about in turn among the rocks. They seemed prisoners of an uncontainable agitation. The boldest ones managed to make a path through that foul-smelling flock and approach the wounded ram. Never could I have imagined that the hooves of a lamb could be capable of rending the skin of the dying, rooting out his eyes or quickly stripping him of his entrails {. . .}.]

Unnerved by this gory display of female exultation at the defeat of their male counterpart, Daniel futilely fantasizes that his own female captive will have escaped by the time he returns to his shelter. Much to his horror, however, he finds her bucking and kicking, eager to join her cohorts in their ritualistic disembowelment of their overthrown leader. His terror at this scene soon whips into a frenzy: "El miedo se transformó en cólera, el desaliento en barbarie. Ejecuté a mi prisionera con la sevicia del desesperado. Apedreé, pataleé, apaleé, hasta que mi propia furia se volvió contra mí y, chorreando sangre, golpeé con la cabeza las paredes del refugio" [Fear turned into rage, dismay into barbarity. I executed my prisoner with the abject cruelty of the desperate. I stoned, kicked, thrashed, until my own fury turned against me and, gushing blood, I beat my head against the walls of the refuge] (94–95). Provoked by the prospective loss of dominion into a brutally animalistic confrontation, Daniel effectively crosses the borderline between self-control and savagery.

With the distinction of civilization and barbarism—the essential marker that serves as the dividing line between man/beast, self/other and Occident/Orient—thrown into hazardous question, it can only be a matter of time before the other fragile binaries collapse as well. Of course, Fernández Cubas is hardly the first to question this construct; among other critics both real and fictional, Crusoe himself referred to the inhuman violence of the Spanish civilizing mission in the "New World." Shortly thereafter even Daniel cannot miss the irony of the supposed distance between civilization and barbarity when he learns that the Island of Grock is actually quite close to the Scottish coast—the nearest border of the British empire: "Había estado a punto de transformarme en un salvaje, y lo que en otros momentos me pudo haber parecido dramático se me antojaba ahora una perversa burla del Destino" [I had been on the verge of becoming a savage, and what at other times could have seemed dramatic, now felt like a perverse mockery of Destiny] (Fernández Cubas 1985, 103–4). Unable to appreciate the drama of the situation when it does not follow the literary script he expects, Daniel begins to recognize nonetheless that the geographical borders that delineate one empire from another are just as illusory and mutable as the moral judgments that separate the "enlightened man" from the "savage beast."

As Daniel observes Grock's dexterity on the island, he comes to realize that the distinction between culture/nature, refigured as the normal/the monstrous, can be inverted. The context of the island shapes Daniel's view of this discourse: "no pude dejar de admirarme y comprender que quien realmente resultaba inapropiado y grotesco en aquel medio inhóspito era yo, y todo lo que antes me pudo parecer monstruoso adquirió los visos de la naturalidad más tranquilizadora" [I couldn't stop admiring myself and understand that the one who really was inappropriate and grotesque in that inhospitable environment was I, and everything that before might have seemed monstrous to me took on the glint of the most reassuring naturalness] (105–6). By the end of the novel, when the scientists kill the redclad Grock because they believe that he is Daniel, and they mistake Daniel for the old shepherd, the narrator recognizes that, from the perspective of the true colonizers of that island, *he* is the monster: "significaba que mi aspecto apenas difería del del salvaje y viejo Grock. No tenía espejo en el que mirarme. [. . .] [P]or primera vez, me reconocí deforme y monstruoso" [it meant that my appearance scarcely differed from that of the savage and old Grock. I had no mirror in which to look at myself. {. . .} For the first time, I recognized myself as deformed and monstrous] (167). Daniel is definitively the colonized, the ostracized, and the monstrous other. The resiting of the discourse of normality/monstrosity within Grock's empire radically affects its re-citing by inverting the terms of domination.

The inversion of power as a repetitious and potentially cyclical process profoundly disturbs Daniel. The protagonist displays his aversion in his reaction to the rebellious sheep and in his dislike of Grock's favorite biblical passage about the prophet Daniel's vision of a mighty ram that dominates all the others and that is finally conquered by an even mightier buck goat: "La lectura de aquel pasaje me llenó de inquietud" [The reading of that passage filled me with uneasiness] (135). If the dominator is just one link in a successive chain of command, then he loses his status as uniquely powerful, as original. Notably, while Daniel is disturbed by this biblical passage, Grock finds it hilarious. Within the text of *El año de Gracia*, the biblical text itself is a repetition of sorts, because it reflects the earlier confrontation between the sheep that Fernández Cubas's Daniel witnessed as well as the struggle between Daniel and Grock.

Finally, Grock's death at the hands of the scientists signals that the two islanders' very identities are switched, so that they come to repeat one another. Longing to pray over the new grave he prepares for Grock, Daniel finds himself intoning this biblical passage that signals repetition, instead of appealing to the original power of God:

> Y seguí escuchándome embelesado, imaginando que, bajo tierra, aquellos ojos cerrados habían vuelto a cobrar vida y me sonreían ahora, entre cansados y felices, por repetirle una vez más su historia predilecta, el enfrentamiento del macho cabrío con el carnero, la postración del pobre y espantado Daniel... ¿Yo mismo? ¿El profeta?... No, Daniel yacía bajo tierra, a mis pies. Vestía la zamarra roja del capitán, la misma con la que me conocieron los hombres del helicóptero [. . .]. (166)

> [And I continued listening to myself entranced, imagining that, beneath the ground, those closed eyes had come alive again and smiled at me now, tired and happy, for repeating his favorite story one more time for him, the confrontation of the male goat with the ram, the prostration of poor, frightened Daniel... Me? The prophet?... No, Daniel lay beneath the earth at my feet. He was wearing the captain's red sheepskin jacket, the same one by which the men in the helicopter knew me {...}.]

The repetition of this story effects a transfer of power similar to the one it treats thematically, for Grock's desire for Daniel to read it to him each week caused the islander to surrender his position of absolute power over the castaway. The red coat becomes the metonymy that signals this type of power, as it is passed from the captain to Daniel to Grock, bringing an ephemeral and transient authority in its wake.

The image of the Bible as a tool of colonizing power is a key strategy of subversive repetition in Fernández Cubas's novel. The Bible is, after all, the archetypal Western text of origins. Bhabha notes that the discovery of the English book—with the Bible being the Good Book, the greatest Book of all—inaugurates the literature of empire: "The discovery of the book installs the sign of appropriate representation: the word of God, truth, art creates the conditions for a beginning, a practice of history and narrative. But the institution of the Word in the wilds is also an *Entstellung*, a process of displacement, distortion, dislocation, repetition [. . .]" (Bhabha 1985, 147). As Fernández Cubas has suggested in stories like "Lúnula y Violeta" and "La ventana del jardín" (*Mi hermana Elba*) as well as "Los altillos de Brumal," within the word hovers the potential displacement and deconstruction of the Word. Bellver has observed that in *El año de Gracia* "The Bible is instrumental in [Daniel's] survival, but as a technique for manipulation rather than as consolation" (Bellver 1992, 223). Similarly, Spires has pointed out the imperialistic implications of Daniel's use of the Bible as a tool of power over Grock (Spires 1996, 171–72, n. 15). Yet Fernández Cubas dislocates the Bible from the hands of the colonizing European: Daniel finds the Word already in place upon his arrival to the island. He merely appropriates it from Grock to gain power over the tyrannical shepherd.

When the power paradigm is thus inverted, Grock, too, reappropriates the Bible as a tool literally to beat his dominator into submission so that he will stay on the island. This certainly qualifies as a displacement of the intended purpose of the Word. Soon after the attack fails, Grock himself becomes a Christ figure when he is killed on the beach: "Al sonido de los disparos siguió enseguida un grito de dolor. Grock alzó los brazos, avanzó aún algunos pasos, de nuevo sonaron varias detonaciones, y el viejo cayó de bruces sobre las piedras para no levantarse jamás" [A cry of pain followed the sound of the shots. Grock raised his arms, advanced still a few steps more, various reports sounded again, and the old man fell headlong on the rocks, never to get up] (Fernández Cubas 1985, 159). With his arms outstretched, the Good Shepherd cries out and is sacrificed in Daniel's stead. This postcolonial version of deliverance thus rewrites the inscription of savior and saved, center and margin.

The protagonist Daniel, like the prophet whose name he bears, is horrified by the transmutational, cyclical, repetitious nature of power such as the one embodied in the vision of the battling rams. Nonetheless, Fernández Cubas's prophet comes to suspect that this might be a more accurate vision of reality than the notion of an inviolate original power. Imagining himself as Grock, alone and awaiting the biannual arrival of the plane to deliver his liquor, Daniel contemplates the cyclical nature of existence:

> Dos años era mucho tiempo. Algún barco podía estrellarse contra el acantilado en pleno invierno, un náufrago internarse por entre las brumas y repetir mi ciclo de esperanzas y sufrimientos. Y yo entonces, en un acto ritual, decidiría sacrificarme en aras de un nuevo Grock. Porque tal vez [. . .] mi antecesor no fuera más que un simple eslabón en una larga cadena de Grocks cuya historia, ahora, no tenía más remedio que hacer mía.
>
> [Two years was a long time. Some boat could crash against the cliff in the middle of winter, a castaway could penetrate the mist and repeat my cycle of waiting and suffering. And then, in a ritual act, I would decide to sacrifice myself for the sake of a new Grock. Because perhaps {. . .} my predecessor was nothing more than a simple link in a long chain of Grocks whose history I now had no choice but to make my own.] (169)

As one more link in the chain of Grocks, Daniel is not the colonizer but a repetition of the colonized. When the ecologists discover him and take him away in their boat, back to "civilization," he is afraid to look back at the disappearing island: "me entregué [. . .] evitando en todo momento mirar hacia atrás. No sé aún si en recuerdo de ciertas maldiciones bíblicas, o por el simple e irracional temor de verme a mí mismo, en lo alto del acantilado, agitando esperanzado una deteriorada zamarra roja" [I surrendered {. . .} constantly avoiding looking back. I still don't know if in memory of certain biblical curses, or for the simple and irrational fear of seeing myself, high atop the cliff, hopefully waving a deteriorated red sheepskin jacket] (174). Like the biblical Lot who was forbidden to gaze back upon the conflagration of the wicked city of Sodom for fear that he would repeat that wickedness, Daniel is afraid to look back upon the island for fear of seeing himself repeated there, as the victimized, polluted by-product of civilization's technological quest for knowledge and power. His siting on the Island of Grock has given him new insight into the working of power.

In keeping with the technological overtones of the power paradigm of "civilization" in *El año de Gracia*, the images of photographs or photocopies capture the idea of identity as nonoriginal and repetitious. Yasmine, the girlfriend that Daniel abandoned in Paris, was a photographer, who, Spires argues, ultimately serves as a mere reflection of Daniel, for she is the inspiration of "a purely solipsistic exercise of constructing a female other in his own image" (Spires 1997, 137).[4] Grock laughingly shows Daniel an "instamatic" photograph of a man, but does not recognize that the image that so highly amuses him is a replica of himself. The snapshot that the men in the helicopter take of Daniel in his red coat eventually leads them to identify Grock in the red coat as Daniel, furthering the chain of repeated and replaceable identities. When the ecologists finally take Daniel to the hospital, his photo is taken, revealing the ravages that the polluted island wrought on him. Upon viewing it, however, the protagonist is unable to laugh, Grock-like, at the identity repeated there. Denying that the permanent changes in his sight and hearing were caused by the illegal contamination of the island, the medical establishment tries to erase the imprint of the pustules on Daniel's appearance. They create a replica of his former self, with the significant modification that he now must wear a mustache to cover some of the persistent scars on his upper lip—in Bhabha's words, it is a difference that makes him "*almost the same, but not quite*" (Bhabha 1994, 86).

Daniel's scarred body bears the physical imprint of empire, whose dominion, disregard, and contamination of Gruinard has changed him irrevocably. Although the protagonist returns to the site of "civilization," his tenure in the excluded zone of the island affects his vision, both literally and metaphorically. Spires has characterized Daniel as "a myopic prophet incapable of foreseeing a future order with no central base of knowledge and authority. His year of (G)race has been in vain. He has thrown away the opportunity provided by his sister to be 'otherwise'" (Spires 1996, 167). Although the ending of the novel is ambiguous and defiant of any absolute interpretation (as Fernández Cubas's texts usually are), I am inclined to argue that Daniel, like the blind prophets of lore, comes to see the decentered authority of his civilization. This new "vision," while it might terrify him, also attenuates his identification with the colonizers, although he is unable to outwardly alter his life in any radical way once he returns to the center of that civilization.

Daniel's attraction to Gruda may be read as subtle evidence of his unrealized desire to embrace the change and difference inherent in the other, instead of staying enclosed on only one side of the self/other binarism. On yet another boat, the protagonist meets Gruda, whose constant, inane laughter unsettles him and evokes Grock's raucous reaction to the biblical story of the ram's struggle for power (much as the harsh sound of her name echoes the shepherd's). Significantly, Gruda is Scottish, thus part of a colonized country; hers is a perspective that Daniel now shares. Nonetheless, her only reason for crossing the borders of historical centers of European civilization, about which she knows nothing, is that she won a supermarket lottery. In this light, Gruda's tittering supplies only a vacuous repetition of Grock's laughter in the face of the loss of power to an other. Critics have argued that Daniel's marriage to Gruda confirms his lack of growth (Gleue 1992, 153) or represents the typical happy ending of the nineteenth-century sentimental novel (Alborg 1987, 7). Indeed, Gruda is a mundane, flighty character. Although her laughter metonymically associates her as a repetition of Grock, she is an inferior copy with whom Daniel cannot communicate his experiences on the island: "Había una parte de mi vida que no podía ni quería compartir" [There was a part of my life that I could not and did not want to share] (Fernández Cubas 1985, 183). At night, while Gruda jabbers out loud in her sleep, Daniel mentally separates himself to relive his other experience on the island. In the end, he is unable to express to her his altered vision of the world.

Daniel's experiences after leaving the island are recounted in the Appendix of the novel, which is like a sequence of chain links that explain the story just told—repeating parts of it, while adding significant additional bits of information. As such, the intratextual borders of *El año de Gracia* emphasize the distinctions between colonial and postcolonial representations of the story of the subject. Having returned to the "civilized" center and observing its depiction of the island, the narrator remarks that "La historia de la Isla de Gruinard no difiere demasiado de la de la Isla de Grock" [The story of the Island of Gruinard does not differ much from that of the Island of Grock] (177). The versions are the same, except that the historical rendition of the events on the Island of Gruinard includes (or excludes) one difference: "no había una sola referencia a la existencia de Grock ni al trágico fin que, quién sabe desde qué secreto despacho, se me había destinado días atrás" [there was not a single reference to the existence of Grock nor to the tragic end that, who knows from what secret office, had been destined for me days before] (177–78). Herein is another *"difference that is almost the same, but not quite"* (Bhabha 1994, 86), except of course that this divergence changes everything—it silences the victim sacrificed to power in order to ensure the propagation of centralized power.

Like the cycle of history that Daniel cursed when he repeatedly failed at building his raft, his story spirals back on itself when he discovers that it has been retold and distorted from still another perspective. The protagonist enters a café in Saint-Malo, and a customer informs him that the owner, Naguib, was rescued from a sinking ship by another boat and that he started his restaurant, called Providence, with money that the captain, tío Jean, had beneficently "given" him as his dying act. The protagonist's reaction to the news is revealing:

> Me quité las gafas y, por unos segundos, mi tambaleante interlocutor se difuminó entre brumas y sombras.
> —Sí. Una historia increíble—me limité a decir.
> Pero en mis palabras no se ocultaba ironía alguna. (Fernández Cubas 1985, 182)

> [I took off my glasses and, for a few seconds, my swaying interlocutor faded into mists and shadows.
> I said only, "Yes. An incredible story."
> But there was no irony hidden in my words.]

Naguib's story is a reconstruction, a markedly altered repetition of the "original" tale that readers hold in their hands. Yet even *El año de Gracia* itself is a repetition, presumably at least a printed copy of the photocopy that the ecologists made of Daniel's manuscript, which he wrote and rewrote by hand during his stay on the island. At last, however, Daniel seems unperturbed when faced with disturbing repetition. There is no irony in his observation that the boat hand's story is incredible, perhaps because he finally understands that history, which is constructed by those with the power to make us believe, must be seen as unbelievable.

Like any good *bildungsroman*, *El año de Gracia* is the story of how the protagonist confronts his fear. His is a fear of repetition, a fear of not being the origin but being an other that is the same and yet different, re-cited in a different site. This need for dominance is exactly what postcolonialism undermines: "Such a reading of colonialist authority profoundly unsettles the demand that figures at the centre of the originary myth of colonialist power. It is the demand that *the space it occupies be unbounded*, its reality *coincident* with the emergence of the imperialist narrative and history, its discourse *nondialogic*, its enunciation *unitary*, unmarked by the trace of difference [. . .]." (Bhabha 1985, 157). *El año de Gracia*, with its postcolonial perspective, undermines the myth of origins by mimicking and mocking those origins, by repeating them differently. This endeavor foregrounds the way imperial attempts to occupy *everyplace* inevitably establish hierarchical boundaries between the center (*someplace*) and the periphery (*no place*); it then challenges the validity of those associations by shifting the sites of dominance. By setting up repetitious chains of power, the postcolonial project of *El año de Gracia* undermines any notion that power and supremacy dwell only within the rendition of imperialist narrative and history. It engages conflicting visions of power in dialogue with one another, interrogating the borders that define them according to the differences they exclude. In the process, Fernández Cubas's novel disorients the subject in order to reorient the story that he tells as one that is almost the same but, importantly, not quite.

El columpio

While subversive reiteration in *El año de Gracia* culminates with a rewriting of canonical literature, in Cristina Fernández Cubas's most recent novel, *El columpio* [The Swing] (1995), the multiple images of repetition converge in history as a reiteration and alteration of the past.[5] In its preoccupation with recounting the past, *El columpio* lays bare the nature of history as change wrought over time. The account of a woman who repeats her mother's past in her own present as she writes *la historia* of her family, this novel highlights the intrinsic relationship between the connotations of the Spanish word *historia* as "history" and "story." Every account of what has happened in the past consists of selected moments in time, a plotting of certain events, and the interactions of chosen characters. Whoever makes these "telling" decisions necessarily imposes his or her perspective on the tale. In the process, other perspectives, other moments in time, other possible plots and conclusions are silenced and excluded. In projecting the formation of history as the shaping of a story, Fernández Cubas underscores the constructed nature of both. Hence in this context the two terms come to be virtually interchangeable. In *El columpio* the author explores how the passage of time affects the evolution of any *historia*, as time governs the playing out of events, the shifting of perspective, and thus the interpretation of the meaning of the tale.

The motif of repetition in *El columpio* —intrinsic to the project of pondering the past from the standpoint of the present—is an essential characteristic of the postmodern context in which all of Fernández Cubas's works are written. In *The End of Modernity*, Gianni Vattimo posits that postmodernity is resigned to the impossibility of overcoming or escaping the basic metaphysical tenets of modernity such as progress, the certainty of cause-effect relations, and an organic view of history. To attempt to "overcome" and get beyond modernity would mean to remain within one of modernity's characteristic modes, so postmodernity has no recourse but to subvert those modes from within their own discourse. In the postmodern view, history "is now perceived as having broken down into an infinity of 'histories' that can no longer be (re)combined into a single narrative" (Vattimo 1991, xviii). Indeed, the narrative, "fictional" nature of history itself cancels out any notion of a sole, absolute version of the truth. Moreover, a crisis in the notion of progress invalidates a linear view of history for postmodernity. "Progress" no longer advances modernity, but serves only as the prerequisite for modernity to exist at all: "In a consumer society continual renewal (of clothes, tools, buildings) is already required physiologically for the system simply to survive. What is new is not in the least 'revolutionary' or subversive; it is what allows things to stay the same" (Vattimo 1991, 7). Hence postmodernity critically rethinks modernity even as it repeats it. In this guise, metaphysics, foundations, the teleological view of history and modernity itself all "may be lived as an opportunity or as the possibility of a change by virtue of which [they] are twisted in a direction which is not foreseen by their own essence, and yet is connected to it" (Vattimo 1991, 173). Although many other theoreticians have described and explained postmodernity (see the introduction to this study for references), Vattimo's emphasis on repetition in relation to time, linearity, and progress particularly illuminates Fernández Cubas's project in *El columpio*. Like her first novel, *El columpio* conjures up the haunting prospect of infinite repetition as the postmodern quandary, but its numerous reiterations of images, of events, and of history itself include subtle discrepancies that ultimately suggest "the possibility of a change."

3 / RE-CITING AND RE-SITTING THE STORY OF THE SUBJECT

This repetition with a difference in *El columpio* engages the construction of history, truth, and identity as an open and dynamic process to be continually reexplored, expanded, and rewritten.

The overlay of distinct versions of history in *El columpio* is similar to the diverse versions of fiction in the author's first novel. In *El año de Gracia*, Naguib's reconstruction of the shipwreck story is just one of the many metafictional aspects, which constitute another kind of repetition as they reflect back upon and yet alter and augment the novel.[6] For example, the narrator states that his manuscript was entitled *El Año de Gracia* and cites its opening lines, which repeat exactly the opening lines of Fernández Cubas's *El año de Gracia* (Fernández Cubas 1985, 84–85). There is at least one difference between the two texts, however, besides one being a copy of a copy of the other and the slightly altered capitalization in their titles. At one point in the novel, the narrator cites a fragment that he wrote earlier in his manuscript, a fragment that does not appear anywhere else in the text we read (140–41). With the "original" fragment inexplicably erased, all that remains is the replica—which casts the very existence of an "original" manuscript into doubt. This omission invites speculation that the narrator might be only a double after all, a hybrid of the implicit author herself—constructed by the readers of her texts—who in turn is a hybrid of the "original," "real" Fernández Cubas, and so forth. One could continue thus indefinitely, circling in the spiral of metafictional reflections that has so delightfully characterized the novel since its very inception (another questionable "origin," because the novel itself is a hybrid of other genres). In this, too, *El año de Gracia* is another repetition—almost the same, but not quite. The juxtaposition of Fernández Cubas's two novels as repetitions of history and fiction blurs the distinctions between the two and unmasks them both as discursive modes of cultural knowledge, carefully constructed according to perspectives of power.

In *El columpio* the first-person narrator reconstructs her late mother's—and thus her own—history by visiting her mother's childhood home in Spain. Her experiences there recast her mother's account in a markedly different light, even as the narrator senses a haunting repetition of her parent in herself. A twenty-five-year-old woman raised in France, the nameless narrator commences her account by recalling her mother's frequent assertion that, while still a child, she encountered her adult daughter in a dimly remembered but seemingly felicitous dream. The mother, Eloísa, would tell how she was found inexplicably shaken and soaked in the garden soon after the anachronistic encounter with her own daughter, and how she then fell into a prolonged, feverish illness. Longing to come to know her deceased mother's beloved brothers, Lucas and Tomás, and cousin Bebo (referred to collectively as "the uncles"), who peopled the woman's many tales of her idyllic childhood, the protagonist travels to the House of the Tower where the men still live in a tiny Spanish town near the Pyrenees mountains.

Although unprepared for her visit because they never received the letter announcing her arrival, the reclusive uncles welcome her as their beloved Eloísa's daughter. In this home that seems unchanged by time, the young woman learns more of her mother's personality, particularly her predilection for the diabolo. This was an old toy made up of a spool that was tossed up and then spun on a whip-like cord suspended horizontally between two sticks, which Eloísa always manipulated with stunning dexterity—to the point of once being accused of wielding the toy to slay a dog. After several days the uncles try to hasten their niece's departure before that Friday evening, when they will hold their weekly meeting to discuss family matters over dinner. Puzzled and hurt by their exclusion of her, the protagonist determines to stay anyway. She pretends to go to bed early that Friday night, but then, after the men try to drug her to sleep, she stealthily escapes the house. Pausing for a final look back at her uncles through the dining room window, she discovers that their ritualistic dinner focuses on an apparently unoccupied place setting, which the three address as Eloísa. The protagonist, baffled by their apparent ability to speak with one another's voices, is further stunned to hear the petulant, angry voice of a little girl who demands to know if the unwanted guest has departed. Astonished at the specter of her uncles' insanity, the woman flees into the rainy night, only to halt when hit by a sharp object—an old-fashioned diabolo.

Suddenly, she finds herself face to face with the young Eloísa. The irate child whips the diabolo cord around the intruding woman's neck, as a thud and a splash are heard, but the girl stops short of strangulation when her victim cries out, "¡Mamá! Por favor. . . , mamá!" [Mama! Please. . . , Mama!] (Fernández Cubas 1995, 124). Suspended time moves forward then, as the young girl's hair and clothes, picture-perfect until that moment, suddenly become drenched by the pouring rain. About to faint, the protagonist hears the splash and thud once again and realizes that she is standing at the edge of a well. After running to the nearby town, the young woman obtains a room at an inn for the rest of the night. Before she catches the bus the next morning, Lucila, the innkeeper, gives her a letter from the uncles, delivered earlier along with her soaking wet suitcase that "parece que salga de un pozo" [seems as if it has come out of a well] (128). The letter affectionately reproaches the niece for worrying them with her impetuous departure in the middle of the night and includes a check as a token of what her mother Eloísa would have inherited had she not abandoned the land to go to France. Realizing that the letter depicts her uncles as only concerned for her well-being, and her own departure as irrational, the protagonist rips up both the letter and the check. On her journey back to France, the narrator mulls over her experiences and the way that her mother, from within her dream, saved her daughter's life.

In *El columpio*, history is depicted as the tension between the repetition of the past and the inevitable alteration—the different perspective—imposed by the passage of time into the present. When the protagonist returns to the site of her mother's past in order to experience her history, she is struck by her uncles' efforts to defy repetition and the passage of time. Thanks to the rents they collect from the nearby urban development, the uncles "podían permitirse el lujo de vivir como siempre, como si nada hubiera ocurrido, como si el mundo pudiera detenerse con sólo que alguien [...] olvidara la existencia del reloj y se negara a arrancar las hojas del calendario" [could permit themselves the luxury of living as always, as if nothing had happened, as if the world could be stopped if someone just {...} forgot the existence of the clock and refused to tear off the sheets of the calendar] (39). They strive to freeze time and preserve everything in the house exactly as it was during Eloísa's childhood. Within the house, the uncles tolerate no alteration of their established routine; they rebuff all the protagonist's efforts to infuse new life into the place with expensive sherry, brighter lightbulbs, or a special dinner. Even the architecture induces the repetition of the same: the dining room boasts a vaulted roof, which causes every word spoken there to echo.

A portrait of the young Eloísa, posing with her diabolo, serves as the consummate symbol of the quest for eternal preservation. For the uncles, the picture suspends time and action by immortalizing Eloísa's past image as the reigning icon in the House of the Tower. Nonetheless, even the whimsical creature in the portrait is only a reflection of Eloísa, much like the faded family photographs that the mother would use to evoke the memory of her happy childhood long ago. Paradoxically, in their attempt to preserve the young Eloísa's presence, the portrait and photographs—as mere copies of the original—also underscore her absence. Moreover, the portrait emphasizes the passage of time even as it seems to paralyze it, by highlighting the anachronistic contradiction that someone of Eloísa's generation should have played with an outdated gadget such as a diabolo: "Si mamá viviese, tendría poco más de cincuenta años. Ninguna mujer de esa edad recuerda el diábolo como un juego de infancia" [If Mama were alive, she would be a little over fifty. No woman of that age remembers the diabolo as a childhood toy] (69). This mention of age points extratextually to a different history, the history of Spain itself. Speculating that the moment of narration takes place sometime in the early 1990s (because the novel is published in 1995), one could surmise that Eloísa would have been born in the 1940s (not unlike Fernández Cubas herself). The narrator notes that the child in the portrait seems to be between nine and twelve years old, situating the suspended time of the uncles' House of the Tower in the 1950s—the period, not so coincidentally, of Franco's strongest control over Spain. Thus the portrait itself harbors clues that defeat its ostensible timelessness, by contextualizing the story in the concrete historical period of the Spanish postwar.

Many writers and historians have characterized Francoism as a deliberate reversion to Spain's past in an attempt to impede the country's progress into the future—a progression that would have required change. Carmen Martín Gaite, in an essay ironically titled "Bendito atraso" [Blessed Backwardness] refers to the Franco Regime's depiction of the ancient as modern, particularly with regard to women: "To endow with newness, that is to sell as modern, that type of ancient, traditional and always new woman is an endeavor to which the propaganda of the time dedicated itself tirelessly" (Martín Gaite 1987, 27). Dressing its rhetoric in the trappings of "progress" and "change" that, for Vattimo, define modernity, Franco's regime in fact inscribed a regression to the past, which it then paralyzed with stasis. With the allusion to the context of Francoist Spain, Eloísa's characterization by a metonymical object inappropriate to her own time ("Eloísa sin su diábolo no es Eloísa" [Eloísa without her diabolo is not Eloísa] { Fernández Cubas 1995, 31}) parallels the regime's depiction of the ideal post–civil war Spanish woman as a paragon of medieval piety.

In *Narrating the Past: Fiction and Historiography in Postwar Spain*, David Herzberger argues that such superimposition of the past over the present characterizes Francoism's transmutation of history into myth. In this endeavor, the fundamental tactic for preventing change was to revert time to an epoch that was depicted nostalgically, mythically, as ideal: "By resorting to myth, Francoist historiographers imprison both time and discourse and thereby cut at the very heart of discovery and change that impel history to begin with" (Herzberger 1995, 36). Moreover, they deliberately weave a narrative of history that is larger than life and that propounds a single version of truth: "historians of the Regime draw forth meaning in history that stands resolutely as the equal of truth, hence historiography assumes the secondary but no less important function of disallowing dissent" (17). This absolutist project of Francoism is echoed by Lucas's affirmation to his niece of the way it *is* and always *will be* in his constructed world in *El columpio*: "Esta es, querida niña—concluyó—, la única verdad. No hay otra" ["This is, dear child," he concluded, "the only truth. There is no other"] (Fernández Cubas 1995, 39). The abundant images and tactics of repetition in *El columpio*, then, reflect the Francoist view of history: "a conception of truth and temporality in which history is viewed less as a complex web of diachronic and synchronic relationships, both formed and revealed through narration, than as an unfolding of time that is *repetitive*, deterministic, and radically unchangeable" (Herzberger 1995, 33; italics mine). The uncles try to arrest time and, through repetition, preserve everything as the same. In doing so, they mythologize the past into the intranscendence of a family centered on the archetypal, angelical figure of woman.

In *El columpio* the House of the Tower and the surrounding town serve as the metaphorical boundary of Franco's control over Spain, for the repetition of the same within the designated borders of both worlds is the key to securing and proliferating monolithic power. Furnished just as it was during Eloísa's childhood, the men's home is an enclosed, static environment that only Tomás ever ventures to leave with any regularity in order to purchase the household necessities. Symbolically, in good weather Bebo is permanently confined to their land, and in the winter to the House of the Tower. The house is the center of fascination for the townspeople, who treat the protagonist with respect and great interest for what she might reveal to them about the reclusive goings-on there. The urban development itself, owned by the uncles, is a site of stagnation where "casi todos son viejos y niños" [almost all the people are elderly or children] and "'El aburrimiento se contagia. . . .' Pero no sólo el aburrimiento. Todo en el valle, hasta mi propia voz, me devolvía a la Casa de la Torre" ["Boredom is contagious. . . ." But not just boredom. The entire valley, even my own voice, brought me back to the House of the Tower] (Fernández Cubas 1995, 82, 85). The house, like Franco himself, occupies the center of everyone's consciousness.

In contrast to Francoist historiography, however, Fernández Cubas's narrative features an alternative perspective, that of the mythologized Eloísa's daughter, who imposes a distinct interpretation on the house in general and her mother's portrait in particular. For the protagonist, the picture reveals a "criatura mal sentada, con un mohín de disgusto, una cuerda borrosa entre las manos y un diábolo desdibujado en el suelo" [small, improperly seated child with a vexed pout, a blurred cord between her hands and a faded diabolo on the floor] (38). This outsider perceives a side to the young Eloísa that undermines the pure, Edenic image of the past that the woman always depicted in her stories to her daughter. The diabolo itself, along with Eloísa's adroit and sometimes dastardly tricks with it, evoke another repetition, this one linguistic: the *diábolo* repeats and transmutes into the *diablo* [devil]. Eloísa's photographic, painted, and narrative portraits of herself depict her as fundamentally angelic; yet, as the daughter discovers, her actions and her emblematic toy belie these repetitions of piety and suggest a significant, diabolical difference. This work of art, then, reveals another reality beyond the Regime's official image of the ideal Spanish woman as pious, gentle, and obedient.[7]

Indeed, Bebo's body bears the mark of Eloísa's rage at his physical advances on her person. Much to Lucas's and Tomás' irritation, Bebo admits to the protagonist that Eloísa scarred his neck with her diabolo once when he gave her a kiss. The adult Eloísa's version of that kiss, recounted to her daughter, never disclosed such violence: "Una vez yo era una princesa cristiana y ellos, tus tíos, unos terribles sarracenos que me tenían presa. Me habían encerrado en lo alto de la torre y querían hacerme renegar de mi fe. [. . .] Pero entonces Bebo, sin avisar a mis hermanos, cambió el argumento de la obra. Les envió a guardar las puertas de la mazmorra, se quitó los ropajes de moro, se puso una cruz y, allí mismo, en el desván, cuando nadie nos veía, me dio un beso" [One time I was a Christian princess and they, your uncles, terrible Saracens who held me prisoner. They had shut me up at the top of the tower and wanted to make me renounce my faith. {. . .} But then Bebo, without warning my brothers, changed the plot. He sent them to guard the dungeon doors, took off his Moor's robes, put on a cross and, right there in the attic, when nobody was watching, he gave me a kiss] (21). By altering the script and rewriting the *historia* of their playful enactment, Bebo also violated the balance of power wherein Eloísa was set apart, pure and untouched, elevated from the men up in the tower.

Similarly, outside of their imaginary games, the young Bebo longs to break the prohibition of blood ties against his ardor for Eloísa by marrying her. Once again, Bebo transgresses and incites the anger of the patriarchal powers that be, his male cousins. In response, Eloísa reveals to her daughter that "Entonces yo me columpiaba con rabia, como si estuviera enfadada, y decía que era inútil, porque, si seguían así, discutiendo tontamente, cruzaría los Pirineos, me casaría con un francés y no volverían a verme" [Then I swung with fury, as if I were angry, and said that it was useless, because, if they kept this up, arguing foolishly, I would cross the Pyrenees, marry a Frenchman, and they would never see me again] (17). Eloísa's reaction of protest is feigned, however, for she only *acts* "como si estuviera enfadada" [as if she were angry] (17) and threatens to topple the whole balance by leaving the center of power altogether.

In fact, she herself is the one who dominates the center of power, where she deliberately invites dissension in order to display her control. As Bebo's scar attests, the young Eloísa seems quick to whip all into submission when the games go too far.

Yet, Eloísa fulfills her facetious threat: she grows up and leaves the sanctified confines of the House of the Tower, and the men never see her again. She marries a man who lives in France, even if he is not really French. Fernández Cubas's portrait of Eloísa's marriage—the history behind the protagonist's story—is sketched with the faintest of strokes, but it allows for the possibility that Eloísa's husband, like many of Franco's dissenters, may have been exiled in France. As the jagged geographical border of the Pyrenees accentuates, France is the definitive outside to Spain. Eloísa, the key representative of power in the House of the Tower, undermines its supremacy as the center by crossing the border to the periphery of France. Unable to accept the alterations that time has imposed, the men sustain their accustomed order in the space of the House of the Tower by denying chronological time and by indulging their illusion in a realm where time does not move and power does not shift.

Fernández Cubas's fictional history of the dynamics of the 1950s poses an interesting deconstruction of the religious and political rhetoric advanced by the Regime's account of what was happening in Spain during that time. If Eloísa figures as the devil incarnate, then the inseparable male cousins evoke the Christian Trinity, three in one. Yet Fernández Cubas's version contradicts the divine dialectical opposition, for in *El columpio* the devil is the one who rules, with the acquiescent cooperation of the Trinity. Unlike the biblical devil (who really was a devilish angel, banished because he believed that he was as great as God), this angelic devil apparently chooses to inhabit the outside and to relinquish her dominion over the Trinity. This contradiction deconstructs the binary oppositions such as good/evil and center/periphery that undergird the master narratives of mankind (I choose this word deliberately), Christianity, Spain, and Eloísa herself.

This archetypal structure of dichotomies is founded on the assumption of the existence of difference as the factor that divides the subject from its object. Drawing on Heidegger, Vattimo argues that the distinction between subject and object is obsolete, since the notion of *their* difference is preceded by an *ontological* difference between Being (reductively speaking, existence itself) and beings (those who exist): "both subject and object equally *are*, and therefore there is no longer any ontological difference between them: the real ontological difference is between Being itself and the realm of subjects and objects—that is, beings" (Vattimo 1991, xiv). Similarly, Fernández Cubas seems to point to the collapsibility of the difference that beings construct between subject and object in order to secure and wield power.

Perhaps Bebo's cardinal sin, then, is his desecration of such boundaries of power structured on notions of difference—a sin for which he is branded by Eloísa's whip in their childhood game. Instead of playing the Moor in opposition to her Christian princess (a difference that forbade amorous union as stridently as did their blood relationship), Bebo dons the robes of a Christian and kisses her. The robes, as a costume to be taken on or thrown off, highlight the constructed nature of the roles Bebo may play.[8] As Judith Butler's theory of performativity emphasizes, this act of easily exchanging one identity for another points to the replaceability, repeatability, and similarity that inheres within constructions of difference. In effect, *the same* can be found on both sides of the constructed border of difference. This sameness is potentially devastating, for it threatens the play of power that difference affords.

Eloísa's daughter eventually sees that her uncles themselves, whose personalities seemed so distinct, evoke mere repetitions of sameness. When she escapes from their home the night of the special "family meeting" after they try to drug her, she pauses for a final look back at her uncles through the dining room window. Amazed, the protagonist observes that Tomás's typical words seem to emanate from Lucas's mouth: "En un momento escuché: 'Bien, bien, bien. . .,' pero Tomás, que sonreía fascinado, no había movido los labios, no había pronunciado palabra alguna. Lucas repitió: 'Bien, bien'. Y Tomás, enseguida, se puso a hablar con voz de Bebo. Luego Bebo dijo algo en el tono ceremonioso de Lucas" [At one moment I heard "Good, good, good. . . ," but Tomás, who was smiling in fascination, had not moved his lips, had not pronounced a single word. Lucas repeated, "Good, good." And immediately Tomás began to speak with the voice of Bebo. Then Bebo said something in Lucas's ceremonious tone] (Fernández Cubas 1995, 116–17). Hence each man only appears to be the author of his voice, when in fact he speaks the words of another.

The uncles' words are interchangeable because they all merely parrot the same discourse, a discourse that originates with none of them. Brad Epps calls this phenomenon "ventriloquism": "It refers, that is, to the slipperiness of reference, to the mystifying ability to take one thing for another, one's words for another's. Ventriloquism, in other words, is an act of speech that hides its sources and throws itself, disembodied, into the bodies of others" (Epps 1996, 55). Francoism pretended to possess the fundamental truth about Spain—Herzberger notes that the Regime aimed "to convert what in reality was a cultural and political proposition about the past into what appeared to be a wholly natural *fact*" (Herzberger 1995, 17). Similarly, the uncles strive to author a unified vision of their world with Eloísa. In fact, however, these patriarchal figures merely recite discursive constructions of history converted into myth, drawing power from the "exaltation of sameness" (Herzberger 1995, 33). Observing all this in secret, from outside the house, the protagonist realizes that the words of the great men are only slippery constructs that are passed along and repeated from one patriarchal figure to another. Who, then, is the head of power? Like Daniel and Grock in *El año de Gracia*, each uncle ultimately turns out to be other than what he appears to be. Although it presumes to reify the origin of authority, repetition, when seen from a different perspective, ends up undermining authority and power by rendering it infinitely replaceable by an "other."

The tension of repetition as a tactic that both enforces and erodes authoritative power continues with the dual image of the attic as, first, the privileged site of knowledge at the top of the tower and, second, a metaphor for Lucas's mind, the supposed locus of power and knowledge in the home. The protagonist herself observes that the central function of attics is to halt time: "Los desvanes son como inmensos arcones en los que el tiempo se ha detenido" [Attics are like immense trunks in which time has stopped] (Fernández Cubas 1995, 70). In addition to being a repository for objects from the family's past, and the site of Bebo's romantic transgression, the attic of the tower serves as the protagonist's hiding place where she reads Eloísa's—and her own—letters in secret. As in *Los altillos de Brumal*, this space abounds with texts that open up the past to the present. If the tower is the phallic symbol of power for the house, then Lucas, whose mind harbors the family's textual knowledge, appears to be the patriarchal head of the household.

Just as the protagonist violates the sanctity of the house by reading forbidden letters in the attic, two cleaning women menace the order of Lucas's mental domain by moving his papers around in his study. When his niece mentions her visit to the attic, Lucas complains that the cleaning women have reduced his mind to a similar jumble: "Han logrado convertir mi cabeza en un auténtico desván" [They have managed to turn my head into a veritable attic] (65). The two Rachels are figured as intruders on the masculine space: "La irrupción puntual de las raqueles era contemplada por los tíos como una invasión, una fatalidad ineludible de la que cada cual se defendía a su manera" [The punctual inrush of the rachels was viewed by the uncles as an invasion, an inescapable fatality against which each one defended himself in his own way] (48). Coming from the outside, the women introduce a different perspective that dialectically opposes Lucas's fragile system of "order": "Y de pronto las raqueles le atacaban por donde menos esperaba. *Su* orden. Porque aquellas mujeres, con sus absurdas tentativas de orden, no hacían más que entorpecer su ordenado intento de desorden, demasiado reciente aún para tenerlo asentado, firme" [And suddenly the rachels were attacking him where he least expected it. *His* order. Because those women, with their absurd attempts at order, did nothing more than hinder his orderly undertaking of disorder, still too recent to be established and firm] (67). Order, then, like disorder, is not an absolute but an artifice whose construction is threatened by a different vision of the way things should be. Despite the repetition that they embody, the two Rachels threaten Lucas's established order by slightly changing it: "Pero entonces aparecían ellas, las raqueles. ¿Podía existir algo más perturbador para sus elucubraciones que encontrarse la cotidianeidad sutilmente alterada?" [But then they, the rachels, would appear. Could there be anything more disturbing for his lucubrations than to find the details of daily life subtly altered?] (67). Repetition that introduces a subtle alteration holds the potential to puncture the closed system of power. As the phallic symbolism of its name suggests, the House of the Tower is a patriarchal space where oppositional feminine presence constitutes a violation.

As metonymies of other women who transgressed the unchanging realm of the House of the Tower, the unopened letters of the adult Eloísa and her daughter symbolize the uncles' efforts to negate any alterations wrought by time and history in their home. Letters epitomize the effect that the passage of time and an altered perspective have on the interpretation of a message or an event, by their nature as texts that are written in one moment and then read, at a point later in time, by someone different. When the protagonist arrives at the inn near her uncles' home, she finds the undelivered letter that she herself had sent them two weeks previously to announce her impending arrival. She later discovers the letter that she had sent informing her uncles of her mother's death, bound up along with the adult Eloísa's letters in a secret compartment of her childhood desk "como si jamás hubiera sido recibida, como si no existiera. O tal vez—se me ocurrió de pronto—como si mi madre no hubiera muerto nunca" [as if it had never been received, as if it did not exist. Or perhaps—it suddenly occurred to me—as if my mother had never died] (Fernández Cubas 1995, 60). By refusing to collude in the inherently temporal contract of sender/receiver, Lucas, Bebo and Tomás attempt to preserve the sacred closure of their atemporal space. Once the protagonist discovers her mother's communication, however, she determines to rescue those words from oblivion; she violates the male prohibition against reading, learning, and change by reading the letters for herself. Upon closer examination she realizes that, just like the letter that she herself had sent announcing her impending visit, her mother's letters have been opened and resealed. Later, she suspects that Tomás might have read and resealed the letters, in an effective gesture of censorship and silencing denial. If a letter necessarily imposes the passing of time on the communication of knowledge, the uncles prevent time from altering their world—and their image of Eloísa—by refusing to acknowledge the letters and sequestering them away in the secret archive of Eloísa's desk.

Just like the letters left unopened and thus unread and repeated by another (or letters opened and suppressed, which seek the same effect), Lucas's project is to write a book of recipes that can never be read by another. Lucas manipulates recipes in order to block any transmission of knowledge via the act of reading: "jamás ser humano alguno podría penetrar en ese archivo perfecto que tenía en mente y en el que las fichas aparecían ordenadas de acuerdo con diversos sistemas: alfabético, asociativo, por materias... Y otro, el más importante, que destruía y anulaba los anteriores" [No human being would ever be able to penetrate that perfect archive that he had in mind and in which the note cards appeared organized according to diverse systems: alphabetical, associative, by subject.... And another, the most important one, that destroyed and canceled out the previous ones] (65–66).

As with the unread letters, Lucas hopes to stonewall the passage of knowledge and power by blocking the message from any receiver. Evocative of the Derridian dictum that reading is writing, Lucas tries to preserve his own authority by preventing any reader from intruding and rewriting his text through repetition in the form of reading and interpretation. Lucas's project seems a ridiculously futile one, but it reflects the restrictive and similarly doomed undertaking of the Franco Regime: "For those who propose a rhetoric of difference, or even for those who wish to defer closure concerning the past, the consequences of the State's position are harsh: both truth and meaning are collapsed into a single concept that steadfastly precludes dissent" (Herzberger 1995, 29). Of course, as Fernández Cubas's metaphor suggests, such an endeavor—if successful—would ultimately arrest communication itself, producing an "algo indisoluble" [indissoluble something] (Fernández Cubas 1995, 65) in static suspension that could never be read, repeated, or altered by another.

Although one function of repetition is to reinforce the original text, repetition also undermines the validity of the origin by copying it and replacing it, as Derrida, Irigaray, Foucault, Butler, Bhabha, and a host of other thinkers have signaled. Lucas's greatest fear is that he might lose his authority, in the sense of both authorship and power, over his book one day if he finds it published under someone else's name (much like what happened to Clara Galván in "En el hemisferio sur" [*Los altillos de Brumal*]): "para prevenir el robo, el fraude, el plagio indemostrable, estaba ideando un nuevo sistema—el mismo al que antes había calificado como 'el más importante'—, una puerta falsa para despistar al enemigo. Y en eso había estado toda la tarde. Creando fichas apócrifas que invalidaran las verdaderas; caminos, atajos, pistas en fin, de una aparatosa lógica que, sin embargo, no conducían a otro lugar más que a un laberinto" [to prevent the theft, the fraud, the indemonstrable plagiarism, he was devising a new system—the same one he had earlier described as "the most important"—, a fake door to throw the enemy off track. He had been working on it all afternoon. Creating apocryphal index cards that would invalidate the real ones; trails, short cuts—clues, in short, to an ostentatious logic that nevertheless would lead nowhere but to a labyrinth] (66).

This image of the labyrinth of texts reiterates Borges's "La biblioteca de Babel" ["The Library of Babel"], in which every possible book has already been written, and Jameson's "prisonhouse of language" from which no one can escape. Fernández Cubas repeats Borges's and Jameson's conviction that any hope for totalizing communication is doomed: "Y ahora era él quien temía perderse por las pistas falsas que acababa de diseñar para extraños. Caer en sus mismas redes y chocar con el espejo—porque en el laberinto había tenido la ocurrencia de colocar además algunos espejos—, y sólo después, cuando fuera ya demasiado tarde, comprender que había sido la primera víctima de su propia estrategia" [And now he was the one who feared getting lost amongst the false clues that he had just designed for others. Falling in his own traps and colliding with the mirror—for in the labyrinth he had had the idea of placing some mirrors as well—and only afterward, when it was already too late, realizing that he had been the first victim of his own stratagem] (67). Lucas's pursuit of unrepeatable verbal power threatens to consume him in the confusion of nonsensical codes, resulting in the collapse of any communication at all. The interjected aside, "—porque en el laberinto había tenido la ocurrencia de colocar además algunos espejos—" [—for in the labyrinth he had had the idea of placing some mirrors as well—] (67), suggests an ironic view (if not by the narrator then by the implicit author) of Lucas's hope to avoid repetition. Not only did he create index cards that were repetitions with a difference from other cards, but the use of mirrors and labyrinths is itself a technique that echoes the textual imagery of a host of authors who have preceded Lucas. Inevitably, Lucas's textual labyrinth of mirrors, like *El columpio* itself, constantly reflects and refers back to other codes whose influence he can never escape, for such is the nature of language.⁹

Although it is impossible to get outside the recurrence of language, *El columpio* and the concept of history itself demonstrate that repetition is always an act, subject to the passage of time, that alters one's perspective and experience. As Epps observes, "difference inheres in repetition: . . . the reiteration of texts, entailing as it does the reiteration of contexts, is always an alteration" (Epps 1996, 25). Perhaps the most telling repetitions in *El columpio* are those that illustrate this shift of perspective, of context, which brings about knowledge, understanding, and change. At one point, having learned from her mother's unopened letters to her uncles that their adult relationship was not ideal, the protagonist gazes out the attic window from high in the tower and imagines that she sees herself arriving, with her own unread letter, two days earlier. Reliving the same incident from the altered perspective imposed by time, the protagonist longs to apply her newly acquired knowledge to her past and save herself from the experience. It is a futile wish, for without the experience of time she never would have gained the knowledge that the stories told by her mother were not the only view of history; "aquella que fui yo" [she who I was] (Fernández Cubas 1995, 57) was different from the "I" in the present. Understanding the power of time distinguishes the protagonist from her uncles, who persist in detaining time and thus relinquish their chance to learn and change.

As the novel's title highlights, the image of the swing epitomizes how movement over time changes one's perspective. The swing, another of Eloísa's favorite childhood diversions, at times seems to be almost a personified force in the novel: "Algo acababa de moverse entre los árboles [. . .]. Algo o alguien que se asomaba y se ocultaba enseguida" [Something just moved among the trees {. . .}. Something or someone that appeared and immediately hid] (43). One day, on a picnic with her uncles, the protagonist climbs on Eloísa's swing and experiences a change of perspective: "Y de pronto fue como si reviviera una de las fotografías de mi madre. Desde el otro lado. Porque allí estaban ellos, los hermanos y el primo, y yo, de pie sobre un columpio de madera, con un traje de organdí [. . .], jugaba a irritarlos, a enfadarlos, a hacer valer mi condición de reina absoluta" [And suddenly it was as if I were reliving one of my mother's photographs. From the other side. Because there they were, the brothers and the cousin, and I, standing on a wooden swing, with an organdy dress {. . .}, playing at annoying them, at making them mad, at asserting my status as absolute queen] (43–44). The woman reexperiences the photograph that she had viewed so often, except now from the point of view of the little girl on the swing inside the picture instead of from the outside gazing inward.

Of course, a change in perspective affords distinct knowledge, and the protagonist's magical transposition indelibly alters her understanding of the scene on the swing. Somehow, she hears Eloísa's childish voice singing about marrying a Frenchman and leaving forever: "Pero no era el tono de mi madre, la dulce entonación de mi madre rememorando su infancia. Sino el grito de una niña malcriada, caprichosa, tiránica. . . 'Siempre serás un bruto,' oí. Y, volviendo en mí, me di cuenta de que estaba de rodillas en el suelo [. . .]" [Yet it wasn't my mother's tone, the sweet intonation of my mother recalling her childhood, but the shout of a spoiled, capricious, tyrannical little girl. . . . "You'll always be a beast," I heard. And, coming to, I realized that I was on my knees on the ground {. . .}] (44). The daughter experiences her mother's perspective in the past and realizes that her mother was not as sweet as she had recounted in her stories. In this scene, time is duplicitous as well as capricious, allowing for at least two possible interpretations of this incident. The uncles claim that Tomás accidentally pushed the swing too hard and that his niece fell off. Alternatively, Eloísa, the transcendent child, may have resented having her position on the swing usurped, so she shoves the interloper off the swing, off her seat of power. The latter reading of the incident with the swing posits two intersecting planes of time: the realm of the present, when the protagonist visits her uncles, and the suspended, unchanging plane of the past, wherein the child Eloísa still reigns supreme over her brothers and cousin.

This intersection of temporal planes is repeated when, at the end of the novel, the protagonist flees in the pouring rain after observing the uncles' covert dinner and bumps into the young Eloísa. Eloísa's tale of her childhood encounter with her grown-up daughter is now experienced firsthand by the protagonist herself: "Agitaba en la mano una de aquellas cuerdas sobre las que ejercía el más absoluto dominio. Y ahora se ponía a silbar [. . .]. Un dolor agudo en la garganta, el silbido de un látigo agitado con destreza en el aire; un chapoteo, un golpe; mis manos [. . .] luchando por zafarse de un terrible reptil enrollado a mi cuello; la sensación de asfixia [. . .]" [She waved in her hand one of those cords over which she wielded the most complete dominion. And now it began to whistle {. . .}. A sharp pain in the throat, the hiss of a whip brandished with skill in the air; a splash, a thud; my hands {. . .} fighting to break loose from a terrible reptile rolled around my neck; the feeling of suffocation {. . .}] (Fernández Cubas 1995, 123–24). This encounter, imprinted in Eloísa's narrative version as a happy dream, is seen from the daughter's perspective as something more akin to a nightmare. On the verge of death, the daughter calls out to her mother for mercy, and the spell of suspended time seems to break:

> como si hasta aquel momento me hubiera encontrado en una zona indefinible, fuera del espacio y del tiempo, de pronto mis palabras habían llenado el jardín de una extraña claridad. Sentí la garganta liberada de la presión de la cuerda y todo, al instante, se convirtió en real. Ella seguía allí, a sólo un par de metros de distancia. Pero la lluvia se deslizaba ahora por su rostro, deshacía los rizos, caía a borbotones sobre el traje vaporoso que se pegaba a su cuerpo de niña. Y ya la sonrisa, la patente arrogancia, habían dejado paso a una expresión de estupor, de sobresalto. [. . .] [M]e contemplaba como a una aparición, como a alguien venido de otro mundo. (124–25)

> [as if until that moment I had been in an undefinable zone, outside of space and time, and suddenly my words had filled the garden with a strange clarity. I felt my throat released from the pressure of the cord and everything, in an instant, became real. She was still there, only a few meters away. But the rain now slid down her face, undid her ringlets, fell in torrents on the vaporous dress that stuck against her child's body. And the smile, the patent arrogance, had now given way to an expression of stupor, of fright. {. . .} {S}he looked at me like an apparition, like someone come from another world.]

As with many of her tales, Fernández Cubas does not allow a clear-cut interpretation of exactly what takes place here. It is conceivable that the young Eloísa was not a tyrant at all, but "únicamente una niña" [only a child] (124), and that the tyrant is the figure preserved on the anachronistic plane that interacts with the adult Lucas, Bebo, and Tomás. As such, the domineering little girl could be merely a male fabrication that parallels the hidden side of the Spanish woman during the Franco years. On the other hand, it is quite possible that Eloísa was a manipulative little girl whose jealous drive for control almost obliterated her own daughter. The men in this story unwittingly support such a view, for despite their efforts to impose an ideal vision of Eloísa, they divulge unsavory aspects of her personality. Moreover, like the biblical Eden, their garden becomes the site of a transgression that ultimately produces transformative knowledge, a secret that Eloísa and her brothers and cousin repressed but that her daughter cannot deny: "el olvido disfrazó con los años algo que su mente de adulta se negaba a aceptar, pero que, sin embargo, necesitaba repetir compulsivamente" [with the passing of years forgetfulness disguised something that her adult mind refused to accept, but that, nonetheless, it needed to repeat compulsively] (135). It is quite possible, then, that Eloísa's *historia* reconstructed her past in a manner that was more comfortable for her to recollect from the distance of the present. Yet its very repetition, while ostensibly affirming the mother's view of the "truth," allows for the possibility of a different interpretation.

Thus the act of narration emerges as the ultimate re-collection of past events that weaves an order and design into the fabric of history. In a duplication of her mother's love for storytelling, the narrator retells and supplements her mother's history within the context of her own story: "ahora comprendía la razón por la que [. . .] nunca pudo contarme con exactitud aquellas imágenes que tanto le habían impresionado [. . .]. Pero de pronto era yo, tan reticente a escucharla, quien podía contarle paso a paso aquella terrible pesadilla que sólo el tiempo, ayudado por la desmemoria, transformaría en un hermoso, impreciso recuerdo" [now I understood the reason why she never could tell me with precision about those images that had so impressed her {. . .}. But suddenly I, so reluctant to listen to her, was the one who could tell her, step by step, about that terrible nightmare that only time, aided by forgetfulness, would transform into a beautiful, vague memory] (Fernández Cubas 1995, 135). The narrator finds that the collision of her mother's past with her own present wrought the greatest transformation of all: the communication of knowledge. For Eloísa, the experience brought a horrific understanding of the power she chose to wield against her daughter: "a través de sus ojos sorprendidos asomaba el horror ante mi grito, ante el castigo que había estado a punto de infligirme, ante lo que podía ocurrirme aún. Y, exhausta, dejaba caer la cuerda [. . .]. Intencionadamente. Previniéndome, avisándome, indicándome el peligro" [in her surprised eyes there appeared horror at my cry, at the punishment that she had been on the verge of inflicting on me, at what could happen to me still. And, exhausted, she let the cord fall {. . .}. Intentionally. Alerting me, warning me, showing me the danger] (135–36). By repeating the experience, the daughter receives the message communicated by her mother in a way that Eloísa was never able to express with her reconstruction of the past. In her turn, the protagonist repeats the story as her mother did, but from a different point of view, altered by time.

Time modifies the vision of things, sometimes bringing clarity and other times confusion, according to how people bring the experience into focus. History, as the narration of time, invariably privileges certain perspectives. In doing so, it advances some stories while silencing others: "Narrative history is, then, also a narrative against narration, a narrative of restriction, silence, illiteracy, and illegibility, a narrative where some invariably narrate (for) others" (Epps 1996, 46). While exploring the influence of time on one's viewpoint within space, *El columpio* oscillates in its perspective from the present to the past and back again, to illustrate the value of history, of change, of knowledge gained through experience. Juxtaposed with this paradigm of growth over time is the plane of frozen time, emblematic of Franco's mythification of Spain and of society's mythification of women, which inhibits the forward motion through time and space that alters perspective in order to promote understanding and change. The overlapping of the past with the present may be seen, on the one hand, as a technique of the marvelous or, on the other, as a trick of the fantastic genre, wherein readers cannot be sure what really happens. The protagonist herself is uncertain of the events: "¿O no había sido ella? Porque lo que sucedió a continuación fue al tiempo muy rápido y muy lento, muy claro y muy confuso" [Or had it not been she? Because what happened next was at once very fast and very slow, very clear and very confused] (Fernández Cubas 1995, 123). Whatever "truth" one attempts to interpret from this situation is ultimately irrelevant, however, because what the protagonist experiences from this perspective radically changes *her*. Thus *El columpio*, like *El año de Gracia*, validates the necessity of a change in point of view, for all the challenges to subjectivity that any quest for change must pose.

In the end, the daughter's altered view of her mother's stories transforms her view of her own history. Upon seeing the stagnation effected by her uncles' efforts to stop time, the protagonist refuses to manipulate the world according to her whim, the way they and her mother created "aquel mundo imposible en que se había detenido el reloj" [that impossible world in which the clock had stopped] (133). On the bus, en route to the train that will take her back to France at the end of the novel, she reads her uncles' letter to her and then rips it up, exorcising herself of "otras muchas cartas, de recuerdos ajenos, de un desván con olor a cerrado [. . .]" [many other letters, of other people's memories, of an attic that smelled closed-up] (133). In contrast to the men, she has read and interpreted the letter she received, although she interpreted much more than the discourse they attempted to impose through it: "Aquellas líneas cumplían una astuta función. La de eximirles a ellos de su locura e ingresarme a mí en una categoría difusa [. . .]. Una caprichosa y temeraria sobrina que bien pudiera hallarse ahora en el fondo de un pozo" [Those lines fulfilled an astute function. That of exempting them from their insanity and of installing me in a diffuse category {. . .} A capricious and rash niece who very well could find herself now in the bottom of a well] (131–32). Rejecting the image of herself that they attempt to construct with their written word, she also rips up the check they had sent to her, thinking of Lucas: "Con mayor frialdad repetí la sentencia de Lucas: 'El dinero te permite diseñar el mundo a tu antojo.' Lo destrocé lentamente, sintiendo un placer desconocido, lanzando al campo los papeles minúsculos que una brisa terca se empeñaba en devolver al interior del coche. Y entonces sí me sentí libre" [With greater coldness I repeated the sentence of Lucas: "Money allows you to design the world at your will." I ripped it up slowly, feeling a strange pleasure, throwing to the fields the miniscule pieces of paper that a stubborn breeze insisted on returning to the inside of the car. And *then* I felt free] (133). She repeats Lucas's words, but with the significant difference of altered intention, brought about by an altered perspective. Of course, repetition is inescapable, as the return of the shreds of the check into the bus whimsically suggests, but in that repetition lies the potential for liberation.

El columpio ends with a final repetition, when the protagonist awakens to hear the bus driver call out "¡Lucila!" (136) and sees the sign for an inn outside her window, just as she experienced when she first arrived at her uncles' town. Her fear of being imprisoned in an eternal return is alleviated, however, when she sees the subtle alteration of a different surname on the inn, accompanied by the sign *"On parle français"* (137). Symbolically, this repetition incorporates another perspective and another discourse—those of the outside, or the other, represented by France—that modify the experience of the same. The *same* does return eternally but, like Vattimo's truth and Being, it repeats only as "what is constantly being reinterpreted, rewritten, and remade—rather than as objects endowed with permanence and stability" (Vattimo 1991, xx). Because Being itself can never be expressed accurately, formulating history involves the endeavor of reinterpreting, rewriting, and remaking "being," the identity of the people whose story it tells. This narration is always subject to the vagaries of time and perspective, always subject to change.

Postmodernity has deconstructed truth and Being as absolute metaphysical values, and as a result the only remaining recourse to them, for Vattimo, lies in "what is handed down through 'linguistic messages from one generation to another,' as a series of texts and traces from the tradition that must always be interpreted once again" (Vattimo 1991, xxxix). If the modern view of history hinges on "progress" and "overcoming" (Vattimo 1991, xvi), then Fernández Cubas's postmodern text repeats this idea by suggesting that time alters the perspective and thus permits learning and change. In her fictional world, however, progress and overcoming are not the products solely of linear time. The central catalyst of the protagonist's development is her interaction with another realm that defies temporal limits, where she regresses and repeats her mother's experience in order to achieve progress and change for herself. Thus linear time is not overcome as much as it is undermined through reiteration. Like the swing, the protagonist moves forward only to move backward and cover the same space again, albeit always with a new perspective that is imposed by the passage of time. This oscillation, the act of repeating, is synthesized with the narrator's reinterpretation and rewriting of her mother's history. As a postmodern text, *El columpio* recasts the modern view of progressive and transformational history as a regression and repetition whose greatest innovation might be the deconstruction of time as a singular experience.

Conclusion

Whereas Fernández Cubas plunders Spain's distant past to consider the impact of colonialism on the construction of subjectivity in her first novel, in her second novel she meditates on the nature of history in general, and postwar Spanish history in particular, as the need to find difference in the repetition and recollection of the past. Iain Chambers has noted that "Representation involves repression: some things are shown, others are hidden; some things said, others unsaid. For in every representation the object represented is initially canceled and then replaced, re-presented, in another context and language" (I. Chambers 1990, 6). In this light, *El año de Gracia* repeats the literary canon, but studies what has been foreshadowed and excluded in the West's literary representation of its own centrality through its alienation of the other. *El columpio*, in its turn, represents a static and arcane Spain like the one depicted by Franco, yet counterpoises it with a different Spain, a periphery-turned-center, which, tempered by time, conveys undeniable forces of change. Thus the motif of repetition, inherent in representation, emerges as the limitation and the liberation of the contemporary subject in Fernández Cubas's two novels.

In the author's exploration of subjectivity, *El columpio* merges with the novelistic endeavor of *El año de Gracia* to accentuate the narrative nature of history and literature, two modes of representation that inescapably influence identity. As constructs, her works suggest, both discourses can be *deconstructed* even as they inexorably are repeated. In these two novels the censorship and deliberate manipulation of discourse, which strive to structure "truth," underscore the edited, incomplete nature of any representation of reality. Yet, through her protagonists who are *changed* over time, Fernández Cubas ultimately stresses the importance of experience and communicating knowledge, no matter how limited, for subjective development and agency.

Crucial to both novels is the configuration of power as a central tactic in the discursive construction and subversion of subjectivity. *El año de*

Gracia portrays the establishment of difference for the affirmation of power, as propagated in binaries such as civilization/barbarism and center/margin. *El columpio* then considers how authoritarian forces negate difference—of past/present, old/new—in order to uphold power and obstruct any alteration that a change in perspective might bring. Both novels suggest that power is not monolithic but mutable, repeatable, and ongoing, as symbolized by the titular image of *El columpio*. Implicit in the shifts of power evinced by the oscillating swing is the passing of time that alters perspective. No less significant to the transformation of identity is the change in the space of the subject, as I discuss in the next chapter in relation to *Con Agatha en Estambul*.

4
The Space of Oppositional Subjectivity in *Con Agatha en Estambul*

"¿Existía Estambul? ¿O no era nada más ni nada menos que un espacio sin
límites que todos, en algún momento, llevábamos en la espalda, pegado
como una mochila? [. . .] ¿O se trataba únicamente de un eco? Un eco
distinto para cada uno de nosotros que no hacía más que enfrentarnos a
nuestras vidas."

[Did Istanbul exist? Or was it nothing more and nothing less than a space
without limits that all of us, at some point, carried on our backs like a
backpack? {. . .} Or was it only an echo? A different echo for each of us,
that did nothing more than confront us with our lives.]
—"Con Agatha en Estambul"

MY STUDY IN CHAP. 3 OF FERNÁNDEZ CUBAS'S TWO NOVELS EXPLORED how the subject can exercise agency, even within the tautology of re-citing the discourses that define it, by repeating those markers differently. Such difference is inherent in repetition, the author's works suggest, because of the altered perspective imposed on the subject by the passage of time. In a humorous take on the disasters that befall the female subjects of *Con Agatha en Estambul* [With Agatha in Istanbul] (1994), Zatlin's "Amnesia, Strangulation, Hallucination and Other Mishaps: The Perils of Being Female in Tales of Cristina Fernández Cubas" considers how the feminine experience shapes perspective. Pérez discusses the unreliability of narrative perspective in these stories (Pérez 1998). Pritchett studies the title story as a journey to a middle ground that transforms the female protagonist (Pritchett 1996). Finally, Glenn traces the verbal and visual artistry of female artists in "Mundo" ("World"), the first story in the collection (Glenn 1998). Whether female or male, reliable or unreliable, key to the formation of any perspective is the subject's locus in space. In the present chapter I examine how the borders that define one's space influence the construction of identity in *Con Agatha en Estambul*. In these tales, the characters project their identities onto their surroundings, construct their identities based on clues from their environs, or even conceive of identity itself as a space to be filled or destroyed, in accordance with the viability of the subject herself.

This collection of stories reflects the extratextual space of post-totalitarian Spain, wherein identity is a complex construction that negotiates multiple boundaries on individual, regional, national, and international levels. The 1978 Constitution recognized that numerous autonomous communities constitute Spain (although the criteria for constructing those communities was often polemical). Rejecting Franco's drive toward homogeneity and his suppression of difference, the new Spain recognized that being Spanish also meant being Galician or Catalan or Andalusian, and so forth. Then, at the start of 1986, Spain joined the EC and officially defined itself as part of a larger space with extended parameters of identity. In addition, the impact of globalization constantly penetrates national borders to bring countries under the influence of one another on a daily basis through media, commerce, and so on. In Fernández Cubas's texts, when the issue of space is prominent, it is frequently a foreign site, or else—barring markers such as language—it is an undefined location, potentially anywhere in the world. The crisis of cultural and individual identity played out against the backdrop of a world community is, to a degree, what gives this author's fiction its universal appeal. In this context of a world in flux, Fernández Cubas's stories construct, interrogate, and redefine the setting of space as a fundamental step in the process of writing the ongoing story of the subject.

"Mundo"

The very title of this story focuses on the symbolic spatial image of *el mundo*, a word whose standard meaning is "world" and whose antiquated meaning is "trunk." When Carolina, the narrator, recounts her entrance into the convent as a young girl, she explains that she carried her mother's wedding dress and her own possessions in her *mundo*. The closed space of this trunk serves as a metaphor for both the convent and the oppressive world at large. Despite the feminine usage associated with the chest, its lid displays a picture composed of masculine imagery: a sailor stands with the sun on one side and a storm on the other, with his boat in the distance, waiting to embark; the picture also contains a sword and a skull, traditional symbols of the phallus and of death. Yet what most stirs Carolina is the face-to-face confrontation provoked by the sailor. This sailor positions the viewer straight ahead with his intent gaze as he holds up a picture of himself, an image that replicates exactly the very image on the lid of the trunk that Carolina sees. Thus she observes a sequence of infinite repetitions of the sailor, who remains enclosed in the frame and does not change (except for the shrinking size of each of his subsequent selves). By implication, the viewer, positioned by the sailor's gaze, is also trapped in an imploding infinity of subjectivity to patriarchal power.

The imprisoning spaces of this picture, as well as the space within the trunk and the convent, reflect the controlled and subjugated status of Carolina herself. This nun, who begins the story with no voice at all, comes to define herself within the cloister by gaining and exercising her voice in relation to the other characters. Eventually, she holds a pivotal role as the key communicator among the nuns, and also between the nuns and the outside world. At the time she narrates her story, Carolina is the most powerful nun in the convent. She claims in her narration that she has no desire to leave the nunnery—to open it or herself up to the potential of change by outside forces. According to her own discourse, then, Carolina as abbess is not a threat to the closed nature of the status quo. At the textual level, however, Carolina's narration introduces real potential for change. Under the guise of propagating the closed structure of power in the convent, Carolina *as narrator* opens her text to permeation by other subversive voices, inviting oppositionality and potential change. Ultimately, her text is opened to the reader, the "other" who must complete the potential communication of subversion by interpreting the oppositional message in her narrative.

Carolina, who has been literally "shut up" in the convent by her father and her priest because she has discovered the secret of their amorous liaisons with the housekeeper (and, she later discovers, because her father wanted control of her inheritance), alters the silence of the convent as she gradually comes to find her voice and define her identity. On her first day in the convent, Carolina is sent by the abbess, Mother Angélica, to take a last look at herself in the mirror, in order to view the self-image that will endure the rest of her life. Because she will never be allowed to look in the mirror again, this fleeting image of a youthful self is intended to impose eternal stasis over the future *unseen* images of change in Carolina. Parallel to the mirror stage of psychoanalytic subject development, this reflection establishes the ideal image of a youthful self that will give Carolina the illusion of wholeness. This specular visage highlights how representation offers, at most, a slanted and limited view of reality. By refusing to let her augment that youthful reflection with any future images, the power structure in the convent denies Carolina the opportunity to expand her vision of herself.

Shortly after viewing the image of her identity in the mirror, Carolina confirms her subjectivity verbally when she signifies herself in opposition to the priest, who brings her father's money to the convent to pay for her expenses. At this moment, she realizes that the priest's patriarchal contract has sealed her fate. Defining herself in resistance to her religious "father" as well as to her biological parent, Carolina discovers her voice: "una voz que no era mía, pero que salía de mí, empezó a hablar. Y me escuché atónita. 'Padre, yo no hice nada.'" [a voice that was not mine, but that came out of me, began to speak. And I listened to myself, astonished. "Father, I didn't do anything."] (Fernández Cubas 1994, 35). When the priest rejects her pleas and condemns her to stay in the convent, Carolina is amazed to find that she possesses a "voz interior que susurra despropósitos" [interior voice that whispers nonsense] (35). Eventually, she stops trying to suppress this voice and allows it free reign: "'Cerdo, cochino, puerco,' murmuré. [. . .] 'Hueles a mierda,' añadí. Y súbitamente tranquila, como si para mí empezara en aquel momento una nueva vida, cerré con toda suavidad el arca, acaricié al marino, di la vuelta a la llave y, muy despacio, muy despacio, la guardé en el bolsillo" ["Pig, swine, hog" I murmured. {. . .} "You smell like shit," I added. And suddenly calm, as if in that moment a new life were beginning for me, I closed the chest with utmost gentleness, caressed the sailor, turned the key and, very slowly, very slowly, put it in my pocket] (37). From a psychoanalytic perspective, this description of private defiance suggests that Carolina has separated from the figure of the "father" as her "other" in order to transfer her desire onto a different object: the sailor, the keeper of the hidden secrets that she whispers into the trunk. Most importantly in her development as a subject, Carolina has discovered the power of her own voice, which she can now begin to strengthen.

Once she has actively entered into the realm of language, Carolina defines her self by exercising her voice in relation to others. With the abbess, Mother Angélica, the young Carolina forges a relationship based on trust, communication, and a mutual passion for secret knowledge. Carolina's favored position gains her access to the mother superior's library where, in the closed space of a cabinet—a secured, compartmentalized image reminiscent of the trunk and the convent— Mother Angélica guards her books about the world under lock and key. This relationship accords Carolina knowledge and confidence to strengthen her voice, which she will eventually use to create her own authority.

Many years later, Carolina's voice becomes even more powerful with the arrival of a mute nun named Mother Perú, who communicates by painting narrative pictures on gourds. Carolina takes on the role of interpreter of pictures and intermediary between the voiceless nun and the enclosed community of women: "Y por eso yo de nuevo tomaba la voz cantante, [. . .] con la autoridad que me confería el moverme a mis anchas en las estanterías del despacho de la abadesa, por mis conocimientos del país de las tres regiones, de las costumbres de ciertos conventos del mundo, de sus milagros, de sus leyendas. . ." [And hence I took the lead, {. . .} with the authority bestowed on me because I could move about at ease among the bookshelves of the abbess's office, because of my knowledge of the country of three regions, of the customs of certain convents in the world, of their miracles, of their legends. . .] (48). By appropriating acceptable roles to promote forbidden and liberating communication, Carolina finds freedom in what Paul Smith calls "the interstices of subject positions" (Smith 1988, 25). Thus she is able to maneuver in the breach between the roles of submissive woman and silent nun, roles which society preordained for her: "Porque lo cierto es que desde la llegada de madre Perú no parábamos de hablar. Como si su mudez irremediable nos relevara de nuestro sacrificio voluntario" [Because what is certain is that since the arrival of Mother Perú we hadn't stopped talking. As if her irremediable muteness relieved us of our voluntary sacrifice] (Fernández Cubas 1994, 48). Carolina's voice, the key that enables communication among the nuns, subverts and supplants the dominant ecclesiastical discourse of silence within the convent.

This undermining of silence relates to Ross Chambers's theory in *Room for Maneuver: Reading (the) Oppositional (in) Narrative*, which highlights narrative as a site of agency and, ultimately, as a means for extending textual agency to readers so that they can defy the limited roles that society offers them. Chambers distinguishes between acts of open resistance and of subtle oppositionality as means of reacting against oppressive power. According to his scheme, acts of overt resistance seek to invert a given power structure, but eventually end up propagating the same power model of oppressor and oppressed after they attain control. In contrast, oppositional techniques are always carried out by the powerless merely to survive, to gain a small measure of control in their daily environment, not to imminently transform the whole system of power. Nonetheless, oppositionality can indeed achieve gradual change, because it works "to shift desire from forms that enslave to forms that liberate, that is from the modes of desire that are produced by and in the interest of the structures of power to forms that represent a degree of release from that repression, which is simultaneously a political oppression" (R. Chambers 1991, xvii). Oppositionality, then, is generated *by* the system of power and works *within* that system to effect gradual change.

According to Chambers's paradigm, Carolina's subversion of the silence in the convent constitutes oppositional behavior that counters power covertly, not to change the overall system of the convent, but to survive better within it. Hence one might argue that, under the cover of the convent, Carolina inspires the women to change their activities so that they may better accommodate themselves. Nonetheless, a reading of inviolate female advancement is problematic in this tale because these women ultimately do not alter the closed structure of the monolithic institution. On the contrary, Carolina's hierarchical ascent in the nunnery corresponds to her manipulation of communicative signs to reinforce the closure of power.

Within the convent, voiced and unvoiced signs coalesce in the images that the mute Mother Perú paints on the symbolic space of the gourds, which become the battleground for power. The gourd constitutes the space of telling stories and the site of Carolina's apprenticeship as a seer of pictures and a spinner of tales. Carolina's struggle to negotiate between words and pictures as modes of communication provides an artistic parallel to the oppositionality between the self and other that permeates all of Fernández Cubas's works. W. J. T. Mitchell describes the ekphrastic duality of text/image as "a relation of [. . .] domination in which the 'self' is understood to be an active, speaking, seeing subject, while the 'other' is projected as a passive, seen, and (usually) silent object" (Mitchell 1994, 157). In its representation of an image, the verbal text privileges itself as the possessor of information necessary to explain the significance of its incomplete, visual, and silent other. The ekphrastic "overcoming of otherness" (Mitchell 1994, 156) illustrates artistically the tension between self and other that shapes the way the subject views its own identity. In "Mundo," Mother Perú is not just any other: she comes from South America, the periphery by which Spain historically defined itself as the center of power. As the author of the pictorial representations, Mother Perú confounds the convent's rites of communication and yet, paradoxically, confers greater authority upon *Carolina*, not herself. Although she is translator and not author, Carolina's status as the sole person with knowledge of both codes needed for communication—the verbal and the visual—endows her with even greater power as the central communicator among the nuns.[1]

Yet Carolina's authority, bolstered by her anticipation of the imminent unveiling of Mother Perú's secret gourd, which is to be a true "obra maestra" [masterpiece] (Fernández Cubas 1994, 51), crumbles when everyone learns that both the artistic nun and her silence are a fraud. For Mother Perú does have a voice after all. The wrath of the abbess at the discovery of this deceit can rival only the fury of Carolina at her loss of power as the privileged seer and speaker. Significantly, this diminution of her voice—of her identity—is quickly followed by the desecration of the beautiful image of herself that she remembers from her final, youthful look in the mirror. Carolina happens upon Mother Perú secretly staring in the looking glass and is forced by the defiant nun to stop observing others and confront her own true image: "Me agarró del rosario con fuerza y me obligó a inclinar la cabeza sobre el espejo. 'Mírate ya. Vieja revieja'" [She yanked me by the rosary and forced me to lean my head over the mirror. "Look at yourself for once. You ancient old hag"] (63). Now it is Mother Perú who usurps power from her other by symbolizing in language the meaning of the image. The safety of the closed structure of space and identity in which Carolina operated has now been pulverized by a subversive voice from the outside that penetrates the inside and articulates the effects of time embodied in the specular image, which before had been seen by others but silenced and concealed from the self. This unsettling "other" voice of Mother Perú reveals that that enclosed protection, which Carolina thought the convent offered her, is as artificial and illusory as that youthful image of herself that the mirror once reflected. Carolina is inspired to take action to improve her situation because of the shocking realization, provoked by the oppositional other, that her identity is not stable at all.

After the power of her voice has been stolen and her self-image shattered, Carolina repositions herself in order to dominate the situation. Rather than trying to change the nuns in the convent, she proposes to seize control of events and manipulate the very people from the outside who now repress her. Carolina wrests the power first from Mother Perú by appropriating the gourd for her own use. The great masterpiece of Mother Perú was, in fact, a testimonial of her years of fleeing from criminals whose crime she had inadvertently witnessed. Carolina burns the gourd with Mother Perú's original images and substitutes another, of her own creation, that implicates Mother Perú as the criminal and not the innocent witness. By stealing Mother Perú's narrative and positioning herself as the painter of pictures and the teller of tales, she extricates herself from silence and subjugation before the angry abbess and the police who seek the impostor. In their eagerness to hear her story, these listeners do not notice the switch in speaking and seeing subjects. The key to Carolina's strategy is her ability to inspire her audience's desire to hear her account: she tells her tale believably using her narratee's discourse, the discourse of a police story. In this way, she recruits the power of her audience to gain power for herself. By reinvesting herself with the force of a narrative voice, Carolina establishes her own authority as the artist/

narrator who can manipulate the images and unfold the tale that others desire to see and hear.

Having donned the discourse of a police story as a means of satisfying the desire of her listeners and of regaining her own power, Carolina then divests herself of the limited feminine confinement of the trunk. After she acquires new authority through the telling of her tale, Carolina leaves the trunk, the former space of her self, empty and silent: "Todos los cajones estaban vacíos y abiertos, incluso los secretos, los que en otros tiempos cobijaron recuerdos y que ahora no parecían sino celdas de un convento desierto [. . .] que yo desinfectaba, fregaba, oreaba, para que no quedase nada de sus antiguos moradores. Ni tan siquiera voces, murmullos" [All the drawers were empty and open, even the secret ones, those that in other times sheltered memories and that now only seemed like cells of a deserted convent {. . .}, which I disinfected, scrubbed, aired out, so that none of its former dwellers would remain. Not even voices, whispers] (64–65). She scrubs the image-inscribed trunk to expunge all traces of the subversive words she once concealed there. Indeed, Carolina's vigorous cleaning erases the mouth of the sailor on its lid, but she reflects, "tal vez me gustaba más así" [perhaps I liked him better that way] (64). She has no need for that masculine image nor its designation of infinite closed spaces, for she has gained authority by manipulating patriarchal discourse for herself.

At the moment of the enunciation of her tale, Carolina is the abbess in control of the convent, and all "evil" forces from the outside that threatened to penetrate the convent have been repelled or coopted. Even the menace of the cats, which one of the nuns used to kill when they invaded the convent gardens, has now been incorporated into Carolina's power structure through the domestication of the black cat, "Nylon." Named for the postwar nylon industry that threatened to render obsolete the nuns' occupation of sewing for the community, the adopted cat Nylon symbolizes an appropriation—another form of oppositionality in Chambers's sense of the word. This reference to nylon also indicates that the time period of "Mundo" is essentially the Spanish postwar. Carolina's refusal to leave the nunnery when finally allowed to do so late in her life corresponds with the arrival of democracy in Spain, when the bishop asked the nuns to leave the convent and vote. In symbolic contrast to the changing system of political power in Spain, this protagonist has no real interest in altering the closed system of control, for she holds a stake in the status quo.

As the abbess, the aged Carolina seduces new nuns into her sequestered space with the power of her words and, apparently, seals them into the absolute, authoritative "truth" of her discourse. She dreams of attracting additional novices with her letters and of initiating them into the discursive history of the convent: "Cuando las cartas que escribo encuentren respuesta [. . .] sí podré narrar [. . .] la azarosa vida de una prófuga que se hacía llamar madre Perú, la llegada al convento de una niña con un traje de boda. . . Historias y más historias. Leyendas" [When the letters I write are answered {. . .} then I'll be able to narrate {. . .} the eventful life of a fugitive who called herself Mother Perú, the arrival to the convent of a young girl with a wedding dress. . . . Stories and more stories. Legends] (Fernández Cubas 1994, 71). It is significant that, when she has secured a position of power, Carolina depends on the written word instead of pictures to communicate. The written word is associated with the discourse of the law, the foundation of patriarchal structure in the Western world. Once in control, Carolina rejects communication through pictures, which she and Mother Perú had invested with a subversive function, in order to continue the patriarchal privileging of the word through the letters in which she records the history of the convent.[2] This narrative role for Carolina in relation to other characters preserves and even propagates the existing power structure.

Although Carolina has failed to open the confining walls of the convent, in fact the space of the *text* has been opened in significant ways. This does not occur at the level of the Carolina's narratees within the story, for neither the nuns nor the police question the authority of the stories she invents. The tales she tells continue to be restrictive, as Glenn observes: "Cells and drawers underscore the idea of enclosure, limitation, and constriction, and both have structural parallels in the sections of Madre Perú's carvings and the twenty-two segments of Fernández Cubas's story" (Glenn 1998, 502). Carolina may reject the trunk as the space of her confessions in favor of relaying her ideas through narration to others; however, the motifs of enclosure and compartmentalization continue to characterize her mode of expression. Nonetheless, readers can maneuver out of the position of this story's narratees, who are positioned as acquiescent objects in Carolina's gaze and comprehend only what she wants them to know.

The space for such oppositional reading surfaces through the other voices and discourses that penetrate Carolina's final story—the text of "Mundo"—to oppose her power by contradicting her overt message. The most forceful of these voices emerges in the closing lines of the tale, "la voz que a veces parece surgir de las adelfas" [the voice that sometimes seems to arise from the oleanders] (Fernández Cubas 1994, 72). The narrator appears to assert her authority by dismissing this voice, which tauntingly echoes Mother Perú's defiant words: "Pero no debemos engañarnos.

La adelfa es una planta venenosa, y nada tiene de raro que el murmullo que a ratos creo apreciar también lo sea. 'Meticona, vieja, revieja. No eres más que una vieja. . .'" [But we shouldn't deceive ourselves. The oleander is a poisonous plant, and it is not at all strange that the rustling murmurs I think I discern from time to time should be so as well. "Meddler, ancient old hag. You're nothing but an old woman. . ."] (72). On a narrative level, Carolina exerts her authority so that her narratee will accept her discourse, just as she convinced the police to believe her before. Nonetheless, the combined subversive voices of Mother Perú and the oleanders open the textual space with the difference and opposition that they establish to Carolina's profession of innocence. The challenge here is for readers to move out of the position of the narratee, who passively accepts Carolina's admonitions, and maneuver into the position of what Chambers would call the interpreting subject, who reads her discourse in the context of the entire text and sees that the "truth" presented by this narrator is not the only "truth" to be told. By interpreting the message of the text differently than the way the narrator attempts to impose, readers ultimately act as the seeing subject, the oppositional other that fulfills the signification of the story as an open text.

This story's representation of misinterpretations and "better" interpretations of texts emphasizes the potential in the act of interpreting well, the power of moving out of the position of object in order to see other perspectives as an empowered subject. Such elastic constructions and deconstructions of meaning point to the breaches through which oppositionality can penetrate any discourse of power. Both visual and verbal representations are proffered in "Mundo" as a training ground for interpretation, establishing a self-other relation that reflects the tension between Carolina and the "others" in the fictional world, as well as that of narrator/narratee and author/reader. Ekphrasis serves as a metaphor of social practice, in order "to expose the social structure of representation as an activity and a relationship of power/knowledge/desire" (Mitchell 1994, 180). Hence Fernández Cubas engages artistic representation and interpretation as a key site where dialectical relations of otherness can be played out to influence readerly desire. Moreover, this story presents a self-reflexive illumination of the narrative act as *discourse* by means of the series of narratees within the tale who acquiesce to the discourse of power offered by their narrators. Fernández Cubas positions artistic representations—both visual and textual—as dynamic players in the process of social change by drawing her readers into the game of subversive interpretation. Through oppositionality, this narrative establishes a new textual image based not on the paradigm of the masculine sailor—one of imploding closures of the self—but one that is open to the difference and danger of otherness.

"La mujer de verde"

If the trunk serves as the central image of space and identity in "Mundo," then the woman in green of "La mujer de verde" ["The Woman in Green"] becomes the depository in which the nameless, first-person narrator and protagonist invests *her* identity in the second story of the collection. In this tale a modern, possibly anorexic woman who is dependent on sleeping pills clutches at the proffered social roles of executive, caregiver, lover, and Cinderella figure. She fails to appropriately fulfill these roles, however, and lashes out violently to defend herself from the menace of a perfection that she will never achieve. The woman in green of the title serves as the catalyst for the nameless protagonist's struggle against the social mores that construct her subjectivity. A hallucinatory image that the narrator obsessively describes and inscribes in her text, each representation of the woman in green invites and requires a rereading of the text. Fernández Cubas's story incites readers to question predefined subject positions by demonstrating that the perspective of this narrator—and the act of interpretation itself—is ultimately always partial and partisan, in need of displacement and a new point of view.

In presenting the formation of the subject, "La mujer de verde" displays the many social roles extended to the "liberated" woman in today's society. According to her own account, the narrator is an important executive who suffers from dietary obsessions—she forgoes food and yet desperately craves it to fill up the emptiness she feels inside her svelte physique. The narrator also depicts herself as the secret lover of Eduardo, her already married boss (she admits, however, that none of the other characters views her as his lover, least of all Eduardo himself). Moreover, the narrator serves as caregiver for the office employees: she buys them personalized Christmas gifts on Eduardo's behalf, allowing him to receive all the credit. Ever conscious of the image that she presents to others, the narrator circumspectly tries to fit in with each of her designated roles: "tengo el papel bien aprendido" [I have the part well learned], she asserts (Fernández Cubas 1994, 79).

As she struggles to comply with all these subject positions of the feminine, the narrator increasingly obsesses with her secretary, Dina Dachs, whom she perceives as the consummate modern woman. At first the narrator describes this employee as average, but soon must admit that certain qualities distinguish her as remarkable: "[hay] una ligera ventaja a favor de Dina. Tres idiomas a la perfección, excelentes referencias, una notable habilidad a la hora de rellenar el cuestionario de casa" [{There is} a slight advantage in Dina's favor. Three languages mastered to perfection, excellent references, a remarkable ability when it was time to fill out forms] (81). In time, she imagines Dina as the exotic embodiment of a theatrical star: "Pienso en un pseudónimo, en un nombre artístico, en DINA DACHS anunciado en grandes caracteres en un teatro de variedades [. . .]" [I think of a pseudonym, of an artistic name, of DINA DACHS announced in big letters at a variety show {. . .}] (81). The immediate stimulus for this fixation is that the protagonist believes that she has seen her secretary in the street, dressed in a green suit with a purple necklace, and looking strangely harrowed: "la mujer, la desconocida tras la que acabo de correr en la calle, mostraba en su rostro las huellas de toda una vida, el sufrimiento, una mirada enigmática y fría que ni siquiera alteró una sola vez, a pesar de mis llamadas" [the woman, the stranger I just ran after in the street, showed in her face the imprint of a lifetime, the suffering, an enigmatic and cold gaze that didn't waver even once, despite my calls] (76). Haunted by the woman's gaze, the narrator confronts Dina to try to help her, but the secretary insists that she is not the woman in green.

In the subsequent weeks, the protagonist repeatedly sees the woman in green, who deteriorates further with each encounter, but none of the other characters notices her. The narrator becomes convinced that the woman summons her for help: "Allí abajo está la mujer [. . .]. Sortea los coches como por milagro. Con el brazo alzado, siempre hacia mí. El deterioro es patético" [The woman is there below {. . .}. She dodges the cars as if by a miracle. With her arm raised, always toward me. The deterioration is pathetic] (87). Thus, even the lovely woman in green is destroyed by a life in the city that is "inhumana, cruel, despiadada" [inhuman, cruel, heartless] (87). The woman in green may be seen to function as the ideal other for the narrator, embodying the impossible realization and eventual doom of the successful executive, the nurturing caregiver, and the skilled lover, all facets of the "perfect woman." It is symbolic that the woman wears green, of course, evocative of youth, sexuality, and fertility. Because these are precisely the qualities of vibrant womanhood that are lacking in the narrator's own life, it is also appropriate that green signals envy. In "La mujer de verde," the narrator struggles to conform to the specter of the social construct of woman, but discovers it to be a mythical and unattainable ideal. She convinces herself that Dina Dachs and the woman in green are one and the same person; as a result, both function simultaneously as the "other" projection of herself—the lure and the menace of the ideal woman.

Emblematic of this displacement of idealism and failure onto the other is the intertext of Cinderella. The narrator frequently mentions her frustration with not fitting into shoes: "Ninguno de los dos pares de zapatos se ajusta a mis medidas. Unos me quedan demasiado estrechos, me oprimen. Para soportarlos debo contraer los dedos en forma de piña. Con los otros me ocurre justamente lo contrario" [Neither of the two pairs of shoes is my size. One is too tight, it squeezes my feet. To wear them I have to curl my toes up like ball. With the other it's just the opposite] (77). This passage recalls the ugly, wicked stepsisters who are too ungainly to squeeze into Cinderella's petite glass slipper and who are spurned by the desired prince as a result. Just as Cinderella's slipper did not fit the stepsisters, the role of the perfect woman that has been mythically constructed by society is unsuitable for the protagonist of "La mujer de verde." Frustrated by her own inferiority in contrast to her secretary's dexterity, she projects the ideal of Cinderella-like perfection onto the woman in green and then watches its destruction. This modern Cinderella's deterioration culminates when the woman in green never recovers her dainty green pump after it falls off her foot: "distingo una mancha verde en uno de los pies, sólo en uno, y enseguida comprendo su ocasional cojera. El otro zapato ha quedado olvidado en el bordillo de la acera. Pero nadie lo recoge" [I make out a green stain on one of her feet, only on one, and immediately I understand her temporary limp. The other shoe was left behind on the curb of the sidewalk. But no one picks it up] (87). When this Cinderella loses her slipper, it symbolizes that the fairy tale *cannot* come true in the modern age (if indeed it ever could). Limping around with no one bothering to rescue her, the ideal woman has degenerated into a literal misfit.

Even as the protagonist's psyche struggles with her shortcomings as a modern woman, she seeks to conform to the situation by taking sleeping pills. Hoping to obliterate the stress of work and the racket caused by her neighbors at home, she frequently resorts to the drugs: "Píldoras para dormir. Ahí estaba el remedio. Un sueño artificial que me ha repuesto de tantos días de agitación y cansancio. Ahora empiezo a ver las cosas de otra manera" [Sleeping pills. Therein lay the cure. An artificial sleep that has revived me after so many days of agitation and tiredness. Now I begin to see things differently] (Fernández Cubas 1994, 89). These sedatives serve as a self-regulating mechanism that reflects Althusser's assessment that "the vast majority of (good) subjects work all right 'all by themselves'" (Althusser 1971, 181). "Good" subjects find a way to tolerate their subject positions, assuming that there are no other positions possible. The artificial sleep induced by the pills alters the narrator's way of seeing things; she can believe that she merely has suffered a temporary lapse in control and that she is now able to fulfill the role of the accomplished, contented woman. Thus the sleeping pills represent the subject's efforts to hold its proper place in compliance with the dictates of society. The drug-induced euphoria is fleeting, however, for the protagonist soon glimpses and then overtakes the green-clad woman in the street only to discover that she now looks like a walking corpse. Confronted with putrefaction as the hidden face of perfection, the narrator realizes that her ideal secretary is fated to become this decrepit phantasm: "escucho por primera vez en mi vida una voz que surge de algún lugar de mí misma. Dina, aunque tal vez no haya muerto aún, está muerta. La mujer de verde es Dina muerta" [I listen, for the first time in my life, to a voice that emerges from some place in myself. Dina, even though she hasn't died yet perhaps, is dead. The woman in green is Dina dead] (Fernández Cubas 1994, 91). Despite her struggle, via the sleeping pills, to make life look "normal," the narrator cannot veil the apparition of doom that she repeatedly confronts.

The narrator's foreboding of condemnation emerges not only in her relationships with "other" women—her secretary, the woman in green—but also in the spaces she associates with them. Early in the story, she tries to pinpoint the woman in green's reflection in the space of a mirror in order to identify her:

> Yo, secándome la cara con la toalla de papel, jugando mecánicamente con las posibilidades de un espejo de tres caras, comprobando mi peinado, mi perfil, y ella, una sombra verde, pasando como una exhalación por el espejo. Rectifico la posición de las lunas, las abro, las cierro y, atónita aún, logro aprisionarla por unos segundos. La mujer está allí. Detrás de mí, junto a mí, no lo sé muy bien. Me vuelvo enseguida, pero sólo acierto a sorprender el vaivén de la puerta. (80)

> [I, drying my face with a paper towel, mechanically playing with the possibilities of a three-sided mirror, checking my hairdo, my profile, and she, a green shadow, passing by the mirror like a vapor. I adjust the position of the mirrors, I open them, I shut them and, still astonished, I manage to capture her for a few seconds. The woman is there. Behind me, next to me, I don't really know. I turn around at once, but I only manage to surprise the swinging of the door.]

This encounter unsettles the narrator because the woman in green eludes entrapment in a single space, just as her identity remains uncertain and un-

4 / THE SPACE OF OPPOSITIONAL SUBJECTIVITY

defined. As the story progresses, the woman in green comes to occupy other, more tangible spaces that evoke a sense of alienation, futility, and disintegration: "He asistido a su proceso de descomposición, a sus apariciones imposibles en calles concurridas, en lunas de espejos, en callejones sin salida" [I have witnessed her process of decomposition, her impossible appearances in crowded streets, in mirrors, in dead-end alleys] (91). The woman in green is seen freely roaming the streets, yet the traffic and the crowd become so menacing that they nearly kill her. Ultimately, those uncaring, crowded streets lead to a veritable dead end, where the woman's face reveals a grimace of death. The fate of the modern woman thus seems tied to the degenerative and increasingly restrictive sites she occupies. The space of this subject, while ostensibly elusive or even unbounded, ultimately shrinks to a place of death.

If overwhelming streets and deceptive mirrors are the spaces of the woman in green, the protagonist's own identity as a subject is situated within the closed spaces of her office, her apartment where she is at the mercy of noisy neighbors, or the shoe stores where she futilely searches for her proper size. Even when the narrator describes herself on the street—a site potentially associated with freedom—she is only there to carry out the role of someone else, as she buys Eduardo's Christmas presents for his employees. Moreover, when the protagonist tries to exert control over her secretary, she does so by overloading her with work to keep her confined in the office as long as possible. In the narrator's perception of female subjectivity, then, any and every space imposes imprisonment and eventual death for women: "Pobre Dina Dachs. Encerrada en su despacho, regresando a su piso, paseando por la calle. Porque Dina, se encuentre donde se encuentre en estos momentos, ignora todavía que está muerta desde hace mucho tiempo" [Poor Dina Dachs. Closed up in her office, returning to her apartment, walking around on the street. Because Dina, wherever she may be right now, does not yet know that she has been dead for a long time] (91). The spaces that invariably contain the women in this story, just like the subject positions that society ordains for them, all prove to be limiting and ultimately lethal.

Believing herself destined to warn Dina of her impending fate, the protagonist seeks out her secretary in her office on Christmas Eve. She discovers Dina dressed for a party in a green silk suit but without the purple necklace of the vision. When Dina rejects all exhortations not to go out, the narrator physically tries to force her to acquiesce:

Ignoro si enloquezco u obedezco la voz del destino. Porque la zarandeo. Y ella se resiste [. . .]. Está asustada, no atiende a razones. Por eso yo, firmemente decidida, no tengo más remedio que inmovilizarla, revelarle la terrible verdad, decirle gimiendo: "Está usted muerta. ¿No lo comprende aún? ¡Está muerta!" Pero Dina no ofrece ya resistencia. Sus ojos me miran redondeados por el espanto y su cuerpo se desliza junto al mío hasta caer al suelo, impotente, aterrorizada. (Fernández Cubas 1994, 96)

[I don't know if I'm going insane or obeying the voice of destiny. For I shake her. And she resists [. . .]. She is frightened and will not listen to reason. So I, firmly decided, have no other recourse but to immobilize her, to reveal the terrible truth, to tell her, groaning: "You're dead. Don't you get it yet? You're dead!" But Dina no longer offers any resistance. Her eyes gaze at me, wide in fright, and her body slides against mine until it falls to the floor, impotent, terrified.]

The narrator envisions herself as the one who must warn Dina that the nature of her subjectivity finally places her in the position of inescapable death.

The argument I have traced thus far, based on the narrator's own discourse about her life, is only one of several possible reflections offered by the mirror of the text. This angle can be displaced by focusing on certain contradictions and chronological inconsistencies in the story. For instance, toward the end of this present-tense narrative there is suddenly a future-tense prolepsis to two days later when everyone will learn the contents of certain papers in Dina's purse. This passage suggests that, in fact, *Dina Dachs* was the lover of Eduardo and that the narrator is not in the place where she pretends to be: "oiré rumores, pasos, sentiré frío [. . .]. *Querido Eduardo*. . . Palabras que recuerdo bien porque son de Dina [. . .]. Frases absurdas, ridículas, obscenas. Promesas de amor entremezcladas con ruidos de pasos, llaves, puertas que se abren, que se cierran, los vecinos del piso de arriba arrastrando muebles, un hombre con bata blanca diciéndome: 'Está usted agotada. Serénese'" [I will hear confused noises, footsteps, I will feel cold {. . .}. *Dear Eduardo*. . . Words that I remember well because they are Dina's {. . .}. Absurd, ridiculous, obscene phrases. Promises of love mixed with noises of footsteps, keys, doors opening and closing, the upstairs neighbors dragging furniture, a man in a white robe telling me: "You're exhausted, ma'am. Calm down"] (96–97). Noisy "neighbors" all around, a man in white urging her to calm down, all those references to taking pills. . . . At this point, textual evidence displaces the speaking subject from her office or apartment into an insane asylum or hospital. What was just read as the somewhat reliable narration of a stressed-out executive now becomes a radically different tale. A reinterpretation of the entire narration, in light of the speaker's insanity, construes the text as the narrator's distorted mental experience of eternally reliving in the present the events that precipitated her incarceration in the madhouse, the ultimate closed space. The speaker can project what will happen two days in the "future," then, because it actually happened to her in the past. In the narrator's mind, past and future converge and collapse into a heinous and everlasting present.

This knowledge alters readers' perspectives of the tale and replaces the earlier interpretation. Whereas the narrator's focalization of her Christmas Eve confrontation with her secretary depicted Dina as wide-eyed in terror, readers may now surmise that, in fact, the secretary's eyes were popping out of her head from the force of strangulation. The narrator choked Dina in order to create the "purple necklace" that she saw around the neck of the woman in green: "observo un cerco amoratado en torno a su garganta y comprendo con frialdad que no le falta nada. 'Todavía es pronto,' digo en voz alta a pesar de que nadie pueda escucharme. 'Pero mañana, pasado mañana, será un collar violeta'" [I observe a bruise encircling her throat and coldly I comprehend that she lacks nothing. "It's early yet," I say out loud even though no one can hear me. "But tomorrow, the day after, it will be a purple necklace"] (98). By suturing her secretary's identity in the present to that of the woman in green in the future, the narrator would destroy the specter of unattainability that previously was the bane of her self-image.

Despite the interpretive transformation precipitated by readers' suspicion of the protagonist's insanity, the apparent "normality" of this narrator throughout much of the text implicitly questions the very concept of insanity. Rereading the text, one notices the changeable, slippery usage of the word *locura*. For instance, before the speaker's insanity becomes apparent, she reflects at one point that "en el mes de diciembre es una auténtica locura mantener la ventana abierta" [in the month of December it is pure insanity to keep the window open] (Fernández Cubas 1994, 86). Later on, after the sleeping pills (or a stronger medication, perhaps, prescribed by the doctors in the asylum?) have helped the protagonist redeem her self-image so that she can laugh in relief to herself, she reflects, "Debo de parecer loca" [I must seem crazy] (90). Only retrospectively do readers realize that she really *may be* "crazy" when she utters these words. Such fluid supplementations of meanings of the word *locura* subtly, almost playfully, question the sociocultural structuring of signification. Is it not "crazy" to take pills to help one adjust to imprisoning social roles that are abhorrently inappropriate for the individual? *Locura* as a fixed concept is further undermined at the end of the story when the narrator presents Dina's view of insanity: "Dina, en el suelo, con los mismos ojos desorbitados por el terror, por el espanto, por lo que ella ha debido de creer la visión de la locura" [Dina, on the floor, with her very eyes bulging in terror, in astonishment, at what she has probably believed to be the vision of insanity] (98). Seeing her own view as the "normal" one, the narrator emphasizes the superiority of her perspective to Dina's. Readers, however, have a third perspective: they realize that Dina does not see anything at all because she is dead.[3] In the end, insanity can be viewed almost quixotically as a concept that is subjective and changeable, according to one's point of view.

The act of murdering Dina, as a manifestation of the narrator's resistance to interpellation, is notably precipitated by the emergence of a new voice that speaks to the narrator. This voice defines itself in opposition to reason: "Me olvido de los dictados de la razón, esa razón que se ha revelado inútil y escucho por primera vez en mi vida una voz que surge de algún lugar de mí misma" [I forget the dictates of reason, that reason that has shown itself to be useless and, for the first time in my life, I listen to a voice that emerges from some place in myself] (91). As opposed to reason, however, is this necessarily the voice of insanity? The narrator insists that "la razón" is "esa razón que se ha revelado inútil" [that reason that has shown itself to be useless]—that reason that tries to define her according to a preordained, impossible subjectivity. Must a defiance of what is inscribed as rational be defined oppositionally as insane? The narrator sees it instead as "la voz del destino" [the voice of destiny] (96). This voice of resistance enables her to seek action, empowerment, and an identity separate from the subject position that she associates with Dina and the woman in green. Yet the protagonist's violent attempt to radically defy the system through resistance ultimately fails, in that it "repeats the methods of power in overcoming it" (R. Chambers 1991, xv). Just as society preestablishes subject positions for women, the protagonist forces Dina to meld with her already envisioned image of the woman in green. Although her voice would speak otherwise, it fails to surpass the all-or-nothing power plays that structure patriarchal discourse.

Thus "La mujer de verde" displaces the narrating subject from a position of authority but, more importantly, it displaces the reading subject out of a single point of view and into the agency of interpreting differently. If Cinderella's slipper evokes restrictive subject positions, and sleeping pills represent acquiescence to them, then the image of the three-sided mirror in "La mujer de verde" serves as the metaphor for agency in this story. Only by playing with the multiple perspectives provided by the three wings of the restaurant mirror could the protagonist glimpse the woman in green. Similarly, readers are placed before the mirror of the text, and must change their perspectives to capture the referent they seek. Yet each new perspective infinitely refracts off the others, so that it is never possible to definitively secure the original referent—the entire "truth" of the story. Always enticing readers to search for more, Fernández Cubas's text opens further with each perspective imposed upon it and defies the closure of a single interpretation.

"El lugar"

Such a vertiginous array of subject positions, evoked by the three-way mirror in "La mujer de verde," can produce a terrible uncertainty as to which role to embrace. This theme is expressed through the motif of finding one's place in "El lugar" ["The Place"], the third story of *Con Agatha en Estambul*. Of all the tales in the collection, this one most prominently highlights the connection between the subject and the space that delineates it. Here a nameless male narrator recounts retrospectively the deep-seated anxiety of his wife, Clarisa, to find her own "place." In her life she found her place in the subject position as his wife, a role that she hoped to extend past death by being interred in his family's pantheon. After the death of his wife the narrator begins to commune with her in his dreams and discovers that she holds a new place in the pantheon, which is a world guided by structures completely different from the logic of his world. This world of death—rooted in his dreaming unconscious yet taking on a life of its own—abounds with drives and power that radically diverge from what the narrator expects. The immersion into an "other" sphere markedly alters the couple's perceptions of absolutist power and human relations. Whereas rigid binaries govern subject/object relations in life, the very act of crossing the border to the other side challenges the structure by which power and the subject are conceptually defined by patriarchy. Moreover, as the protagonist and his wife discover, the excluded space of death defines its subjects according to radically different rules.

Zatlin has noted the structural similarity between "El lugar" and "Los altillos de Brumal" (Zatlin 1996, 38), wherein a woman discovers a remarkable, liberating world within a seemingly closed space. As Bretz indicates in her analysis of *Los altillos de Brumal*, such contrasting realms lend themselves to Julia Kristeva's paradigm of the semiotic and the symbolic orders in psychoanalytic development (Bretz 1988). According to Kristeva's model, laid out largely in *Revolution in Poetic Language*, before the subject is constituted by its entry into language and the phallic structure of the symbolic order, it preexists in the fluid and dynamic drives of the semiotic realm, which has a figuratively feminine association. This space of the unconscious is the prelinguistic fount of creativity that precedes the gender differentiation of the subject and that possesses drives that can penetrate the symbolic in order to alter its rigid constitution. All of this is possible because the subject is, by its very nature, always in process and incomplete. The dual worlds of life and death in "El lugar" would appear to conform to the semiotic/symbolic model. Nonetheless, in chap. 2 of this study I argue that, far from privileging the feminine, Fernández Cubas's *Los altillos de Brumal* in fact *undermines* the viability of associating one gender or another with binary oppositions such as good/bad, liberating/confining, semiotic/symbolic. "El lugar" ultimately questions the foundations of such an opposition as well—this time by exploring the nature of spatial construction. The space of "El lugar" collapses the absolute distinctions initially established to divide life (which might parallel the symbolic order) and death (similar to the semiotic order). The narrator of "El lugar" discovers a greater flexibility and agency as a result of his liminal experience with the world of his unconscious, an "other" world that radically alters his perception of power, control, and human relations. Moreover, in provoking him to take on "feminine" as well as "masculine" qualities in his being, the events that transpire here ultimately undermine the viability and inviolate nature of each side of the dichotomy. In the end, the continuous flux of the self-defining process within spatial relationships in this story reveals that "nada es definitivo" [nothing is final] (Fernández Cubas 1994, 149), for to gain any insight at all into the structuring of the subject is to focus on the process of its subversion, its agency, and its *search* for a space.

The story of the search for a space begins with Clarisa, who believes that she has found her place in life by being a housewife. Her husband recalls his consternation when he observed her newlywed ecstasy at blending her identity with the surroundings in their home: "Nunca la había visto así. Con los ojos entornados, emitiendo aquel murmullo de complacencia. No se sabía dónde acababa su vestido y empezaba el sillón [. . .]. Tuve la impresión de que Clarisa se había confundido con su entorno" [I had never seen her like that. With her eyes half-closed, emitting that murmur of pleasure. You couldn't tell where her dress ended and the chair began {. . .}. I had the impression that Clarisa had become confused with her environment.] (102). According to the narrator's representation of the events, his wife's identification with the home —her total fusion with it— is her desire and decision, not his. Clarisa pronounces that "Aquí está mi sitio" [My place is here] (103), and she soon abandons her university

4 / THE SPACE OF OPPOSITIONAL SUBJECTIVITY

studies to take care of her husband and home even though, the narrator reports, he did not want her to do so.

Clarisa obsesses with identifying herself according to the space that encloses her. For this woman, the word *place* becomes the discursive conjuration of a replete identity that excludes uncertainty and lack: "El *lugar*, para Clarisa, era algo semejante a un talismán, un amuleto; la palabra mágica en la que se concretaba el secreto de la felicidad en el mundo. A veces era sinónimo de "sitio"; otras no. Acudía con frecuencia a una retahíla de frases hechas que, en su boca, parecían de pronto cargadas de significado, contundentes, definitivas. Encontrar el lugar, estar en su lugar, poner en su lugar, hallarse fuera de lugar. . . No había inocencia en su voz" [*Place*, for Clarisa, was something like a talisman, an amulet; the magic word that embodied the secret to happiness in the world. Sometimes it was a synonym of "location"; other times, not. She frequently turned to a series of expressions that, coming from her, suddenly seemed laden with meaning, powerful, definitive. To find the place, to be in one's place, to put in one's place, to find oneself out of place. . . There was no innocence in her voice] (105).

While she is alive, Clarisa searches for her place in order to stave off the uncertainty of undefined subjectivity. She defines her place in relation to the masculine center, her husband. Indeed, the house and her husband *become* her space, so that she holds no separate identity: "Su lugar éramos la casa y yo, su marido" [The house and I, her husband, were her place] (106). In opposition to her place in life the woman can only imagine a frightening, foreclosed realm: "Lejos del lugar—en sentido espacial o en cualquier otro sentido—se hallaba el abismo, las arenas movedizas, la inconcreción, el desasosiego" [Far from the place—in a spatial or any other sense—was the abyss, moving sands, vagueness, unrest] (105–6). Clarisa's greatest fear is that death will rupture the security of her fixed, enclosed identity, especially when she visits the space of death, the pantheon of her husband's family.

The pantheon appears to be a compartmentalized area sealed off from the rest of the world. The protagonist manages to transgress its border in his dreams where, immersed in his unconscious, he repeatedly meets his late wife and advises her on how to get by in her new world. One night, when he reminds her to curry the favor of his formidable Aunt Ricarda with the gifts he enclosed in her casket, she informs him that his aunt, who had been the wealthy tyrant of a Cuban plantation and of their entire family, is only the maid within the pantheon.[4] This unexpected information signals that the husband's dreams—and his wife—have spun out of his control: "Era la primera vez que el sueño se desmandaba, cobraba vida propia y lograba sorprenderme. Hasta entonces—y sólo ahora me daba cuenta—Clarisa se había limitado a pronunciar frases esperadas, plausibles, tópicas [. . .] que posiblemente sólo mi saber inconsciente ponía en su boca" [It was the first time that the dream went out of control, took on a life of its own and managed to surprise me. Until then—and only now was I realizing it—Clarisa had limited herself to uttering expected, plausible, commonplace phrases {. . .} that possibly only my unconscious mind put into her mouth] (Fernández Cubas 1994, 137). The narrator can no longer pretend that his nightly conversations are mere fabrications, and he finds himself fascinated by the passage that his unconscious opens into a completely new world with an altered vision of life. In the Kristevian paradigm, the narrator's access to the pantheon through dreams might be viewed as a reverse journey from the symbolic to the semiotic, one that will change his identification as a subject.

Just as the force of the semiotic far surpasses its physical enclosure within the brain, so do the happenings of the pantheon incarnate a power that extends vastly beyond the physical limits of its space. The deceased Clarisa tries to express this transcendence of boundaries to her husband: "El panteón, por otra parte—*la casa*, decía ella—,era mucho más espacioso de lo que pudiera aparentar desde fuera, y, aunque no se iba a molestar en enumerarme las dependencias—le faltaban las palabras para nombrar lo que hasta hacía poco desconocía y, además, estaba casi segura de que yo no podría comprenderla—, me quería enterar únicamente de que había sitio de sobras" [The pantheon, on the other hand—*the house*, she would say—,was much more spacious than it would appear from the outside and, although she wasn't going to be bothered to list rooms for me—she had no words to name what until recently she did not know and, besides, she was almost certain that I wouldn't be able to understand—she wanted to inform me only that there was more than enough room] (138). Clarisa's inability to describe accurately the world of the pantheon corresponds to a significant limitation in understanding the semiotic pointed out by theoreticians such as Judith Butler or Teresa de Lauretis (see my discussion in chap. 2); namely, although subjects might perceive the semiotic retrospectively through the symbolic structuration of language, their speech can never really define the semiotic because it is prelinguistic.

As a space that extends beyond its own limitations, the pantheon quintessentially figures the act of border crossing and thus destabilizes the lines along which those divisions are drawn. The feat of crossing borders—symbolized primarily by Clarisa, because her husband is never able to truly penetrate the pantheon—calls into question the way one frontier contours the boundary of all that it is not. In its embodiment of one pole of logic, the pantheon contradicts the rules that order the narrator's patriarchal world. On one level, just as Kristeva's paradigm opposes the feminine semiotic to the masculine symbolic, the domain of the dead in "El lugar" inverts the hierarchies that govern the realm of life. Thus, people who possessed qualities of aggression and exerted overt control when they were alive hold positions of servitude in the pantheon. In contrast to the tyrannical bad temper of his father's side of the family, his mother's lineage, the Miró-Miró, was "una gente sencilla y bondadosa" [a simple and kind people] (114) when they were alive. The dead Clarisa reveals that in the pantheon not only is Ricarda Roig-Miró the maid, but the formerly meek Miró-Miró "son los peores" [are the worst] (139).

Whereas the semiotic is connected with the feminine because of its association with the child's union with the mother and its opposition to the phallic structure of the symbolic, the pantheon similarly bestows greater power on those who are not trained in the tyrannical tactics of patriarchal force. Power is still an issue in the pantheon, which simply inverts the rules of patriarchal logic. To the alarm of the narrator, the burial crypt completely transforms his wife's subjectivity and elevates her to a position of power. As with Carolina in "Mundo," Clarisa's growing strength manifests itself in her manipulation of her own voice: "Pero ahora Clarisa hablaba con voz propia, o, lo que era peor, no parecía demasiado inclinada a hablar" [But now Clarisa spoke with her own voice or, what was worse, she did not seem much inclined to talk] (Fernández Cubas 1994, 140). Then, after announcing to her husband that the powerful Miró-Miró faction has been subdued, Clarisa chills him by raising her voice in the otherworldly sound of raucous laughter. The woman's mirth echoes Grock's laughter, in *El año de Gracia*, at the paradox of sameness/difference, wherein each image of repetition conceals otherness and each sign of difference disguises similarity. Whereas the symbolic order relies on discourse to wield its power, the semiotic order makes use of other tactics such as silence, negation, and rejection to manifest itself within and distinguish itself from phallic language. Clarisa's manipulation of her voice and her silence marks her rise to power in the world of the pantheon and reveals that her subjectivity, no longer dependent upon her husband for signification, has evolved past the point of his control.

With this incursion into the semiotic, the power relationship has been inverted so that now it is the husband who depends solely upon his wife as the object of his signification, a process crucial to his subjectivity because he has yet to pass into the other realm. Clarisa's posthumous transformation accentuates the limitations of the patriarchal structure that dominates the protagonist. Prompted immediately after his wife's death to augment his masculine nature with experiences associated with the feminine, the protagonist seeks out the womanly spaces of the market and the notions store to purchase gifts that will facilitate her entry into the pantheon. The disconcerting experience of losing his power over Clarisa in death makes the narrator recall nostalgically how much he used to control her: "con una sorprendente habilidad sobre la que no me hacía demasiadas preguntas, yo sabía cómo retenerla, aprisionarla, retomar el hilo del sueño una, dos, hasta varias veces en la misma noche. Bastaba con llamarla, pronunciar su nombre y ella, obediente, acudía a la cita" [with a surprising ability about which I did not ask myself too many questions, I used to know how to retain her, to imprison her, to take up again the thread of the dream once, twice, even several times in the same night. It was enough to call her, to utter her name and she, obedient, came to the rendezvous] (140). This recognition belies his former depiction of his marital relationship as one entirely chosen and preferred by his wife. Readers can never know how much of her dependency Clarisa chose for herself, since her life is filtered through her husband's perspective. Importantly, the narrator discovers that his overt methods of domination are ineffectual on the other side of the divide.

Despite its apparent correspondence with the dichotomies of feminine/masculine or semiotic/symbolic, this tale diverges from such neat divisions when the inversion of power in the pantheon causes the narrator to reassess the way the gender dynamic functions in his own world. The protagonist comes to suspect that his mother, whom he always considered to be meekly subservient in carrying out his stern father's orders, was the one who ultimately exercised control in his family: "quizá, no había tales órdenes ni el fatídico mal genio, pero ella, la mediadora, temía que sin su intervención se desatara aquel proverbial mal carácter, la ira o la furia que a lo mejor sólo existían en su imaginación" [perhaps there never were such orders or the ominous bad temper, but she, the mediator, feared that, without her intervention, that proverbial ill nature, the wrath or fury that perhaps existed only in her imagination, would come undone] (116). In effect, his mother can be seen as having exercised oppositionality, appearing to comply with the ruling power while covertly "using the characteristics of power *against* power and *for* one's own purposes" (R. Chambers 1991, 10).

Once the center of the mother's oppositional self-definition disappeared with the death of her husband, the space of her subjectivity diminished: "con la muerte de su esposo, parecía como si mi madre hubiera perdido automáticamente la razón de ser en este mundo. [. . .] [S]in terrenos ya que proteger o resguardar, se encerraba cada vez más [. . .]" [With the death of her husband, it seemed as if my mother had automatically lost her reason for being in this world. {. . .} Without terrain to protect or defend any longer, she closed herself off more and more {. . .}] (Fernández Cubas 1994, 117). Now deceased as well, the mother employs the same tactics of "gentle" manipulation in the pantheon. Her power to come between the protagonist and his father recurs hauntingly in his dream of death when she interposes herself to cut him off from Clarisa. The narrator's experience as the dominated one in relation to the world of the pantheon reveals to him the limitations of unidirectional power, making him aware of the vulnerability that one feels as a subservient subject. He also comes to recognize the potential of subtle, oppositional control as the only recourse to power from an inferior position.

Suspecting that his death will subordinate him because he is a Roig-Miró who exercises phallic power, the narrator tries to secure his future by exercising what Chambers would call the oppositionality of seduction. In contrast to the overt power wielded from a position of superiority, Chambers discusses seduction, "not as an exploitive effect of power but as an oppositional response to alienation, that is, as a way—the only nonviolent way, perhaps—of turning the alienating other from attitudes that are oppressive (including self-oppressive) to a more sympathetic 'understanding'" (R. Chambers 1991, 17). Toward this end, the narrator deposits certain former possessions of Clarisa in a green suitcase that he delivers to her doctor with the request that the man slip the objects into his casket as a final favor to him upon his death.[5]

The two men seal their pact with a silent toast: "Fue un extraño brindis de copas vacías. Un brindis silencioso, sin homenajes ni discursos. Porque era como si en el aire flotara un epitafio, una sentencia: 'Nada es definitivo, ni tan siquiera en la eternidad.' O, dicho de otra forma: Clarisa había encontrado *su* lugar. Bien. Pero yo, desde ahora, estaba haciendo lo posible por asegurar el mío" [It was a strange toast of empty glasses. A silent toast, without homages or speeches. For it was if an epitaph, a pronouncement, were floating in the air: "Nothing is final, not even in eternity.' Or, said another way: Clarisa had found *her* place. Fine. But I, from now on, was doing everything possible to secure mine] (Fernández Cubas 1994, 148–49). In tribute to the new power paradigm that he prepares to embrace, this toast embodies qualities associated with the feminine: the glass is an empty receptacle, a lack, and the toast is silent, evocative of the inverted code of power in the pantheon. In that realm he will be the displaced one, just as Clarisa was excluded from those who "mattered" in patriarchy. By offering these gifts of her former self, he hopes to curry

Clarisa's favor, in effect, to mediate her desire so that he can purloin some of her power for himself.

In "El lugar," then, the male narrator is prodded to open the border of enclosed, definitive, masculine space to the fluid rule of the feminine. Yet does this inversion of power really change the logic that undergirds the all-or-nothing dialectics of patriarchy? After all, the characters in the pantheon wield the same tactics of oppositional power that they did when they were alive; the only difference is that the identities associated with the center/periphery are reversed. Like Kristeva's semiotic, the pantheon supersedes power associations based on sexuality alone—Aunt Ricarda's subservience effectively trounces that proposition—but it still defines power based on binary qualities associated with gender constructions. The narrator's struggle to identify himself with the feminine underscores that such an identification is a discourse constructed on otherness.[6] Teresa de Lauretis underscores the problematic nature of such privileging of femininity prevalent in poststructuralist psychoanalysis:

> [W]e are cautioned [that] this femininity is purely a representation, a positionality within the phallic model of desire and signification; it is not a quality or a property of women. Which all amounts to saying that woman, *as* subject of desire or of signification, is unrepresentable; or, better, that in the phallic order of patriarchal culture and in its theory, woman is unrepresentable except as representation. (de Lauretis 1987, 20)

Fernández Cubas's preoccupation with space as always constituted by the otherness that it excludes implicitly questions a model such as Kristeva's, which is defined by terms of gender opposition. Even if the semiotic is not essentially female, but only a feminine representation, it still marks off a space that inevitably establishes an exclusion, the exclusion of the masculine. "El lugar" may be read, then, as the "outside" that haunts dialectical discourse with the very terms that it eliminates.

As one of the author's few tales narrated by a man, this story defamiliarizes a mainstream feminist depiction of patriarchal subjectivity. The border crossing of Clarisa's posthumous place usurps the dominion of the protagonist so that he perceives what it is like to be enclosed in a controlled space and defined as a lack, as the powerless, as an objectified reflection of the center. Yet such liminality also destabilizes the terms by which each side defines itself. Thus, through her imagery of a simplistic inversion of the masculine/feminine dialectic of power, Fernández Cubas reveals how absolutist definitions fix the subject into stasis by excluding the object from active subjectivity. As a narrative text, moreover, this story fundamentally demonstrates the exclusion inherent in any univocal definition of the subject: Clarisa as an individual woman is absent from the text because, in the end, she figures only as the narrator's object, his representation of Woman. However, the narrator's experience of power on the other side of the divide throws his subjectivity into flux and alters his view of himself and of woman, his other. Transgressing the boundary that encloses objects into passivity and static exclusion, then, "El lugar" opens the space of subjectivity to the fluctuations of power and the productivity of change. In doing so, it argues for a viable space for human beings as subjects, not as mere representations of objectified otherness.

"Ausencia"

After the exploration of the ideological positioning of the subject as it relates to space in the first three stories, the space under examination in "Ausencia" ["Absence"] becomes the subject herself. Suffering from a mysterious amnesia, the protagonist is able to empty herself of her own identity and thus examine, from a distance, all the elements that construct her subjectivity. This story begins with the protagonist sitting in a café, not knowing who she is, and trying to reconstruct her identity on the basis of the space that surrounds her. She studies her clothes, her purse (which she decides must be hers because it matches her outfit), and her reflection in the mirror over the bar. She attempts to extrapolate her identity from diverse surroundings and scenarios, finally visiting the apartment of Elena Vila Gastón, whose name she finds in her wallet. In this home she discovers many clues to her personality, including that she has a companion, Jorge, who needs to be picked up from the airport the next night. She decides that she would like to be Elena Vila Gastón, for this woman has a very pleasant, comfortable life. The following morning, she goes to work and stuns her secretary by looking at her kindly and smiling. Suddenly, however, the protagonist begins to be annoyed and irritated with everything, and recognizes this feeling as the way she has always been.

The most striking element of this story is the second-person narration, which draws readers into identifying with the main character but also signals a division in the identity of the protagonist herself. The trajectory of Elena's self-discovery closely parallels the psychoanalytic paradigm of subject development through language. In Lacan's scheme, for instance, the split state of this subject separates the discursively constructed "I" in the symbolic order from the prelinguistic "you" in the imaginary order. In this way "Ausencia" points to the limitation of being able to express the experience of the imaginary order only through language. As the subject strives to recapture, through language, some initial state of completion like the imaginary, each successive utterance creates an additional barrier between that original being and the subject formed in language. The protagonist cannot escape the discourse that she generates and from which she herself is generated. After exploring the ideological construction of its identity, the "you" in Fernández Cubas's story complies with her proffered subject position and abandons her "absence" from the strictures of subjectivity for a frustrated presence in language and ideology. The "you" to whom the story is directed also beckons the identification of readers, however, who may see the futility of the protagonist's acquiescence and critically interpret the discourses that define her. The investigation of the subjectifying power of language in "Ausencia" ultimately urges readers to identify not with the "you" interpellated into psychoanalytic and social discourses, but with another position of interpreting subject as a means of exercising agency.

The narration of this story commences with the newly divided subject that uses the present tense to address its "you," from whom it has split apparently just moments earlier with the onset of amnesia. This speaking subject informs the "you" that its identity has suddenly become unknown: "'lo que menos importa en este momento es recordar lo que estás haciendo allí, sino algo mucho más sencillo. Saber *quién* eres tú" [what matters least right now is to remember what you are doing there, but something much more simple. To know *who* you are] (Fernández Cubas 1994, 153). Although the main narrative speaker in this story is "you," and no "I" is specifically verbalized, the first-person subjectivity is implicit in the very act of conversing with an other. Émile Benveniste theorizes that the pronominal relationship, which two people accept as positions for themselves in discourse, demonstrates that "the basis of subjectivity is the exercise of language" (Benveniste 1971, 226). The implicit "I" in this narrative may be seen to represent the ideological part of the subject that is constituted in language with its entry into the symbolic order. In Lacanian terms, the identification of the self as an "I" supposes a conscious separation from the other, a repression of the imaginary order into the unconscious, and the compliance of the subject with socially constituted subject positions. In contrast to the implicit "I" in this story, the "you" represents the essence of the subject, not yet constructed ideologically, that can be seen as preformed in the imaginary order.

The "you" of this narrative subsequently undergoes a process of examining her social construction in order to define her identity as a subject. Gender figures as the fundamental category of identification when, first and foremost, the protagonist recognizes her femaleness even before she confronts her reflection in a mirror: "Tú eres una mujer [. . .]. Lo sabes antes de ladearte ligeramente y contemplar tu imagen reflejada en la luna desgastada de un espejo [. . .]. El rostro no te resulta ajeno, tampoco familiar. Es un rostro que te mira asombrado, confuso, pero también un rostro obediente, dispuesto a parpadear, a fruncir el ceño [. . .]" [You are a woman {. . .}. You know it before leaning over slightly and contemplating your image reflected in the worn glass of a mirror {. . .}. Your face does not seem strange, but not familiar either. It is a face that looks at you startled, confused, but also an obedient face, ready to blink, to wrinkle its forehead {. . .}] (Fernández Cubas 1994, 153–54). This identification suggests that gender is a state that preexists the specular identification that evokes a sense of self, and that the incipient subject is willing to comply with the orders extended to her.

After her first glimpse in the mirror, the "you" is careful to determine her location in space as a means of discovering who she is, but her presence in a café reveals little. Then she searches in her wallet to learn her name, Elena Vila Gastón, and attempts to discover her age as a way of determining her relation to time. Scrutinizing her mirror image further, she begins to recognize it even though she still cannot reconcile it to the linguistic marker of her name: "Es la cuarta vez que te contemplas ante un espejo y quizá, sólo por eso, aquel rostro empieza a resultarte familiar. 'Elena,' en cambio, te sigue pareciendo corto, incompleto, inacabado" [It is the fourth time that you gaze at yourself before a mirror and, perhaps only for that reason, that face begins to look familiar. "Elena," on the other hand, continues to seem too short, incomplete, unfinished] (158). In search of further clues to her self, Elena tries to estimate her social class on the basis of her clothing: "Te pones la gabardina y te miras de nuevo. Es una prenda de buen corte forrada de seda, muy agradable al tacto. 'Debo de ser rica,' te dices. 'O por lo menos tengo gusto. O quizás acabo de robar la gabardina en una tienda de lujo'" [You put on the raincoat and look at yourself again. It is a well-cut garment lined in silk, very pleasant to the touch. "I must be rich," you tell yourself. "Or at least I have good taste. Or maybe I just robbed the raincoat from a luxury shop"] (158). All these details, carefully observed, hint at Elena's positioning as a subject in space and time, according to certain social codes. However, she does not identify with the picture she begins to construct.

Elena's distancing from her self also entails her alienation from the discourses that construct her subjectivity: she questions language, numbers, and the very origins of her knowledge. As when the narrator of "La ventana del jardín" confronts the sameness/difference of the code of Tomás/Olla, this protagonist's language becomes defamiliarized and devoid of logic: "Abres un estuche plateado y te empolvas la nariz. [. . .] [C]uriosamente, te has quedado detenida en la expresión 'empolvarse la nariz.' Te suena ridícula, anticuada, absurda" [You open a silver compact and powder your nose. {. . .} [C]uriously, you have paused at the expression "to powder one's nose." It sounds ridiculous, antiquated, absurd] (154). When she calculates her age by comparing her birthdate to the newspaper date, Elena questions how she acquired the knowledge of counting. Yet to interrogate her knowledge so radically is to risk losing her way completely in an endless deconstruction of social order, without any center at all: "¿Hablarán tu idioma? O mejor: ¿cuál es tu idioma? [. . .] Algo, dentro de ti, te avisa de que estás equivocando el camino. No debes preguntarte más que lo esencial" [Will they speak your language? Or better yet, what is your language? {. . .} Something inside you warns that you are heading down the wrong path. You shouldn't question more than the essentials] (154–55). Analyzing more than is absolutely necessary threatens to completely destroy her uncertain existence by annihilating its center. Derrida himself notes that there must be a center in order for humans to live. However, his deconstructionist theory demonstrates that such a center is not absolute, but actually a function of the subject's worldview and hence dependent on individual perspective.[7] In reconstructing her self, the protagonist senses that she must accept a center of identity. Her subjective center—one among many, the story subtly suggests—establishes her as a Spanish woman whose logic of the world conforms to a specific linguistic and numerological pattern.

Elena's defamiliarized perspective of her self and her discourse has the effect of immersing her in a childlike world where language is unfamiliar. Distanced from speech as a commonplace tool, she remembers a similar experience from her girlhood when she would visualize words to represent their character: "De pequeña solías *ver* las palabras, los nombres, las frases. Las palabras tenían color. Unas brillaban más que otras, algunas, muy pocas, aparecían adornadas con ribetes, con orlas [. . .]. Como Ausencia. De pronto ves escrita la palabra 'ausencia.' La letra es picuda y está ligeramente inclinada hacia la derecha" [As a child you used to *see* words, names, sentences. Words had color. Some shone more than others, some, very few, appeared adorned with borders, with trimming {. . .}. Like Absence. Suddenly you see the word "absence" written. The writing is pointed and it slants slightly to the right] (Fernández Cubas 1994, 156). This artistic visualization of words accentuates them as a creation. By attaching visual instead of lexical associations to the meanings of words, Elena, similar to Tomás/Olla, applies an alternative logic to the construction of signification while she enters the system of language.

4 / THE SPACE OF OPPOSITIONAL SUBJECTIVITY 169

As the fundamental vehicle of speech by which one communicates to others, the paramount mark of identity is the voice. In an echo of the other stories in *Con Agatha en Estambul*, this protagonist ponders alterations in her voice as a sign of subjective change and redefinition. This newly reborn protagonist is quite taken with the sound of her own voice and uses it to imagine who she is: "Te has quedado admirada escuchando tu voz. En la vida, en tu vida normal, sea cual sea, debes de ser una mujer de recursos. Tus palabras han sonado amables, firmes, tranquilizadoras" [You pause, admiring, listening to your voice. In life, in your normal life, whatever it is, you must be a woman of means. Your words sounded kind, firm, reassuring] (157). Once again, the meaning she extracts from words derives less from semantics than from style, from the way they sound. Elena feels a certain distance from this voice, however, for she does not yet identify with it as an intrinsic part of her being. In her experience of developing as a subject, she must recognize the separation of herself as a subject from others before this speaking voice of language can become part of her.

In the psychoanalytic process of her development, the protagonist has already passed through the mirror stage in the imaginary where the infant begins the phase of separation from ideal union with the mother. Even though Elena identifies with the appearance that she sees reflected in the mirror, she is still unsure of her subjectivity: "aunque empieces a sentirte segura de tu aspecto, no lo estás aún de tu identidad" [even though you begin to feel sure of your appearance, you aren't yet sure of your identity] (159). Trying to forge ahead in development, Elena calls her home in the hope of being able to discern her identity through its relationship to others. She needs the person who answers, be it husband, child, or cleaning woman, to provide a clue as to who Elena really is. Indicative of the mechanization that dominates postmodern society, however, the only "other" who responds to Elena's call is the sound of a voice on an answering machine:

> [U]na voz femenina, pausada, modulada, vocalizando como una locutora profesional, repite el número que acabas de marcar, ruega que al escuchar la señal dejes tu mensaje y añade: "Gracias." [. . .] "Gracias," repites. Y ahora tu voz suena débil, sin fuerzas. Tal vez te llames Elena Vila Gastón, pero cuán distinta a la Elena Vila Gastón—si es que era ella—que con una seguridad implacable te acaba de ordenar: "Deje su mensaje." (159–60)

> [{A} feminine voice, deliberate, modulated, vocalizing like a professional announcer, repeats the number that you just dialed, asks that you leave your message after the beep and adds: "Thank you." {. . .} "Thank you," you repeat. And now your voice sounds weak, without strength. Perhaps your

name is Elena Vila Gastón, but how different from the Elena Vila Gastón—if it really was she—that with implacable confidence just ordered you to "Leave your message."]

Elena suffers a new crisis because she cannot reconcile the emerging, uncertain image of her self with the artificial sound of "her" voice on the recording. The exchange via the answering machine dramatizes her predicament as a split subject because, pinned in the position of "you," she cannot identify with the voice of the speaking "I." That "I" is eminently conscious of its status as a *locutora profesional*, for speaking is an imposed role that it accepts as a way of life. Since Elena, listening in silence at the other end of the telephone line, is not yet constituted as a subject in the symbolic order of language, she certainly cannot mediate herself as a subject against others.

This alienation from the voice of her other "I" provokes Elena to go to confession as a pretense for listening further to her own voice. Realizing with relief that she completely recognizes her surroundings, she refuses to question that knowledge. Indeed, she imagines that alienation from her space would be worse than alienation from her self: "te imaginas consternada, a ti, a Elena Vila, por ejemplo, sabiendo perfectamente que tú eres Elena Vila, pero sin reconocer apenas nada de tu entorno" [you imagine yourself dismayed, you, Elena Vila, for example, knowing perfectly well that you are Elena Vila, but hardly recognizing anything in your surroundings] (Fernández Cubas 1994, 160). This vision highlights the intricate relationship between the subject and its space. Whereas "Ausencia" explores the formation of the subject, the final story in this collection will investigate the discontinuities produced in the subject when it ventures outside its defining space.

Although Elena enters the confessional booth in the church hoping to recognize her self in the sound of her voice, she has no memory of having committed any sins: "a falta de una lista de pecados más acorde con tu edad, los inventas. Has cometido adulterio. Una, dos, hasta quince veces. Has atracado un banco. Has robado en una tienda la gabardina forrada de seda [. . .]" [for lack of a list of sins more suitable to your age, you invent them. You have committed adultery. Once, twice, even fifteen times. You have held up a bank. You have stolen from a store the raincoat lined in silk {. . .}] (161). Caught in an amusing predicament, the protagonist tries to manipulate the ecclesiastical discourse in an attempt to comply with the subject position of a mature confessant. In this enumeration of riotous, extravagant sins, Elena begins to understand the nature of reciting lines and role-playing: "Pero tu voz, lenta, pausada, te recuerda de repente a la de

4 / THE SPACE OF OPPOSITIONAL SUBJECTIVITY

una locutora profesional, a la de una actriz [. . .]. [N]o te cabe ya la menor duda de que tú eres la mujer que antes ha respondido al teléfono" [But your voice, slow and deliberate, reminds you suddenly of a professional announcer, of the voice of an actress {. . .}. {Y}ou no longer have the least bit of doubt that you are the woman who answered the telephone before] (161–62). The quality of performance, of complying with a role, is the common link now between her voice and that on the machine. In essence, by submitting to the discursively formed roles that are available to her in society, Elena accepts their proffered subjectivity.

Having begun to identify with a distinct subject position, Elena returns to "her" space in her apartment, where a sense of familiarity can begin to reconstruct for her the history of her subjectivity. She looks at the objects and photographs in her house, including pictures of a man whose name she knows is Jorge, and she feels comfortable there, recognizing it as her place—like Clarisa in "El lugar." Situating herself in the house that shows her subjectivity as it is constructed in language, ideology, and culture, Elena is able to identify increasingly with the position of that speaking "I." Now in the space of the speaking subject, she plays the messages on her answering machine and hears the silent response that she had given when she was in the bar, still in the position of "you": "En el contestador hay varias llamadas. Una es un silencio que reconoces tuyo, al otro lado del teléfono, en los lavabos de un bar, cuando no eras más que una desconocida" [On the machine there are several calls. One is a silence that you recognize as yours, on the other side of the phone, in the rest room of a bar, when you were nothing more than an unknown person] (166). Kaja Silverman notes that, for Benveniste, this transferability from speaker to listener emphasizes the changeability of subject positions as a result of their inherent definition in language: "These roles are endlessly reversible, as are the signifiers which depend on them; the person who functions as a speaker for one moment functions as a listener for the next. [. . .] [T]he signifiers 'I' and 'you' have only a periodic meaning" (Silverman 1983, 44). By highlighting the temporal nature of these subject positions, Benveniste underscores the radical discontinuity that is implicit in subjectivity. Elena embodies the discontinuity and progressive redefinition of the self as she moves from the position of "you" to that of "I."

When she progressively identifies with her speaking-subject position in language, Elena notes a creeping, familiar sensation of uneasiness, which she associates with her "real" self. This frustration with her self permeates every aspect of her subjectivity: "El malestar que ya no tenía que ver sólo con Jorge, sino con tu trabajo, con tu casa, contigo misma. Una insatisfacción perenne, un desasosiego absurdo con los que has estado conviviendo durante años y años. Quizá gran parte de tu vida" [The discomfort that no longer had to do just with Jorge, but with your work, with your house, with yourself. A constant dissatisfaction, an absurd disquiet with which you have been living for years and years. Maybe for much of your life] (Fernández Cubas 1994, 166). The disturbing sensation intensifies as voices from her past come back to her: "'Vila Gastón,' oyes de pronto. 'Siempre en la luna... ¿Por qué no atiende a la clase?' Pero no hace falta remontarse a recuerdos tan antiguos. 'Es inútil'—y ahora es la voz de Jorge hace apenas unas semanas—. 'Se diría que sólo eres feliz donde no estás...'" ["Vila Gastón," you hear suddenly. "Always on the moon... Why don't you pay attention to class?" But it's not necessary to go back to such old memories. "It's useless"—and now it is Jorge's voice from hardly a few weeks ago. "One might say that you're only happy wherever you are not..."] (167). Representing the discourses that construct her subject positions as obedient student and as girlfriend, these voices speak to her as a "you" to position her in their paradigm. Silverman emphasizes the necessity of identifying with the position of "you" in the process of accepting subject roles: "the pronoun 'you' only means something to the degree that the viewer identifies with it, recognizes him or herself in the subject of speech" (Silverman 1983, 49). By associating herself with that position as a receiver of speech, Elena accepts the subjectivity that such discourse would impose.

Elena is glad to experience the "absence" as an escape from the frustrating oppression of her presence as a subject, but in the end she succumbs to the positioning of all those discursive voices that hail her. The speaking subject then condemns its other "you" to the inescapable unhappiness of her fixed identity: "Tal vez tú, Elena Vila Gastón, seas siempre así. Constantemente disgustada. Deseando ser otra en otro lugar. Sin apreciar lo que tienes por lo que ensueñas. Ausente, una eterna e irremediable ausente [. . .]" [Maybe you, Elena Vila Gastón, are always this way. Constantly annoyed. Wanting to be another in another place. Not appreciating what you have because of what you dream about. An absentee, an eternal and irremediable absentee {. . .}] (170). Significantly, imprisonment in one place is intricately tied to the stifling nature of Elena's identity. In this context, the word "absent" is infused with new meaning: the true essence of her self—that creative, uninformed and hence, as yet, unformed subject—is what is lacking in the structure of her subjectivity in discourse. By allowing herself to be interpellated into the "you" position that is hailed by ideological discourse, to use Althusser's terminology, Elena permits herself to be defined, confined, and subdued in subjectivity.[8]

4 / THE SPACE OF OPPOSITIONAL SUBJECTIVITY

In exploring the discursive construction of the subject, this story presents a series of infinite supplements of "I" and "you," mirror reflections of subjects and objects that define one another. In addition to the principal, implicit narrating "I" speaking to the "you," a new sequence of speaking subject/object relationships is opened up when the narrating "I" pronounces that the "you" speaks to herself: "'Ausencia,' te dices. 'Eso es lo que me está ocurriendo. Sufro una ausencia'" ["Absence," you tell yourself. That is what is happening to me. I'm suffering an absence"] (156). The division of subjects and objects multiplies further when the "I" talks to the "you" about "Elena" in the third person: "¿eres tan valiente? ¿Es Elena tan valiente?" [are you that brave? Is Elena that brave?] (163). This triangular relationship is reminiscent of the image of the three-sided mirror in "La mujer de verde," where each side of the mirror returns a different reflection of the subject, separating it into layers of supplementations. In such an endless play of reflections through the multiple mirror of discourse, the subject becomes divided, duplicated, and distorted into an infinity of subject positions whose original referent cannot be traced.

In the end, however, the protagonist returns to her old, disgruntled subjectivity and neglects to embrace the difference that she experienced when she was "other" than Elena Vila Gastón, when Elena was an undefined identity. As in the tale of "Mundo," not much has truly changed at the end of this story. Once again, the real potential for agency and alteration lies at the extratextual level of this story, for readers can choose not to be hailed by that "you." They can read Elena's experience against itself, reject the stultifying limitations of the subjectivity to which she succumbs, and recognize the liberating potential in the otherness that she eventually chooses to ignore. This oppositional reading can change identity, as Chambers argues: "The change in the reader that occurs as a result of oppositional reading thus necessarily has the character of a conversion from 'autonomous' identity (the addressee as a 'you' defined, in a dual relationship, as not the addressing 'I') to a sense of self that depends on a triangular system of otherness, in which dualities are mediated by a third which prevents any of the terms from claiming an autonomous identity or a 'positive' status" (R. Chambers 1991, 17). Through the mediation of the text, readers can step away from the immobility of the "you" in the process of ideological hailing and into the agency of the interpreting subject.

"Ausencia" foregrounds the formation of the subject as discursive *construction* by highlighting Elena's tracing of her identity according to a specific sequence—gender, specular image, voice, language—and her refusal to question that order too radically. In doing so, the text implicitly questions the assumptions that Elena does not dare to destabilize. Why must she be a woman, first of all? What, in fact, constitutes a woman? How does she extract meaning from language and numbers? How does her understanding of mathematics formulate her quantification of the world? How does her language shape her comprehension and expression of the world? The emptying of Elena's identity emphasizes that a subject's position is a space, filled with discursive interpolations, that shapes its view of the world. From this perspective, the psychoanalytic story of the subject is just one of many possible discursive ways of plotting the tale—not the masterplot that orders the way a subject *must* be. In light of the many critical deconstructions of Freudian and Lacanian psychoanalysis as a just-so story that retrospectively inscribes the masculine as the original center, "Ausencia" may be seen to recite the trajectory of psychoanalytic construction as a fiction, as one construction of logic among many—even if it is a widely read and accepted story of the subject.

"Con Agatha en Estambul"

At one point in "Ausencia," Elena shudders to imagine herself knowing her own identity but "sin reconocer apenas nada en tu entorno" [hardly recognizing anything in your surroundings] (Fernández Cubas 1994, 160). The title story of this collection unfolds precisely that strange experience of a subject who finds herself in a space that is not her own. The first-person narrator of "Con Agatha en Estambul" ["With Agatha in Istanbul"] is a nameless middle-aged woman who has been married for fifteen years to a man named Julio. One day she spontaneously decides to grant her husband's casually expressed wish, and she buys them both round-trip tickets to spend fifteen days in Istanbul to escape the madness of the Christmas season in Barcelona. Upon their arrival, however, the protagonist cannot even see this other space because it is covered in fog. Her confusion at her blurred surroundings is augmented by a series of bizarre events that happen to her there. Because the writer Agatha Christie once stayed in her very hotel, the protagonist decides to become a sleuth herself and search for clues to explain the mysteries of her new environment.

Istanbul imposes a tension between the narrator's epistemological endeavor to seek out the rational knowledge that will explain her perplexities, and the ontological uncertainty of being as it is defined in this other space. Brian McHale ties the epistemological mode to modernist fiction, with the detective novel as its "genre *par excellence*," and describes this mode's typical questions as: "What is there to be known?; Who knows it?; How do they know it, and with what degree of certainty?" (McHale

1987, 9). The preoccupation of the narrator of "Con Agatha en Estambul" with tracing clues seems futile and even funny because, first of all, the "mysteries" she investigates are often trivial and ridiculously overblown. Moreover, as Pérez perceptively observes, in these stories "The epistemological quicksand upon which characters and readers alike stand sinks further as narrators admit their ignorance, speculate, provoke doubts as to their own agendas, and proffer conjectures in lieu of anything more tangible, while other characters prove evasive, deceptive, or unwilling to cooperate with the narrator's quest for factuality" (Pérez 1998, 33). This scenario is a daunting one in and of itself but it becomes still more complicated, for the dominant challenge in this story is not to uncover the "absolute truth." Instead, the quest laid before the narrator could be described, in McHale's terminology, as an ontological and postmodernist one of discovering what world she is in, how it differs from her old world, which of her selves can be found in each world, and if ever these divergent paths shall meet.

The first surprise that the other space of Istanbul offers is the subversion of vision as the primary sense by which knowledge is perceived. When the narrator and her husband arrive in Istanbul, the entire city is buried for days beneath a dense fog, similar to the scene that greeted Daniel in *El año de Gracia*. Unable to see the place for herself, the narrator depends on the visual depictions of postcards, photographs, and movies, referents that become more real than the actual realm that encompasses her. Indeed, she has seen so many representations of the city that she begins to suspect that representation is all that exists: "¿Existía Estambul? La sensación de irrealidad que me había embargado en el aeropuerto, nada más bajar del avión, no había hecho en aquellos días sino acrecentarse. Pero ahora ¿estaba yo realmente allí? O mejor: ¿qué era *allí*? A mis espaldas unos cuantos grabados reproducían retazos de aquella ciudad que se negaba a mostrarse en conjunto" [Did Istanbul exist? The sensation of unreality that had overpowered me in the airport as soon as I stepped off the plane had only increased in the days since. But now, was I really there? Or better yet, what was *there*? Behind me several pictures reproduced bits and pieces of that city that refused to show itself entire] (Fernández Cubas 1994, 176). The possibility that representation might be the only reality accessible to her plunges the protagonist into the postmodern crisis of ontological uncertainty of what other realities and worlds might exist. Thus for her, the trip to Istanbul becomes a struggle between, on the one hand, the irrationality, doubt, and curious liberty that she encounters in this misty, ontological space and, on the other hand, the epistemo-logic of knowing in her ordinary world.

In addition to subverting her dependence on vision, Istanbul further alters the protagonist's linguistic identification as a subject when she discovers that she can suddenly, inexplicably speak Turkish. While in "Ausencia" Elena found herself devoid of the knowledge that she ought to possess for her subject position, the narrator of "Con Agatha en Estambul" discovers that she controls knowledge of a foreign place that is totally inappropriate—indeed, impossible—for her subject position as an outsider. The narrator stuns her husband by spontaneously speaking Turkish to the waiter in a restaurant: "el camarero se acercó a la mesa, yo dije '*Iki kahve ve maden suyu, lütfen*,' el hombre sonrió y Julio se enmudeció de la sorpresa" [the waiter approached the table, I said "*Iki kahve ve maden suyu, lütfen*," the man smiled and Julio was speechless in surprise] (176). Not even the narrator herself understands how she has mastered the code to ask for coffee and water in Turkish. Her familiarity with the discourses that rule that place changes her subjectivity as a foreigner and draws her further into the world of Istanbul. In effect, she is discovering the answer to the ontological question, pinpointed by McHale, of "which of my selves can know this world" (McHale 1987, 10). The narrator's knowledge of Turkish posits a new self for her, one shaped inside the cultural boundaries of that world.

The protagonist finds freedom in her experience of radical otherness to her former self. After spraining her ankle and having it swell up to an enormous size, she hobbles through the streets and identifies with a native street child with a deformed leg: "Me sentía una coja congénita, una residente, estambuleña de toda la vida" [I felt like a congenital cripple, a resident, a lifelong Istanbulite] (Fernández Cubas 1994, 203). Feeling "contenta, extrañamente libre" [happy, strangely free] (202) in the misty world where overt rationality and consideration of other people are not the point of living, the narrator spontaneously purchases a flask of Chanel perfume called *Egoïste*. Her husband, annoyed at her odd behavior and lengthy ramblings in Turkish during their stay in this city, is completely offended when he catches a whiff of the strong-smelling perfume:

> Empezó a olfatear sin disimulo, como un sabueso. Parecía estupefacto, irritado, ofendido.
> —*Egoïste* —dije yo. Y le mostré el frasco.
> Julio lo miró con incredulidad.
> —Deberías pensar en los demás —gruñó secamente.
> Y abrió el cristal de la ventana. (208)

> [He began to sniff openly, like a bloodhound. He seemed stupefied, irritated, offended.

"*Egoïste*," said I. And I showed him the flask.
Julio looked at it incredulously.
"You should show some concern for others," he growled dryly.
And he opened the window.]

This humorous passage illustrates a change that the ontological space has wrought in the narrator: no longer preoccupied with following the paths of other people in an epistemological search for knowledge, she now concerns herself with exploring the new, unpredictable world of Istanbul and with understanding the self that fits in this world. Such a project may be egotistical, but it is an exploration of her subjectivity that is long overdue.

During the long hours that the protagonist spends cooped up in the hotel because of her injured ankle, she fixates on a strange fish in a tank, which comes to represent the transformability into different selves that she experiences in this story. The woman is astounded at the ability of the fish to change from an ordinary being into a fantastic one: "a ratos se diría que el pez dejaba de ser pez—enorme y feo—para convertirse en un rostro grácil, infantil incluso. Un rostro de dibujos animados. Tuve que esperar a la tercera transformación para reconocerlo. 'Campanilla'" [from time to time one might say that the fish stopped being a fish—enormous and ugly—to become a face that was graceful, even infantile. A cartoon face. I had to wait for the third transformation to recognize it. "Tinkerbell"] (191). The remarkable ability of the fish to transmute from one self into another enthralls the narrator, who spends enormous amounts of time watching for its metamorphosis. She hopes to capture the image of the fish in precisely the instant when it is also, simultaneously, Tinkerbell. The fish may represent, then, the transformational process occurring within the protagonist herself.[9] Her goal is to capture the blend of her own two selves—the rational, epistemological one and the transcendent, ontological one—as a means of combining the characteristics of the two worlds she occupies.

Despite the changes taking place in her, however, the protagonist's enchantment with the unpredictable world of Istanbul conflicts with her epistemological tendency to search for the absolute, rational truth to explain her circumstances. Like the narrator of "El lugar," this speaker tries to believe that her knowledge of the new place has logical explanations. Thus she rationalizes her uncanny ability to speak Turkish: "Aquellas palabras, que manejaba con indudable soltura, yo las había visto con anterioridad. En el avión, ojeando—distraídamente, creía yo—, un capítulo dedicado a frases usuales de una guía cualquiera [. . .]" [Those words that I wielded with indubitable skill—I had seen them previously. On the plane, flipping—distractedly, I thought—, through a chapter, dedicated to typical phrases, from some guidebook {. . .}] (Fernández Cubas 1994, 179). Like the narrator of "La ventana del jardín" who found himself in a similarly "other" space, the narrator of "Con Agatha en Estambul" subjects the anomaly of her knowledge to a process of logical explanation, retracing her steps to seek out the clue to the puzzle. For this sleuth, however, the difference is not just outside her but within her.

In additional attempts to experience the detectivesque adventure of discovering the "key," the protagonist constructs a number of "mysteries" out of apparently normal events. At times her proclivity to turn up clues is hilarious because it surfaces unexpectedly in the middle of her narration of other events. For example, while pondering a strange voice that she hears, the narrator suddenly exclaims that she has found the answer—but readers are not even sure what the question is: "Enseguida, como si alguien en el cuarto hubiera prendido una luz, vi un número salvador, un rótulo parpadeante, al tiempo que mis labios—esa vez sí fueron mis labios—pronunciaban una cifra: 'cuarenta y cuatro.' Me puse a reír. 'Eso era. Ajá'" [Right away, as if someone in the room had turned on a light, I saw a saving number, a blinking tag, while my lips—that time it *was* my lips—uttered a number: "forty-four." I started to laugh. "That's it. Aha!"] (201). As it turns out, her discovery is not the explanation of the voice she hears, but her husband's shoe size, information that will help her buy a shoe for her enlarged foot and walk around the town. In a scrambling of reason that recalls many Fernández Cubas tales, this narrator's non sequiturs and sudden leaps in logic ludicrously construct a new type of rationale that only she understands.

The two drastically different sizes of the protagonist's feet symbolize her state of having one foot in each world, so to speak. Her deformed foot is one of the elements that make her belong to the misty, ontological world of Istanbul. Yet she adapts to her condition of not fitting into her designated "space," symbolized by her "normal" foot. In contrast to the narrator of "La mujer de verde" who never finds shoes that fit her properly, nor finds a space to accommodate her self, the narrator in "Con Agatha en Estambul" is undaunted by her podiatric anomaly. Instead of recriminating herself for falling short of the feminine ideal of small feet, she simply co-opts a man's shoe in a shoe store for her own use. By means of such resourcefulness, the protagonist applies her methodical, epistemological tenacity to find a way to penetrate deeper into the ontological world of Istanbul.

The narrator even converts her uncanny ability to speak Turkish into a detectivesque adventure, by studying a textbook as if she were searching for the clues that would lead to the eventual treasure of fluency. After pro-

4 / THE SPACE OF OPPOSITIONAL SUBJECTIVITY

gressing in the book with relative ease for six chapters, however, she finds it difficult to continue. The methodological approach to knowing a language can take her only so far before its value is questioned: "La lección siete se estaba revelando sorprendentemente ardua, espinosa. No sólo me resultaba infranqueable, sino que, de pronto, ponía en tela de juicio todo lo que creía haber aprendido hasta entonces" [Lesson seven was turning out to be surprisingly difficult, thorny. It not only seemed insurmountable but, suddenly, it called into question everything that I believed I had learned up until then] (196–97). The epistemological rules of language that she studies stymie her progress and threaten all the ontological awareness she has absorbed through her immersion into otherness.

Yet the greatest mystery that the protagonist creates and pursues is the truth of the relationship between her husband and Flora, another guest in the hotel who spends time with Julio while the invalid is immobilized by her sprained ankle. As a wife, the narrator suspiciously analyzes Flora's gaze toward her husband: "Una mirada luminosa, segura, seductora. La mirada de una mujer con proyectos, con planes [. . .]" [A luminous, sure, seductive gaze. The gaze of a woman with designs, with plans {. . .}] (Fernández Cubas 1994, 193). Naturally, the narrator casts herself as the sagacious, fortuitous detective who stumbles on the sinister plot and manages to impede its successful completion. Employing the discourse of a detective ("Pero entonces. . . lo vi" [But then. . . I saw it] [210]), the narrator believes that the key to the insidious mystery in Flora's gaze is hidden in her uncanny ability to alter her appearance by changing the direction of her gaze with her profile: "La elegancia de sus rasgos, la perfección de sus facciones, quedaban, sin embargo, desmentidas en cuanto alguien, como yo ahora, la sorprendía de cara, de frente [. . .]. *El enigma de un rostro*, murmuré" [The elegance of her appearance, the perfection of her features, were nevertheless belied as soon as someone, like me now, surprised her head-on, from the front {. . .}. *The Enigma of a Face*, I muttered] (211).[10] The narrator also finds it suspicious that Flora follows Julio to a distant town after she herself had tried to throw the seductress off track by lying about her husband's destination.

Ultimately, the detective's search for truth lands her in a great mess, when her accusations of infidelity provoke a big fight with Julio. Her incensed husband provides an entirely different perspective of the protagonist's behavior, which he considers to be bizarre and unreasonable:

Te empeñaste en beber whisky tras whisky, nos soltaste un rollo descomunal sobre Patricia Highsmith. . . [. . .] El resto te lo has pasado dopada con esas tremendas pastillas rojas y con cara de imbécil. Moviéndote por la ciudad seguida de una corte de los milagros, empeñada en chapurrear un idioma que desconoces, en usar un perfume pestilente. Y encima, lo que faltaba, un ataque de celos. (221)

[You persisted in drinking whiskey after whiskey, you made up a big story about Patricia Highsmith... {...} The rest of it you've spent doped up with those huge red pills, looking like an imbecile. Going about the city followed by the court of miracles, insisting on butchering a language you don't know and on using a foul-smelling perfume. And to top it off, just what we needed, an attack of jealousy.]

As in so many Fernández Cubas stories, pills and alcohol emerge as a possible, "rational" explanation of the "abnormal" events that the protagonist experiences. Ironically, although Julio is infuriated by her objective pursuit of knowledge that unjustly incriminates him, the behavior he criticizes is precisely that which characterizes her entry into the blurred, ontological world of Istanbul—a subjective experience that he does not share.

The narrator's epistemological appropriation of the detectivesque discourse of Agatha Christie (not of Patricia Highsmith, as Julio intimated) highlights the intricate and often nebulous relationship between representation and reality. By its very nature, fiction foregrounds the ontological perspective of other possible worlds in coexistence with the extratextual, "real world." As Brian McHale expresses it, "Propositions about the real world fall under the modality of necessity. Propositions in fiction, by contrast, are governed by the modality of possibility; they require, in short, 'suspension of belief as well as disbelief'" (McHale 1987, 33).

With a typically postmodern twist, the boundaries between the worlds of representation and reality often blur in "Con Agatha en Estambul," most notably with the figure of Agatha Christie.[11] The very hotel where the protagonist and her husband are staying stakes its livelihood on the suggestion that the writer of detective fiction has now become a real, ghostly protagonist who eerily beckons guests toward the revelation of hidden secrets.[12] When the narrator attempts to recount the story of Agatha in Istanbul to Julio and Flora, she loses herself in the labyrinthine passageways of the tale: "hice lo que ningún desmemoriado debería hacer: seguir hablando como si tal cosa a la espera de recuperar el hilo" [I did what no forgetful person should do: continue talking as if it were nothing in the hope of finding the thread again] (Fernández Cubas 1994, 186). After more ramblings, it finally occurs to her that "no había ningún hilo por recuperar" [there was no thread to recover] (187); the ontological world of representation is not one whose order can be tracked by epistemological means.

4 / THE SPACE OF OPPOSITIONAL SUBJECTIVITY

Nonetheless, the protagonist pursues her epistemological quest when she decides to investigate the mystery of Agatha's ghost. She peeks through the keyhole of the locked door to the room reputed to have been the writer's, but the "treasure" she glimpses on the other side of that lock is one of her own invention, as she imagines Agatha at work in her hotel room. The protagonist's representation of the writer replaces Agatha Christie's life, for her mental projection of an elderly Agatha does not reflect the youthful age that the famous writer would have been when she stayed in that hotel: "Le oscurecí el cabello, cambié la anacrónica pluma de ave por una estilográfica y la hice pasear por el cuarto angosto. Fuerte, erguida. 'Eso era. Ajá.' Pero aquella ensoñación, la nueva Agatha, no resistió más que unos segundos. Enseguida reparé en que la mujer canosa y despeinada no se resignaba a abandonar su escritorio" [I darkened her hair, changed the anachronous quill pen for a stylus and made her walk about the narrow room. Strong, erect. "That's it. Aha!" But that fantasy, the new Agatha, did not last more than a few seconds. I saw right away that the gray-haired, tousled woman would not resign herself to abandon her desk] (199). The ontological creativity of her mental representation of Agatha finally defies the epistemo-logic of following the facts of the writer's life. Ontology then becomes the total dominant of the narrator's representation when the boundary that separates her time and space from Agatha's disappears: "Fue una sensación breve, inexplicable. Agatha, a través de la puerta cerrada, me estaba sonriendo *a mí*" [It was a brief, inexplicable sensation. Agatha, through the closed door, was smiling at *me*] (199). The ontological existence of possible worlds has enticed the narrator to transgress the limitations of her own boundaries and to enter into Agatha's world or, inversely, to invite Agatha to ingress into the narrator's world and shake up its monotony.

As an extension of the ontological questioning of worlds, this story also interrogates reality. The ontological space of Istanbul prompts the narrator to ask after the nature of the reality she experiences. Pritchett views this city, "located precisely between Europe and Southwest Asia," as a middle ground, a threshold between worlds that functions as a site "where transformations occur" (Pritchett 1996, 254). As part of the process of transforming the protagonist, this space prompts her to consider her role in creating reality. She imagines that the outlines of the city really do not exist at all, but only materialize when called upon to do so by the viewer: "Cuadros que se iluminaban de repente, cobraban vida, y que, tan pronto nos habíamos alejado, volvían a sumirse en aquella oscuridad inmerecida" [Pictures that suddenly illuminated, came alive, and that, as soon as we had gone away, sank again into that undeserved darkness] (Fernández

Cubas 1994, 177). In perceiving the city as a representation conjured up by the viewer, the narrator underlines the crucial role of the subject in the reception process: the text does not coalesce into form until it is envisioned by readerly desire. Istanbul comes to represent, then, the transcendent space that causes the individual to confront her subjective reality: "¿Existía Estambul? ¿O no era nada más ni nada menos que un espacio sin límites que todos, en algún momento, llevábamos en la espalda, pegado como una mochila? [. . .] ¿O se trataba únicamente de un eco? Un eco distinto para cada uno de nosotros que no hacía más que enfrentarnos a nuestras vidas" [Did Istanbul exist? Or was it nothing more and nothing less than a space without limits that all of us, at some point, carried on our backs like a backpack? {. . .} Or was it only an echo? A different echo for each of us, that did nothing more than confront us with our lives] (222–23). Of course, this Chinese box effect of fictions encased within realities ultimately extends to readers, who realize that being an expert in representation helps them to understand reality, which is only one of many "possible worlds" that constantly merge and diverge in untraceable distinction.

Indicative of the narrator's split subjectivity in separate worlds, and evocative of numerous Fernández Cubas texts, is the sound of another voice besides the protagonist's own that speaks to her mind. Calling it "la voz de la sabiduría de los cuarenta años" [the forty-year-old voice of wisdom] (217), she hears it prodding her to delve into the "mystery" of Flora's interest in Julio. As the clues of their liaison multiply, the wife hears the voice berating her: "Agatha en tu lugar hubiese hecho algo—oí. Era la voz. Esa voz que surgía dentro, que era yo y no era yo, que se empeñaba en avisar, sugerir y no aportar, en definitiva, ninguna solución concreta" ["Agatha, in your place, would have done something," I heard. It was the voice. That voice that arose within, that was and was not me, that persisted in warning, suggesting and definitively not contributing any concrete solutions] (200–201). The voice even helps her invent an entertaining murder mystery with Flora as the insidious criminal. This voice emerges in Istanbul perhaps as the mark of the protagonist's other identity, the voice that incites her to lose her old self in the ontological blur of Istanbul.

The woman becomes frightened, however, when she has a huge fight with her husband because she pursued the voice's suspicions of Flora. Angry with the voice because she must return to Barcelona on a separate plane from her husband and believing that it abandoned her after getting her into foolish trouble, she reminisces nonetheless about the exciting, unexpected adventures she had in Istanbul. Suddenly, she hears a voice once more: "'Aventura. La vida no es más que una aventura. Asume los hechos. Asúmete. Y empieza a vivir.'" [Adventure. Life is nothing more than an adventure. Accept the facts. Accept yourself. And start to live] (Fernández Cubas 1994, 231). To the narrator's surprise, the voice that urges her to take this perspective on life is not the forty-year-old voice of wisdom, nor that of Agatha, but that of the narrator herself: "La mirada del caballero, a mi derecha, me hizo comprender que había sido yo y sólo yo quien estaba hablando de asunciones y aventuras. Y enseguida entendí que [. . .] la voz formaba ya parte de mí misma" [The look from the gentleman to my right made me realize that it had been I and only I who was talking about takeovers and adventures. And right away I understood that {. . .} the voice now formed part of me] (232). Thus she incorporates the other voice, the other self, and the other ontological world into her being.

In celebration of her expanded subjectivity, the protagonist takes out the *Egoïste* perfume and sprays herself liberally. The sole passenger at her side moves to another seat, most certainly daunted by the overpowering scent of her perfume and, no doubt, by her muttering aloud about *asunciones* and *aventuras*.[13] The protagonist takes advantage of the now vacant adjoining passenger seats to stretch out her limbs: "Tumbada en los tres asientos, recordando, fabulando. Decidiendo, en fin, que aquellos pocos días, en Estambul, yo me lo había pasado en grande" [Stretched out over the three seats, remembering, inventing. Deciding, in short, that during those few days in Istanbul, I'd had a ball] (233). Embracing the complex nature of her subjectivity that weaves in and out of possible worlds, she can enjoy the expanded space that her newly conscious voice procures for her.

For the narrator of "Con Agatha en Estambul," the trip to that city serves to immerse her in a nebulous space where borders are blurred and absolutes are relative. Her fascination with the detective novels of Agatha Christie causes her to try to apply epistemological methodology to her own life, seeking out solutions to problems like her swollen foot, and searching for clues to mysteries like the relationship between Julio and Flora. Yet the epistemological detective hunt that she undertakes proves to be a confabulation of a nonexistent reality. In effect, her epistemological map is blurred by the mist of the ontological world in which she finds herself. Thus, she realizes that the absolutes of epistemology eventually cede to the uncertainties and possibilities of ontology, and that every reality is, in a sense, another representation to be read. In her representation of her own experience, the narrator, as a writer, actually reads the events of her life. At the same time, by projecting her text out to her readers for representation, she asks that they write the meaning and complete the signification of her story. Ultimately, then, writing and reading—two possible worlds that blend epistemology and ontology—converge into one and the same act in the exercise of exploring the space of open subjectivity.

CONCLUSION:

As entertaining and distinct as each of the tales in *Con Agatha en Estambul* is, in many respects they can be seen as uniting to tell the same story, the story of subjectivity. The spatial images, multiple voices, questioning of *locura*, and ontological subversions are woven throughout the collection, so that the texts reflect one another and intertextually penetrate the borders of one another's designs. Yet each story is not simply a replica of the one before; on the contrary, their order suggests the overarching plot of a cohesive tale. "Mundo" ironically revives the traditional setting of a convent to indicate that, even in post-totalitarian Spain, repression and fear of difference still permeate the subjective unconscious. "La mujer de verde" depicts a contemporary career woman who, in many ways, is just as repressed as the nun in the first story. "El lugar" reveals that constricted subjectivity is not the lot of women alone, but that both genders strive to accommodate themselves in an often inadequate space of subjectivity. "Ausencia" dramatizes the oppositional elements of subjectivity through the interpellation of I/you subject positions, but in the end its protagonist returns to the limitations of her former speaking self. At last, in "Con Agatha en Estambul," the protagonist embraces a space of difference whose blurred borders give her free reign to discover agency in changing her subjectivity.

In addition to telling a cohesive tale, these stories perform a common function: they inspire readers to interpret oppositionally in order to appreciate the subversions and surprises that the text has to offer. Readers then understand that it is unnecessary, and even detrimental, to simply accept whatever discourse might appear to dominate. Instead, they change their interpretive stance in relation to the text, which in turn projects alternative images of subjectivity to readers. Thus, what begins as an attempt to extract readerly pleasure becomes a process of acquiring readerly power. This transformation occurs in the space of the text via a change in readerly desire: "reading will consequently be [. . .] a 'space' where there is room for oppositional maneuver in that the discursive practice of irony works seductively to shift desire" (R. Chambers 1991, xvi). Thus the act of reading, with all its oppositional potential, constitutes the ultimate space, whose ever-changing contours liberate readers from the confines of a static subjectivity. Such an emphasis on narrative communication and interpretation inevitably calls into question the point of view from which the self observes and constructs its other. Perspective thus emerges as the subject of my final chapter, on *El ángulo del horror*.

5
Plotting Desire: The Visual Construction of the Subject in *El ángulo del horror*

> "'Es un ángulo,' continuó. 'Un extraño ángulo que no por el horror que me produce deja de ser real... Y lo peor es que ya no hay remedio. Sé que no podré librarme de él en toda la vida...'"
>
> ["It's an angle," he continued. "A strange angle that is no less real for the horror that it produces in me.... And the worst part is that it's too late for a cure. I know that I won't be able to free myself from it in my whole life...."]
> —"El ángulo del horror"

WHILE THE SUBJECT DEFINES ITS PERSONAL SPACE IN RELATION TO ITS oppositional other, a dynamic that I explore in chap. 4, in this chapter I interrogate the necessity of such a relationship of duality as shown in *El ángulo del horror* [The Angle of Horror] (1990). In all of Fernández Cubas's works, subjectivity is a process that takes two, wherein the desire for the other motivates, castigates, and inevitably formulates the self. This duality is synthesized and expressed in the relation of seeing subject and seen object, a dynamic of optical collusion that the author always duplicates at the textual level by proffering a distorted interpretation to readers and enticing them to search for a clearer view. Hence the visual construction of the subject—a motif underscored by the title's focus on angles—becomes in narrative a matter of plotting desire. Peter Brooks envisions the reading of plot as "a form of desire that carries us forward, onward, through the text. Narratives both tell of desire—typically present some story of desire—and arouse and make use of desire as dynamic of signification" (Brooks 1984, 37). "Plotting desire" incorporates its own double vision, then. As an adjective, "plotting" refers to desire that plots, that surges forth in search of its other to define itself in an ongoing process. As a gerund it describes the tendency of narrative to trace out that desire as its own object and, in so doing, to mark the contours of meaning that give shape to the self. Desire and vision conjoin in *El ángulo del horror* as the central motivation and mechanism for constructing the subject in dynamic interaction with the differences and similarities of its other.[1]

"Helicón"

With its focus on doubling, the opening story of *El ángulo del horror* playfully undermines the hegemony of a central gaze that sees the subject/object pursuit as only a one-way process. The first-person male narrator of "Helicón" ["Helicon"], Marcos, recounts his struggle to fortify his timid masculinity through his relationship with his new girlfriend, Angela. His efforts to impress her with his popularity on the bar scene and to get her drunk on their first date are impeded by Angela's rejection of alcohol for a banana milk shake. Her subsequent discovery that the shake contains a double banana launches her into an extensive treatise on the horror of all things double, for exact replicas often obscure any distinctions between the two parts. Upon hearing this, one of Marcos's friends at the bar inevitably mentions Marcos's own twin brother, Cosme, a bizarre man who is said to reside in a sanatorium.

Only Marcos knows, however, that Cosme is a farce that he fabricated when Violeta, his former amorous fixation, intruded on one of his sessions of filth, abandon, and inspirational musical creation with his helicon. Unable to admit that he, Marcos, could indulge in such antisocial behavior, he claims to be Cosme, Marcos's twin brother. Some time later, when Marcos, in a state of physical disarray, roams the city one night during a drunken spree, a woman he believes to be Angela finds him and locks him in a passionate embrace. Later, when he discovers that this is really Eva, Angela's twin sister, he decides that Angela must harbor the same hedonistic, degenerative identity as her sister, the other side of her controlled and somewhat uptight persona. He rejects Angela as flawed and unfit for him, but then calls up Eva to ask her out on a date.

"Helicón" is the story of Marcos's desire for a woman—focused first on Violeta, then Angela, then Eva—which is essentially his desire to strengthen his own masculinity in relation to the women in his life. This desire also manifests itself as the desire to tell, to reflect his image in the mirror of the text. Many critics have commented on the relationship between desire and narrative as an inherently Oedipal one, as Teresa de Lauretis summarizes: "All narrative, in its movement forward toward resolution and backward to an initial moment, a paradise lost, is overlaid with what has been called an Oedipal logic—the inner necessity or drive of the drama—its 'sense of an ending' inseparable from the memory of loss and the recapturing of time . . . and the restoration of vision" (de Lauretis 1984, 125–26).[2] Georges Bataille has observed that the desire for the other parallels the desire for death, the first being the nearest approximation toward continuity that can be experienced in life.[3] Much like the desire for the other, the desire to narrate constitutes a parallel drive toward the end in an endeavor to recover or construct a continuity perceived to be lost in the past. "Helicón" posits a narrator who carefully structures his perspective in order to recount his pursuit of the desirable other and his rejection of the undesired one.

On the surface, "Helicón" seems to support the Oedipal trajectory of the male desiring subject who pursues the female object of desire. Such polarities of gender are mythically and culturally inscribed into the act of narration itself as the enunciation of desire:

> [A]ll these [opposite pairs] are predicated on the *single* figure of the hero who crosses the boundary and penetrates the other space. In so doing the hero, the mythical subject, is constructed as human being and as male; he is the active principle of culture, the establisher of distinction, the creator of differences. Female is what is not susceptible to transformation, to life or death; she (it) is an element of plot-space, a topos, a resistance, matrix and matter. (de Lauretis 1984, 119)

Sexual difference forms the foundational dynamic of plot structures, even as gender is the initial mark of identity distinction in society, as Fernández Cubas suggests when the amnesiac Elena intuits her own femaleness even before she recognizes her mirror reflection in "Ausencia" (in *Con Agatha en Estambul*). In the plotting of desire, the *subject*—figured as the masculine hero—pursues his *object*—figured as the feminine obstacle, object, or traversed space.

The fundamental connection between the mythic text and the plot text is their function of explanation, the incorporation of the transgressive into the established norm. As de Lauretis, summarizing Lotman, points out: "plot (narrative) mediates, integrates, and ultimately reconciles the mythical and the historical, norm and excess, the spatial and temporal orders, the individual and collectivity" (de Lauretis 1984, 120). Thus plot always posits a center, a dominant perspective that explicates and appropriates its dialectical other. The key to this structuration in "Helicón" is the narrative perspective that determines what is excessive and must be interpellated into the normalizing plot. In this story Angela represents the excess, for she eludes Marcos's demand for her to be a passive, cooperative object of desire. Whereas Marcos would weld her into the amalgam of Woman, as an exact replica of every other woman, Angela persists in voicing an alternate viewpoint that focuses on the *difference* inherent in every double, in every manifestation of the same. The dominant narrative perspective purports to defuse Angela's dissension by collapsing her into a single identity with her twin sister Eva. Yet his rejection of Angela for her sister at the end of the story subverts their similarity and suggests that there is a marked difference between the two: as an object of desire, Eva duly reflects the specular image of virility that Marcos seeks. In the plot he constructs, the narrator tries to recapture and re-present this past encounter in a more pleasing light for himself as desiring subject. The constant motif of doubling—manifested in images as well as in other characters' perspectives—posits his viewpoint as a decentered mirage, however, and thus advances a re-vision of subjectivity as a dynamic process, open to the dissension and difference of other points of view.

During Marcos's initial date with Angela, he continually strives to get the woman he encounters to reflect his desired image of himself. He chooses a bar where the bartender, Aureliana, knows him and can reinforce his desired image of a "cool" patron. Despite the carefully chosen setting, Angela will not perform her designated role in the drama of inebriation and facile seduction: "Me disgustó que Angela no probara el alcohol. Eso ponía las cosas un poco difíciles. Yo diciendo tontería tras tontería, y ella, cada vez más sobria, más nutrida y vitaminada, observándome [. . .]" [It annoyed me that Angela wouldn't try the alcohol. That made things a little difficult. I, saying one stupid remark after another, and she, increasingly sober, nourished and vitaminized, observing me {. . .}] (Fernández Cubas 1990, 15). Instead of fulfilling her obligations as the object of desire, Angela inverts the paradigm of the look so that she is the observer. Marcos's discomfiture with being the object of Angela's gaze is only intensified by Aureliana, who announces that she put a double banana in Angela's milk shake and unwittingly triggers Angela's obsessive discussion of doubles.

The topic of twin bananas leads Angela to meditate on the repulsiveness of twin egg yolks, a specter of the double that profoundly disturbs her. Trivial as they may seem, these yolks embody inexorable repetition for Angela: "Dos. Exactamente iguales. Repulsiva e insospechadamente iguales. [. . .] Y su fin, el lógico fin para el que nacieron, para el que estaban destinadas, parecía todavía más angustioso: fundirse fatalmente en una tortilla [. . .] y volver a lo que nunca fueron pero tenían que haber sido. Un Algo Único, Indivisible. . ." [Two. Exactly the same. Repulsively, unexpectedly the same. {. . .} And their end, the logical end for which they were born, for which they were destined, seems even more agonizing: to fuse together fatally in an omelet {...} and return to what they never were but had to have been. A Single, Indivisible Something...] (17–18). This mirror image of seeing oneself exactly replicated in the other disturbs Angela because it threatens to obliterate individuality.

In response, the woman projects the need to assert what Mikhail Bakhtin or Judith Butler would term the difference inherent in simultaneity, in reiteration. If this motif of duality is read as a metaphor of women who are culturally, socially, even mythically constructed as mere repetitions of Woman, Angela resists the role of duplicitous sameness to which destiny (or patriarchy) would reduce her. Later, she informs Marcos of how she rescued the yolks from their fate of duality and allowed them to express their distinction: "las eché por el fregadero. Una tras otra. Una por el sumidero de la derecha; la otra por el de la izquierda. En ese punto culminante alcanzaron la felicidad. Venció la diferencia, ¿sabes? . . . Porque una, la primera, pereció burdamente aplastada contra la rejilla. La otra, en cambio, sinuosa, incitante, se deslizó con envidiable elegancia por la tubería" [I tossed them down the sink. One after the other. One down the drain on the right; the other down the left. At that culminating point they attained happiness. Difference triumphed, you know? . . . Because one, the first one, perished clumsily splattered against the drain catch. The other, on the other hand, sinuously, seductively slid with enviable elegance down the tubes] (24–25). Although Angela's compulsion to create difference in the domain of eggs may amuse readers, her obsession with double objectification highly unsettles Marcos: "Lo único que pretendía era acabar con el amenazante monólogo de Angela" [The only thing I was trying to do was put a stop to Angela's menacing monologue] (19). He would rather ignore the detail of difference because he needs women to be the same, a homogenous reflection of him as the virile, active subject.

Angela's ideas threaten her suitor because they distract her from complying with her role as man's object, and also because they point to a certain agency inherent even in views of subjectivity as repressive, inescapable repetition. If objects are differentiated and capable of enacting their own distinctions, the story suggests, then they may well be able to act as subjects and traverse the dividing barrier of subject/object, converting the unidirectional relationship of power into one of reciprocity. Blind to Angela's point of view, however, Marcos persists in seeing even her deconstruction of the duality of the egg yolks as a confirmational reflection of his own desired image of superiority: "Era obvio que, tras aquel desigual desfile de modelos en el fregadero, Angela veía en mí la reencarnación de la yema B, la sinuosa maniquí del sumidero de la izquierda" [It was obvious that, after that unequal parade of models in the sink, Angela saw in me the reincarnation of yolk B, the sinuous mannequin of the drain on the left] (25). Thus Marcos not only constructs Angela, "aquella maravillosa mujer que yacía en mi lecho" [that marvelous woman who was lying in my bed] (25), as an object for his pleasure, but he distorts the meaning of her words in his narrative and denies her the autonomy that she so desperately seeks. In plotting his desire, Marcos ignores his own peculiarities and shortcomings in his representation of Angela as a rather strange woman, prone to obsessions, who succumbs to him in bed. Confusing sex with conquest, Marcos believes himself to be reaffirmed as the powerful one in the male/female binary.

Nonetheless, Angela herself is not immune to the tendency to define the self in total opposition to the other, as her contrasting characterizations of the two egg yolks suggest. In light of Angela's assertion that one yolk "pereció burdamente aplastada contra la rejilla" [perished clumsily splattered against the drain catch] while the other "se deslizó con envidiable elegancia por la tubería" [slid with enviable elegance down the tubes] (Fernández Cubas 1990, 25), it is not difficult to imagine which yolk serves as *her* object of identification. Angela repeats this obsessive search for difference within sameness with her fixation on a newspaper clipping about two middle-aged twin sisters who committed suicide together and were found dead in their apartment:

> [L]a vida tenía que haber dejado forzosamente sus huellas en aquellas antiguas muñecas encantadoras, hoy cincuentonas momificadas. Angela estaba dispuesta a jurar por su honor que no murieron en idéntica posición. Una de ellas—¿María Asunción acaso?—, rígida, perfecta, como en el fondo debió de haber sido siempre. La otra—¿María de las Mercedes?—, un tanto más desmadejada y omisa, como nunca pudo dejar de ser. . . . (22)

> [{L}ife inevitably must have left its mark on those delightful old dolls, now mummified fifty-something-year-olds. Angela was prepared to swear on her honor that they did not die in an identical position. One of them—María Asunción perhaps?—, rigid, perfect, just as deep down she must have always been. The other—María de las Mercedes?—, a little floppier and lax, just as she could never help being. . . .]

The twin Marías—whose prototypically Catholic names make them representative of the Spanish Everywoman, another manifestation of "the same"—display their difference in opposition to one another, just like the double egg yolks. In both anecdotes, Angela constructs identity according to a division of rigid perfection versus weak laxity—or lack.

The oppositional characterizations that Angela assigns to every double that disturbs her reflect, not coincidentally, her distinction from her twin, Eva. Even the sisters' names evoke contrasting biblical archetypes: Angela (like María de la Asunción {Mary of the Assumption}) is celestial, pure, associated with light and goodness, whereas Eva is the fallen woman who seduces Adam into eternal damnation (Glenn 1992, 138). Yet, these identities subsume their own oppositions, for Lucifer was a fallen angel of darkness and Eve was created as the perfect, original woman. Each one thus embodies its antithesis. Angela longs to assert her singularity in spite of her likeness to her sister, perhaps because she fears the other within herself. Consequently she separates her look-alike on the basis of good/bad, strong/weak, perfect/imperfect. These qualities essentially repeat the hierarchical pattern of the male/female dichotomy; what Angela truly strives to assert, then, is her position of superiority in the binary. Even as she struggles to surmount the system of duality founded on sexual differentiation, she cannot escape the oppositional discourse that undergirds those terms.

By taking the construction of differences upon herself, nonetheless, Angela takes on an agency that undermines Marcos's masculine domain as the active subject. Marcos comes to detest her, wildly imagining that she is some misplaced psychologist playing with him as her object of study: "Angela, de mujer deseada, pasaba a convertirse en mujer odiada" [Angela, from the desired woman, was becoming the hated woman] (41). Marcos vehemently resists the feminine inversion of the examining gaze, much the way the narrator of "El provocador de imágenes" (*Mi hermana Elba*) was repelled by Ulla's monstrous power. Indeed, these subversive women threaten the underlying sexual premise of the whole subject/object structure that permeates mythical, psychoanalytic, and cultural discourse. As de Lauretis observes: "[N]arrative itself takes over the function of the mythical subject. The work of narrative, then, is a mapping of differences, and specifically, first and foremost, of sexual difference into each text; and hence, by a sort of accumulation, into the universe of meaning, fiction, and history, represented by the literary-artistic tradition and all the texts of culture" (de Lauretis 1984, 121). In Fernández Cubas's narrative, however, Angela's insistence on the difference that underlies reiteration and her assertion of the individual subjectivity of each female double of man violate her role as acquiescent object and convert her into assertive subject. Thus she undermines the constitutive binary of sexual difference on which the patriarchal construction of subjectivity is founded.

In this manner, Angela's interpretation serves as a counternarrative to Marcos's discursive construction of self/other relations. Significantly, although "Helicón" reproduces exactly the text of the newspaper clipping, Marcos subsumes Angela's interpretation of it beneath his own voice and perspective by means of free indirect discourse. Whereas he cited her directly to present the story of the egg yolks (in order to accentuate her bizarre obsessiveness, no doubt), in the indirect account of the dead twins the man attempts to undermine the impact of this competing narrator, whom he criticizes as "un tanto monotemática" [somewhat monothematic] (Fernández Cubas 1990, 21). Nonetheless, as a manifestation of what Bakhtin calls "double-voicing" in free indirect discourse, Angela's suppressed voice resonates behind Marcos's words. Of course, beyond Marcos's voice is that of the implicit author, whose point of view readers construct from the composite of the story's multiple overlay of voice and vision. Asserting his narrative control, Marcos seems blissfully unaware that he, too, may be the object of a critical gaze from a source other than Angela.

The twist in this story is that, despite his annoyance with Angela's preoccupation with doubles, Marcos himself relies on a double to excuse parts of his character that he would rather not recognize before his friends. For Marcos, too, has a hidden side to his identity: every now and then he foments his sense of masculinity by playing his helicon, reveling in the fact that "El instrumento más gigantesco y fascinante [. . .] obraba en mi poder" [The most fascinating and gigantic instrument {. . .} was working in my power] (29). In addition to being an enormous tuba that envelops the entire body, the helicon also evokes the mountain where the Greek muses dwelled, thus symbolizing a source of power and inspiration. Indeed, the narrator personifies it, referring to it as "Helicón" as if it were a proper name. Nonetheless, the unwieldy shape of the instrument renders it a humorously distorted phallic symbol, at best. Each musical session with the tuba is a ceremony that culminates Marcos's ritualistic preparation, which entails ceasing to bathe or clean up the house for days in order to immerse himself in a state of viscous, putrid abandon. These rites invoke and restore his ephemeral sense of primordial power, which apparently transmutes to timidity when he is not able to sustain his dominance in daily interactions with others—particularly *female* others.

For long before the protagonist fixated on Angela, another subversive woman, Violeta, resisted the plotting of his desire and discovered his essential duality. The fiasco began when Marcos gave Violeta the duplicate keys to his apartment (for he, too, is obsessed with doubles) with the expectation that she would behave according to the accepted code of femininity: "Cuando un hombre entrega las llaves de su piso a una mujer—la réplica de las llaves de su piso, para ser exactos—lo hace [. . .] íntimamente convencido de que esa mujer [. . .] llamará antes a la puerta" [When a man gives the keys to his apartment to a woman—the replica of the keys to his apartment, to be exact—he does so {. . .} utterly convinced that that woman {. . .} will knock first] (26–27). Nonetheless, Violeta breaks the rules of what a woman possessing a man's keys should do and sneaks into his apartment unannounced. Unbeknownst to the narrator, it seems, when he bemoans his error the imagery he selects is hilariously phallic (a little joke, perhaps, on the part of the "implicit" female author): "¿Cómo no pensé en introducir mi llave en la parte interior de la cerradura o sujetar, por lo menos, la cadena de seguridad?" [Why didn't I think to insert my key in the inside of the lock or at least to put on the security chain?] (28). This unwitting metaphor of the sexual act (and even of "abnormal" sexual behavior) inadvertently underscores Marcos's status as the passive, violated object, the role normally assigned to woman in the binary of sexual differentiation. Wielding the keys—the symbol of a replicated and displaced phallus—and thus the control of the situation, Violeta manipulates her power in order to penetrate his space.

The sneaking Violeta is shocked when she intrudes upon Marcos's session of filth and sonorous inspiration with the helicon. With his double sense of self laid bare before Violeta's disgusted eye, the protagonist comes to see himself as the other, as the object: "Y al observarme, al sentirme observado, desnudo, despeinado y pringoso, al aspirar la atmósfera nauseabunda que señoreaba la casa, comprendí por primera vez que *abyección* era el término exacto, propio e insustituible" [And upon observing myself, upon feeling myself observed, nude, my hair uncombed and greasy, upon breathing the nauseating air that dominated the house, I understood for the first time that *abjection* was the exact, proper, and unsubstitutable term] (Fernández Cubas 1990, 30–31). Reflected in Violeta's eyes, Marcos observes himself differently, as the marginalized, the outside, the unacceptable other. Unable to bear the horror of his own aberration, which this gaze imposes on him, Marcos inverts the power paradigm by turning himself into Violeta's specular reflection and howling in unison with her as an acting subject: "Entonces Violeta gritó, y yo, presa del terror frente a mí mismo, me uní como en un espejo a su alarido" [Then Violeta screamed and I, seized by terror at myself, united with her scream as if in a mirror] (31). In his complicitous duplication of her horror, Marcos tries to reposition his identity at the center of power: he claims to be Cosme, Marcos's twin, and later—as Marcos—tells everyone that his brother has been admitted to a "sanatorium" (*not* a "manicomio" [mental hospital], he insists [44]). Cosme as a double is born, then, from the union of Marcos's and Violeta's screams of horror at the specter of abject otherness: "aquel triste día entre Violeta y yo nos inventamos a Cosme" [that sad day, between the two of us Violeta and I invented Cosme] (33). Drawing on Kristeva's theory of "abjection" as a series of exclusions whereby the Self acquires identity in contrast to its Other, Pérez observes that "By no coincidence, Marcos invents Cosme as a means of abjecting or expelling that part of himself which delights in nudity and filth" (Pérez 1995–96, 162). As Marcos's duplicitous trick reveals, the subject's relation of fascination and repulsion to the abject in the other may in fact conceal the horrific specter of abjection within the self.

It is significant that in "Helicón," as in other Fernández Cubas stories, monstrosity and insanity figure as quintessential labels of abnormality in the exploration of otherness. When telling their friends about Cosme, Violeta's discourse exploits these binary definitions (and others, such as that of a potentially sadistic sexual predator) to their extreme in order to heighten the titillating horror of confronting the other—much to Marcos's satisfaction: "Pronto me enteré, no sin cierto deleite, de que mi monstruosa réplica no se había contentado con amenazar de palabra a la inocente intrusa. Un amago de estrangulamiento, desgarrones brutales en su delicado traje de seda, y una pasión y un deseo capaces de aterrorizar a la mujer más bregada componían ahora el cuadro de sufrimientos y penalidades por los que había pasado la dulce heroína" [Soon I learned, not without certain delight, that my monstrous replica had not been content with threatening the innocent intruder with words. A threatening gesture of strangulation, great brutal tears in her delicate silk suit, and a passion and desire capable of terrorizing the fiercest woman now composed the portrait of suffering and hardships that the sweet heroine had endured] (35). In her narration, Violeta casts herself as the heroine but only in the sense that she is acted upon; her task is to withstand the advances of the virile male and to enhance her own virtue in resistance to his menacing otherness. Despite Marcos's condescension toward this "dulce heroina" [sweet heroine], her confabulations complement the image he wants to project of Cosme, because he needs to distance himself as far as possible from the undesirable, unacceptable otherness he harbors within himself: "Violeta se estaba enfangando tanto como yo, y a mí no me quedaba más que dar por zanjado el asunto. Así que interné a Cosme en un sanatorio, condené al helicón al eterno ostracismo en la oscura soledad del armario ropero y me juré a mí mismo que aquellas extrañas sesiones que tanto me alborozaran no volverían a repetirse en la vida" [Violeta was getting as dirty as I was, and there was nothing left for it but to consider the matter resolved. So I admitted Cosme to the sanatorium, condemned the helicon to the eternal ostracism of the dark solitude of the wardrobe and swore to myself that those sessions that so overjoyed me would never be repeated again in my life] (35). With this ostracism to darkness or the insane asylum, Marcos resorts to time-honored tactics of suppressing the monstrosity of otherness.

Indeed, the narrator feels the same fear of being equated with Cosme that Angela harbors of being confused with her twin sister, Eva. He suspiciously critiques Angela's reaction to the news that his brother is insane: "No añadió 'en cierta forma es como si una parte de Marcos estuviera enloqueciendo. . .', pero adiviné enseguida que era eso precisamente lo que estaba pensando Angela" [She didn't add "in a way it's as if a part of Marcos were going crazy. . . ," but I immediately guessed that that is precisely what Angela was thinking] (Fernández Cubas 1990, 23). For these characters, even worse than absolute duplication is to be contrasted with one's double in such a way that their very *difference* renders them deficient: "¿qué tenía de extraño que ella, Angela, se avergonzara de su doble, de ese reflejo distorsionado que se veía obligada a soportar a diario, de la posibilidad de que los demás detectaran en la otra lo que no habían podido percibir en ella?" [was it so strange that she, Angela, would be ashamed of her double, of that distorted reflection that she was forced to endure on a daily basis, of the possibility that everybody else would detect in the other what they hadn't been able to perceive in her?] (48).

In fact, Marcos suspects that he himself is less desirable than Cosme. One night when Marcos drunkenly wanders the streets, an old woman dumps garbage down on him from her window; soon after, a disheveled woman whom he believes to be Angela runs up to him, calls him Cosme, and clutches him in a passionate, brutal kiss. Disturbed, Marcos contrasts this encounter with Angela's typical kiss: "Un beso insípido, cortés [. . .]. Un beso distante años luz de los que reservaba para mi hermano Cosme" [An insipid, courteous kiss [. . .]. A kiss light years away from the ones she reserved for my brother Cosme] (43). Despite the protagonist's anxiety at being equated or subordinated to his vile, fictitious twin, none of his friends assumes that he is insane like his brother. In fact, they confirm Marcos's "normality" in opposition to his brother's eccentricities. Yet, when Marcos finally discovers that Angela has a *real* twin who is just as erratic as Cosme, he judges her exactly as he feared that she would condemn him: "Ya no podía ignorar que Eva, entre otras cosas, era la cara oculta de su hermana" [I could no longer ignore that Eva, among other things, was the hidden face of her sister] (50). In plotting his desire, Marcos assumes that Angela and Eva must be the same—homogeneous objects that lack the virtue of differentiation.

5 / PLOTTING DESIRE: THE VISUAL CONSTRUCTION OF THE SUBJECT

The play of opposites reaches a climax in this story when Marcos sets up a showdown with Angela in a bar, where he plans to manipulate her into submission. Still unaware that Angela's inconsistent behavior is due, in part, to the fact that "she" is really "they," two people, he tries to gain the upper hand by arriving an hour late and then spying on her as she waits: "La observé complacido. Su desaforada pasión por la simetría la había conducido a sentarse frente al espejo, junto a dos sillas vacías" [Gratified, I watched her. Her outrageous passion for symmetry had driven her to sit in front of a mirror, next to two vacant chairs] (46). He believes that he has the liberty of choosing which chair he will fill, which role he will enact: Cosme or Marcos. His smugness quickly becomes stunned surprise, however, when he realizes that there is no mirror reflecting Angela's image, but that the double is her flesh-and-blood twin. Although Marcos initially devalues Angela as tainted by her association with her double, he inadvertently recognizes their difference when he learns that Eva has fallen in love with Cosme. Sticking his head out of the phone booth in the bar, where he talks unobserved to Angela on the restaurant phone while watching her without her knowledge, he then stares at Eva, who "[s]e estaba hurgando la nariz con toda la tranquilidad del mundo" [was picking her nose, serene as could be] (49). Like Narcissus mesmerized by his own reflection, the protagonist gravitates toward this alternate mirror image that returns, instead of a threatening difference, a gratifying likeness to himself.

Thereafter Marcos behaves subtly like an empowered Cosme: "me hice con una llave herrumbrosa y la introduje en la cerradura del armario ropero. ¿Me atrevería? Lo abrí. Helicón, el causante de todos mis desafueros, seguía allí, desterrado desde el día en que cobardemente me asusté ante el mundo, ante los amigos, ante mí mismo" [I got hold of a rusty key and inserted it in the wardrobe lock. Would I dare? I opened it. Helicon, the cause of all my excesses, was still there, exiled since the day I cowardly was frightened before the world, before my friends, before myself] (51–52). Now it is he who takes action, who wields the key. Finding the suppressed double within himself confirmed in a new female object of desire, the protagonist embraces the previously denied, "cosmic" side of his personality and starts playing his helicon again.

As underscored by the title of this collection, *El ángulo del horror*, the angle of vision is crucial to the construction of the subject, of what one sees. Despite all the narrator's efforts to control her, Angela persists as an excess that questions the validity of reducing all women into a single, undifferentiated object. Her perspective, juxtaposed with his, reveals that the narrator's point of view is not the only one, and he re-views his masculine construction of the feminine subject from an angle of horror. Whatever their alternative perspectives may be, each character in this story defines himself or herself through the dialectic of desire between subject and object. Yet, even as desire moves toward its end, its process is in fact never-ending: "If desire is the question which generates both narrative and narrativity as Oedipal drama, that question is an open one, seeking a closure that is only promised, not guaranteed. For Oedipal desire requires in its object . . . an identification with the feminine position" (de Lauretis 1984, 133–34). No woman in this story completely acquiesces to Marcos's desire, whether it be physical or narrative. Indeed, he can only squirm beneath the power of a feminine gaze that finds him lacking. Thus the line that divides the roles of male/female and subject/object is revealed to be simply another border that was meant to be crossed, another taboo that cannot exist without its own transgression.

In the end, however, if interpreting the dynamics of desire in "Helicón" comes down to seeing double, is it possible to privilege any single perspective in the text? Angela clings to the difference inherent within each double because she reads it as the saving grace of her superiority over her sister. Is this really any different from the way Marcos defines men as more powerful than women? The names of each side of the binary might shift—male/female, Marcos/Cosme, Angela/Eva—but the dialectical relation always endures, as one more repetition of similarity and difference. This dizzying array of double images and double perspectives forces readers to constantly change their position in relation to the text in order to modify their view of it. Who, then, is the subject and who is the object in the dynamic of reading? "Helicón," even as it fans our desire for an end, finally eludes any satisfying closure. If it did not, we would not desire to pursue it, to play it, nearly so much.

"El legado del abuelo"

The desire for an end figures as the need to explain death itself in "El legado del abuelo" ["Grandfather's Legacy"], which in many ways is the least complex of the four tales in *El ángulo del horror*. Here an adult narrator recounts his childhood experience of his grandfather's death, focalizing all the upheaval, uncertainty, pain, and suppressed anger from the perspective of a young boy who does not yet know the intricate social codes of discursive expression. Thus the way the churlish grandfather is described posthumously as kind and doting by the boy's mother (Teresa), her older siblings (particularly Uncle Raúl), and the maid (Nati), jars with

5 / PLOTTING DESIRE: THE VISUAL CONSTRUCTION OF THE SUBJECT

the candid evaluation of dislike provided by the child. The old man's surly treatment of the child and petty theft of the money in his piggy bank incite the boy to retaliate. One day, when the invalid suffers a heart attack, the boy withholds his pills, demanding to be allowed to play with the grandfather's jealously guarded Chinese box. In fact, then, the boy himself causes the old man's death. When the child finally pieces this together, he silences his knowledge in order to protect himself. Several days after the death, the adults' euphemistic eulogies cede to angry resentment when they cannot find their father's will. The siblings suspect the boy's young mother of having sequestered the inheritance that the grandfather always hinted at, because she had been the one taking care of the old man for so many years. In vain, Teresa and Nati turn the house upside down in search of some legacy, while the boy resents the increased emotional distance that he perceives in his mother as she sinks into hopelessness at her situation.

At one point, the two women remember a Chinese box with a tiny key that the grandfather always treasured. The boy tells them that he has harbored the box in his room since the day of the death, and he explains that its contents are only an old pipe and some photographs. He decides that the photographs of his grandfather's young children were the real legacy, one that those grown-up children could not appreciate, and he is angered when they never consider the sentimental value of the family photos. Never actually perusing the contents of the box themselves, the women briefly ponder and then dismiss the peculiarity of the grandfather's having saved a pipe, since he never smoked. Disgusted with what he perceives as his mother's increasing weakness and disregard for him as well as her purely monetary interest in her deceased father, the protagonist identifies emotionally with his grandfather as someone else whom Teresa treated unjustly.

At the end of the story, after many years of estrangement from his mother, the protagonist as a young adult happens upon the Chinese box again and studies its contents. This time he realizes that, underneath its patina of grime, the pipe is made of solid gold and bears a loving inscription from the grandfather to Teresa. Stunned, the protagonist realizes that the tyrannical invalid had truly loved and appreciated his daughter and had bequeathed the pipe for her to be able to live comfortably. Unaware of her legacy, however, Teresa has given up on life, has grown old before her time, and for many years has resided in a retirement home with much older people. This new perspective reveals that rejection—the fate that his grandfather had always feared but escaped because Teresa took care of him—was exactly the legacy the protagonist imposed on his mother.

Because its view at the end completely alters the meaning of the narrative, "El legado del abuelo" dramatizes the drive toward the end, toward death, as a retrospective structuration of meaning. The death of the grandfather propels the narrative as an endeavor to explain the ultimate finale of life, to understand and integrate it into the realm of discourse. In this way it parallels Peter Brooks's idea that "plot is the internal logic of the discourse of mortality" (Brooks 1984, 22). The act of narration stands out as the plotting of events over time in an effort to create order and meaning: "It is the ordering of the inexplicable and impossible situation as narrative that somehow mediates and forcefully connects its discrete elements, so that we accept the necessity of what cannot logically be discoursed of" (Brooks 1984, 10). Thus part of this story concerns the young protagonist's apprenticeship with language, his journey toward learning the discourse "for what cannot be logically discoursed of."

The narrator's desire to understand death and its relation to life is both the motivation and the denouement of his tale. Indeed, the desire for death may be the *only* motivator of narration, as Brooks stresses: "what we seek in narrative fictions is that knowledge of death which is denied to us in our own lives: the death that writes *finis* to the life and therefore confers on it its meaning" (22). This retrospective process of coming to know the end is integrally dependent on time and shifting perspectives, as Fernández Cubas underscores in her novel *El columpio*. Whereas a plethora of perspectives that question absolute vision figures in all of Fernández Cubas's texts to some extent, in "El legado del abuelo" this motif is so crucial that it essentially *becomes* the story, the story of a changed perspective.

The ingenuous point of view from which the child perceives everyone's reaction to the grandfather's death humorously highlights the artificiality of the way the adults treat death in this story. The boy cannot reconcile his household's lamentations with the resentment they all felt toward the tyrannical old man when he was alive: "hasta la Nati, refrotándose las manos en el delantal, alzaba los ojos al cielo, decía: 'Pobre señor' y *gemía*. El desconsuelo de la Nati fue lo que más me sorprendió al principio. Estaba cansado de oírla rezongar en la cocina cada vez que el abuelo hacía sonar la campanilla de su cuarto o el timbre de la cama, de escucharla gritar: '¿Qué mosca le ha picado ahora a ese tipo?'. O llamarlo 'tiña', 'peste' [. . .]" [even Nati, wringing her hands on her apron, would look up toward heaven and say "Poor man" and *wail*. Nati's grief was what most surprised me in the beginning. I was tired of hearing her grumble in the kitchen every time Grandfather would ring the bell in his room or sound the buzzer on the bed, tired of listening to her yell "What bug is biting that man now?" Or call him "bloodsucker," "plague" {. . .}] (Fernández Cubas

1990, 55). The adults represent the old man with their words according to an ideal construction, and remember their own actions toward him in an enhanced way as well. Such power of discourse to transform reality is instigated, for the child, by death itself: "Me di cuenta enseguida y comprendí que, de las muchas desgracias que podían suceder en vida, la peor de todas era la Muerte" [I realized right away and understood that, of all the misfortunes that could happen in life, the worst of all was Death] (57). The child intuits that a fundamental goal of language is to express and explain death, even if that representation effects a great distancing from the "reality" of the death itself.

Indeed, the dissonance between discourse and death cause great confusion for the little boy as he attempts to learn to communicate with adult lingo. Having listened avidly to his mother's and Nati's discussions of the death, he tries to fulfill his assigned job of communicating the news by telephone to numerous relatives: "mi madre había repetido hasta la saciedad lo que tenía que decir y en aquellos instantes, en los que por nada del mundo quería disgustarla, transmití el mensaje palabra por palabra, como si tratara de una contraseña secreta [. . .]. —El abuelo está con la abuela—dije" [my mother had repeated over and over what I had to say and in those moments, in which I wouldn't have displeased her for anything in the world, I transmitted the message word for word, as if it were a secret password {. . .}. "Grandfather is with Grandmother," I said] (65). At first this laconic code, uttered completely out of any context on the telephone, unsettles and confuses even the adults. The child identifies with their astonishment: "[Yo] también, como ahora mi tío, pensé en algo peor. No tanto en que el abuelo se hubiera ido a no sé dónde a reunirse con la abuela, sino en que la abuela, desde ese lugar situado en no-se-sabe-dónde, hubiera decidido de repente venirse a pasar unos días con nosotros" [I, too, like my uncle now, thought of something worse. Not so much that Grandfather would have gone to I don't know where to reunite with Grandmother, but that Grandmother, from that place in who-knows-where, should have suddenly decided to come to spend a few days with us] (66). The child's untrained perspective humorously defamiliarizes the signification of the message that society has assigned and highlights the constructed nature of language, which depends on context and expectations of meaning in order to create communication.

Moreover, the protagonist's infantile point of view underscores the function of appearances to veil what hovers beneath. Nati's and Teresa's worried discussion of how to dress the grandfather thoroughly puzzles the boy: "Lo de vestir al abuelo, aquel día, a aquella hora y en aquellas circunstancias, me pareció lo más extraño que había escuchado hasta entonces. Porque, por más que me esforzara, recordaba al abuelo siempre igual, embutido en un pijama de rayas [. . .]" [Dressing Grandfather, on that day, at that time, and in those circumstances, seemed to me to be the strangest thing I had heard yet. Because no matter how I tried, I always remembered Grandfather the same way, stuffed into his striped pajamas {. . .}] (59). Finally, however, the child recalls a single occasion—the death of a friend—when he saw his grandfather fully dressed: "lo vi por primera vez con abrigo y sombrero [. . .], me pareció mucho más alto, fuerte y terrible que de ordinario. Tuve entonces la impresión de que el abuelo era en realidad así, como aquel día, y que los otros, es decir, toda la parte de su vida que yo conocía, no había hecho más que fingir [. . .]" [I saw him with an overcoat and hat for the first time {. . .}, he seemed much taller, stronger, and more terrible than normal. Then I had the impression that Grandfather really was that way, like that day, and that the other days, that is, all his life that I knew, he had only been pretending {. . .}] (60). Notably, this transformation in the grandfather is provoked, for the child, by death. The need to deal with death is the fundamental cause of the disjuncture between being and appearance, as if the end were a truth that must be concealed: "aquella tarde la ropa parecía cobrar una importancia capital" [that afternoon clothes seemed to take on a capital importance] (67).

The pajamas become a metonymy that is literally and figuratively inseparable from the grandfather and also serve as a metaphoric "cover" for oppositionality. The old man's constant wearing of the pajamas symbolizes his refusal to be active in life, which in turn has made him put on weight so that the pajamas are the only clothing that fit him. As a result, Teresa and Nati resort to dressing him in a Bedouin robe that the old man had brought back from the war in Africa. Their hope is that, "para quien no lo supiera, podía pasar por una túnica" [for whomever didn't know, it could pass for a tunic] (Fernández Cubas 1990, 69). Thus even the death shroud is not what it would appear to be and stands as something other.

Death as the ultimate other is underscored here by the dynamics of additional "other" relations. Uncle Raúl becomes furious when he sees that his father is "vestido de moro" [dressed like a Moor] (68), precisely the people the old man hated and fought against during the war. This "aside" engages the traditional dialectic of *cristiano/moro* that, when inverted, enrages the tyrannical Eloísa in *El columpio*. As Fernández Cubas's fiction signals, it is another key historical and cultural construction in Spanish identity.

5 / PLOTTING DESIRE: THE VISUAL CONSTRUCTION OF THE SUBJECT   203

Moreover, when Teresa defends the inappropriate attire that misrepresents the side of the binary that her father embraced, she falls back on the dialectical opposition of gender as the impediment to her acting otherwise: "Porque no se debía olvidar que tanto la Nati como ella eran mujeres y que el abuelo, su padre, era, al fin y al cabo, un hombre. Por eso, debajo de la túnica, le habían dejado el pantalón a rayas del pijama" [Because it should not be forgotten that both she and Nati were women and Grandfather, her father, was, after all, a man. For that reason, beneath the tunic, they had left his striped pajama bottoms on] (69). The African robe masquerading as a tunic is indispensable, then, to cover up the pajama bottoms, which, the boy imagines, conceal his grandfather's identity in order to project a fictive persona. Finally, the pajama bottoms are required to veil a father's masculinity from his daughter—in a humorous twist on the prohibition on nakedness that a drunken Noah once violated in the Bible. These multiple layers of meaning tied to the pajamas purport to conceal what should not, cannot, or will not be seen. Significantly, the foundational prohibition is that of the phallus, suggesting that perhaps the most basic stratum of otherness here is indeed that of gender. In Fernández Cubas's imagery, however, the garments' reversible association with one side or the other of the binary that they represent implicitly unravels the seam between each pair of constructs that they oppositionally stitch together.

At a loss for how to deal with the intricate maneuvers that death requires, Teresa appears childlike in her confusion and helplessness, which encourages her son to identify with her perspective. The narrator characterizes his mother's guilelessness by her gaze: "Mi madre había cambiado de aspecto y sus ojos, a ratos, recordaban los de una niña, sorprendida e indefensa, perdida en un laberinto frondoso del que no se confía en encontrar la salida" [My mother had changed in appearance and her eyes, at times, reminded me of a little girl's, surprised and defenseless, lost in a leafy labyrinth whose exit she was not sure of finding] (58). The boy's desire for his mother as a puerile equal also idealizes her as a reconstruction of glamorous women he has observed in popular culture: "la forma en que sostenía el pitillo, la dedicación que ponía en aspirar y expulsar el humo me recordaban a las artistas de cine y de la televisión, las fotografías de las revistas de moda [. . .]. Me sentía muy a gusto allí, en el sofá, al lado de mi madre, envueltos en humo, en aroma de café, y deseé que aquel momento en que nos habían dejado solos no acabara nunca" [the way she held her cigarette, the dedication she put into inhaling and exhaling the smoke reminded me of the stars in the movies and on television, the fashion pictures in magazines {. . .}. I felt very comfortable there, on the sofa, beside my mother, wrapped in smoke and in the aroma of coffee, and I wished that that moment when they had left us alone would never end] (68). Of course, the phallic symbolism of the cigarette in the boy's identification with his mother is psychoanalytically suggestive—not to mention the fact that his father died while she was in the hospital giving birth to him. It is sufficient to say that the child basks at the center of his mother's regard.

Nonetheless, the gaze of this idealized other soon shifts to different objects. His mother's look becomes as self-centered as everyone else's, in the child's eyes, when the euphemisms of death are displaced by the financial priority of the questionable inheritance: "Porque ahora los ojos de mi madre se parecían tremendamente a los de tío Raúl, tía Marta y tía Josefina. Mirándose con recelo, acusándose unos a otros [. . .]" [Because now my mother's eyes looked very much like those of Uncle Raúl, Aunt Marta and Aunt Josefina. Looking at one another with suspicion, accusing one another {. . .}] (Fernández Cubas 1990, 74–75). Feeling "como si yo me hubiera vuelto invisible otra vez" [as if I had become invisible again] (79), the child's adoration of his mother becomes abhorrence. Hence Teresa becomes one more in the parade of characters in Fernández Cubas's works who do not gaze at their objects—male or female—the way those objects desire. The child in "El legado del abuelo," unseen by his mother, believes that he now holds no importance for her: "Ahora que había perdido su expresión de niña era obvio que no me necesitaba para nada" [Now that she had lost her little girl's expression it was obvious that she didn't need me at all] (80). This disillusionment and abandonment spur him to outgrow his own infantile ignorance and to learn the codes of the adult world.

The household's preoccupation with the inheritance leaves the boy with plenty of freedom to explore on his own. He learns to take the bus and wander the streets alone, and to recognize and cynically condemn the self-serving discourse of his mother and Nati: "Pero ya estaba cansado de todas estas historias. De que dijeran '¡qué tontería!' cuando de nuevo les estaba contando la verdad. Ellas, que no hacían más que mentir. Que hablar de cariño, de dolor, de las razones sentimentales por las que habían tapizado a grandes flores los sillones, las sillas, el sofá del abuelo. . . Pero de mi boca no surgiría una palabra. Y escondería la caja. Callaría [. . .]." [But I was tired now of all those stories. Of them saying "How silly!" when once again I was telling them the truth. They, who did nothing but lie, talk about love, about pain, about the sentimental reasons why they had upholstered the armchairs, the chairs, Grandfather's sofa, in big flowers. . . . But not a single word would come out of my mouth. And I would hide the box. I would be silent {...}] (88–89). The women had torn the furniture cushions apart in search of the inheritance, an inheritance that the boy possesses but wants to conceal (he slips up later and mentions that he has the box, but he never shows it to them). Moreover, the child wields his knowledge of the adult codes when he deliberately hides his role in the old man's death: "Pero yo mismo me tapé la boca. Porque lo que me asustaba aún más, si cabe, era que [...] apareciera una de aquellas dos mujeres en mi cuarto y descubriera que lo sabía todo" [But I shut my own mouth. Because what scared me even more, if possible, was that {...} one of those two women would appear in my room and discover that I knew everything] (84). Silence, he realizes, is itself a kind of discourse that serves to misrepresent and distance the other from what will not be expressed.

The emotional distance the protagonist feels toward "aquellas dos mujeres" [those two women] increases with the years, as his sense of personal superiority—born of disillusionment and alienation—causes him to reject his mother and identify with his grandfather. Believing the old family photos in the Chinese box to be the grandfather's true legacy, the boy has identified himself as "el único destinatario de aquel legado" [the only recipient of that legacy] (Fernández Cubas 1990, 93). Disillusioned by the duplicitous discourse of the adults that he himself has manipulated against them in revenge, the boy grows up believing that he has seen the truth about his mother and found her lacking. Years later he is displaced as the object of desire of his idealized other once again when he rediscovers the Chinese box and its pipe of gold, whose inscription "me hizo dudar de todo lo que hasta entonces había dado por cierto. [...] Y constaté que nada me había servido creerme el receptor del legado del abuelo. Porque había hecho precisamente de mi madre lo que él siempre temió que hicieran consigo" [made me doubt everything that until then I had considered certain. {...} And I observed that I had believed myself to be the recipient of Grandfather's legacy in vain. Because I had done to my mother precisely what he always feared they would do with him] (95–96). Now an adult, he sees the pipe, as a sign, differently. His maturity over time has taught him to recognize that the pipe is made of gold and to perceive its obscured message for Teresa.[4] Hence the protagonist learns that any interpretation of a text depends on the perspective from which it is seen.

This knowledge afforded by a viewpoint altered over time embodies the fundamental distinction between the "experiencing self" and the "narrating self" of the story.[5] The new perspective of his life radically changes his vision of his mother and of himself: "Veía mi mirada de rey destronado, escrutando a mi madre, acusándola en silencio, convirtiéndome en el juez de una situación que únicamente los nervios, las circunstancias y mi obsesiva presencia podían provocar" [I saw my gaze of a king dethroned, scrutinizing my mother, accusing her in silence, making myself the judge of a situation that only nerves, circumstances, and my obsessive presence could provoke] (96). Having spent his life in pursuit of desire, longing to be the object of desire in the gaze of his mother, he now sees how he victimized her as the object of *his* gaze. In a parallel manner, knowing the end changes the meaning of the text for readers, who can review the signs with a new perspective and see the irony of the narrative discourse. Retrospectively, readers understand that the narrator's declaration early in the story that everyone viewed the grandfather's death as "un hecho insólito y extraordinario" [an unexpected and extraordinary event] (56) duplicitously silences the truth: the death seemed strange but was not, for the protagonist himself provoked it.

The distance between the narrating and experiencing selves highlights the fundamental role of shifting perspectives as one of the elements that creates meaning. At first only marked by verb tenses (past versus present), and then informed by the different perspective afforded by knowing the end, the effect of time on the text is underscored by the capricious factor of memory. As the recuperation of the past in the present, memory is shaped indelibly by time, which the narrator recognizes when he recalls the tassels of his grandfather's robe "con las que, cuando era tan pequeño que casi no me acordaba, habíamos jugado los dos al teléfono. O tal vez no había jugado nunca y tan sólo hubiese querido jugar. O algún amigo mío, quizá, me habló de otro batín, de otro abuelo y de unas borlas como aquéllas con las que él y su abuelo hacían como si se llamasen por teléfono" [with which, when I was so young that I almost didn't remember, we both had played telephone. Or maybe I never played and only would have liked to play. Or some friend of mine, perhaps, told me of another bathrobe, of another grandfather, and of some tassels like those with which he and his grandfather pretended to call each other on the telephone] (Fernández Cubas 1990, 59). Thus memory is the reconstruction of the past as the subject perceived it to happen. Time blurs perceptions, all the more so in that its past and present manifestations are always dependent upon perspective and invested with desire.

The dual levels of perspective proffered by "El legado del abuelo"—those of the young boy and those of the adult narrator—dramatize the effects of time on the subject as he progresses toward greater knowledge and death, toward greater knowledge *of* death. Plotting desire, then, is a way to understand the way one has come to be. If desire is what drives one toward the end, to reorder events over time in order to create meaning

5 / PLOTTING DESIRE: THE VISUAL CONSTRUCTION OF THE SUBJECT

retrospectively, however, to satiate that desire would be to unite with death itself: "with the possibility of total realization of desire, the self encounters the impossibility of desiring, because to desire becomes, and can only be, the choice of death of that same self" (Brooks 1984, 51). So it is that desire is also what constantly drives one back to the beginning, to reread and search for new meanings, always from an altered perspective and place in time.

"El ángulo del horror"

As the title story of the collection, "El ángulo del horror" ["The Angle of Horror"] synthesizes and epitomizes the visual construction of the subject through its desire for the other and drive toward the end. Indeed, its focus on perspective—on an unexpected, often bizarre and even horrific angle of vision—can be seen as a metaphor for all of Fernández Cubas's fiction. One's angle of sight shapes everything one perceives and thus mediates in relationships of power, gender, colonialism, history, and subjectivity itself. "El ángulo del horror" explores the dynamics of the gaze as perhaps the most fundamental delineator of the subject in relation to its object.

The multiple and complex implications of the gaze are posited in a surprisingly simple plot in this story. An eighteen-year old young man, Carlos, returns home on vacation from his studies in England in order to visit his two sisters, Julia and Marta, and his parents. The family and particularly Julia, who focalizes the third-person narration, worry when Carlos mysteriously becomes listless and apathetic right after his arrival and locks himself in his room. Finally, he allows the devoted Julia to enter, and he tells her of a dream he had in England in which he saw their house from a completely different and dreadful perspective, an angle of vision that has permanently contaminated his point of view. As Julia listens to his haunted tale, Carlos realizes that he is able to look at her directly and see her as she is, undistorted, in contrast to his vision of everything else.

Not long afterward, he goes downstairs and chats normally with the family, who plan to commit him to an asylum to try to help him. Then he goes into the bathroom and returns to his room. Suddenly, Julia realizes what might have happened and rushes to his room just before her brother, having deliberately overmedicated himself, breathes his last breath. Horrified, Julia sees not Carlos but Death itself languishing there; now everything *she* perceives is contaminated and corrupted by the terrible vision of implicit and impending death. Running outdoors to escape, the girl is comforted to learn that at least she can still look normally at her younger sister, who has followed her. At that moment, Marta comprehends that "a ella, Julia, le estaba ocurriendo *algo*" [*something* was happening to her, Julia] (Fernández Cubas 1990, 115), and the expression in her eyes alters just as Julia's gaze began to change, days before, with the realization that *something* was happening to Carlos.

At the end of the tale the dangling expectation of another repetition of the angle of horror, this time passed from Julia to young Marta, foregrounds the motif of repetition of the same-yet-different, which weaves throughout the author's work. As I have argued in my analyses thus far, the tension between sameness and difference underlies every binary opposition that Fernández Cubas explores and deconstructs. Yet, why must all human relations hinge on this duality? Is it endowed with some overarching power, as the origin that must repeat its authority before it can be deconstructed? In terms of subjectivity, it would seem that sameness/difference is the fundamental measuring stick by which the subject defines itself in relation to its others.

In his studies on the subject, Mikhail Bakhtin contends that the self and the other incarnate the master distinction of perspective that applies to all relationships from the personal to the philosophical to the political. Drawing on Einstein's concept of relativity, which demonstrated that perspective is a relational concept dependent on two bodies in dialogue with one another, Bakhtin creates an overarching metaphor of dialogue to describe relational dynamics. In the context of the abundant social "languages" or "heteroglossia" that pervade novels, Bakhtin highlights the enriched perspective attained by this juxtaposition of differences within a text: "Every language in the novel is a point of view, a socio-ideological conceptual system of real social groups and their embodied representatives. . . . Against the dialogizing background of other languages of the era and in direct dialogic interaction with them (in direct dialogues) each language begins to sound differently than it would have sounded 'on its own.' . . ." (Bakhtin 1981, 411–12). Applying Bakhtin's perspectivism to the level of "embodied representatives" themselves—human subjects—Michael Holquist coins the term "dialogism:" "Dialogism argues that we make sense of existence by defining our specific place in it, an operation performed in cognitive time and space, the basic categories of perception. . . . We perceive the world through the time/space of the self *and* through the time/space of the other" (Holquist 1990, 35). Thus the unitary self is incomplete because it cannot *see* itself fully. It is logical, then, that subjects so frequently long to be the object of the gaze, for this duality is a fundamental step toward understanding their subjectivity: "In order to be perceived as a whole, as something finished, a person or object must be shaped in the time/space categories of the other, and that is possible only when the person or object is perceived from the position of outsideness" (Holquist 1990, 31). Bakhtin's theory reveals that the subject needs its other to supplement its vision of itself; moreover, it defines every other it sees according to relations of similarity to and difference from itself. Although the focus on self/other may seem to reify binaries as foundational, Bakhtinian thought undermines dialectical relationships. For him, it is never *one* as opposed to the *other*, but one and the other only come to signify at all in a third factor, the *relationship* between them of mutual simultaneity and separateness.

"El ángulo del horror" accentuates the desire to see and be seen as fundamental to knowledge. Indeed, the opening line features a frustrated Julia who spies in search of her brother's secret: "Ahora, cuando golpeaba la puerta por tercera vez, miraba por el ojo de la cerradura sin alcanzar a ver [. . .]" [Now, when she was knocking on the door for the third time, she was looking through the keyhole without being able to see {. . .}] (Fernández Cubas 1990, 99). As Carlos's adoring sister, Julia is baffled by his refusal to recommence their customary adventures together, and she posts herself outside his door in the hope that "ella vería. Vería al fin en qué consistían las misteriosas ocupaciones de su hermano, comprendería su extrema palidez y se apresuraría a ofrecerle su ayuda" [she would see. She would finally see what her brother's mysterious concerns were about, she would understand his extreme pallor and would hurry to offer him her help] (100).

If seeing is understanding, Carlos obscures his own vision in order to block out the knowledge transmitted by his altered view of the world, which he cannot bear to accept: "en sus ojos parecían concentrarse los únicos destellos de luz que habían logrado atravesar su fortaleza. ¿O no eran sus ojos? Julia abrió ligeramente uno de los postigos de la ventana y suspiró aliviada. Sí, aquel muchacho abatido, oculto tras unas inexpugnables gafas de sol [. . .] era su hermano" [the only gleams of light that had managed to penetrate his fortress seemed to concentrate in his eyes. Or were they not his eyes? Julia opened slightly one of the shutters and sighed, relieved. Yes, that depressed boy, hidden behind impenetrable sunglasses {. . .} was her brother] (105). The play of light and darkness in Carlos's room highlights the literal menace of vision and the metaphorical threat of knowledge. Once Carlos finally invites her in, Julia is delighted to be reconfirmed by his gaze and his esteem: "Un destello de orgullo iluminó sus ojos. Carlos, como en otros tiempos, iba a hacerla partícipe de sus secretos, convertirla en su más fiel aliada, pedirle una ayuda que ella se apresuraría a conceder" [A glint of pride lit her eyes. Carlos, as in other times, was going to share his secrets with her, make her his most faithful ally, ask her for assistance, which she would hasten to give] (105–6). Julia longs to be seen by her brother, from the outside, because her relationship with him is crucial to what she believes she knows about herself.

Yet Carlos's vision has been irremediably altered by the shift of time/space from which he contemplates the world. He first sees the angle of horror in the realm of his dreams, while he is in England. Thus, at least implicitly, this altered view is associated with a double displacement, oneiric and geographical, from the daily reality he knows in Spain. Essentially, Carlos has come to see "the same" from the perspective of difference, from the outside, as he explains to his sister: "Era [. . .] la casa en la que hemos pasado todos los veranos desde que nacimos. Y, sin embargo, había algo muy extraño en ella. Algo tremendamente desagradable y angustioso que al principio no supe precisar. Porque era exactamente *esta casa*, sólo que, por un extraño don o castigo, yo la contemplaba desde un insólito ángulo de visión" [It was {. . .} the house where we had spent every summer since we were born. And yet there was something very strange about it. Something tremendously unpleasant and upsetting that at first I couldn't put my finger on. Because it was exactly *that house*, except that, by some strange gift or punishment, I was seeing it from an unwonted angle of vision] (108–9).

Once he has found this perspective, Carlos can never return to the position from where he saw things before: "Un extraño ángulo que no por el horror que me produce deja de ser real. . . . Y lo peor es que ya no hay remedio. Sé que no podré librarme de él en toda la vida. . ." [A strange angle that is no less real for the horror that it produces in me. . . . And the worst part is that it's too late for a cure. I know that I won't be able to free myself from it in my whole life. . .] (109). Carlos's angle of seeing/knowing recalls Judith Butler's point that what is excluded from any body forms its boundary as much as the body itself. Carlos has crossed the border to see the center—his home in Spain—from the perspective of the outside.

Although reluctant to accept the knowledge Carlos tries to share with her, Julia's altered view of him changes the way she sees herself. At first the girl tries to look away from her brother in denial of the new vision of him. Discomfited by this view of her older brother as no longer "fuerte, sano y envidiable" [strong, healthy, and enviable] (Fernández Cubas 1990, 109), Julia suddenly glimpses her own image from his perspective, reflected in duplicate in the two lenses of Carlos's dark glasses: "Dos cabezas de cabello revuelto y ojos muy abiertos y asustados. Así debía de verla él: una niña atrapada en la guarida de un ogro, inventando excusas para salir quedamente de la habitación, aguardando el momento de traspasar el umbral de la puerta, respirar hondo y echar a correr [. . .] y ella sentía debajo de aquellas dos cabezas de cabello revuelto y ojos espantados dos pares de piernas que empezaban a temblar [. . .]." [Two heads of tousled hair and very wide, frightened eyes. That's how he probably saw her: a little girl trapped in an ogre's lair, making up excuses to leave the room quietly, waiting for the moment to cross the threshold, to take a deep breath and start to run] (110).

With the trick of reflection, of doubling, Julia is able to see herself through the eyes of the other. She realizes that this self-image reveals her own perspective shaded by the discourse of fairy tale and myth, which inscribes binary oppositionality as the fear of difference. From that angle, the little girl trapped in the monster's lair longs to cross the threshold—the border—and escape from the threatening other and his space. Yet Julia also comprehends the perspective of Carlos and realizes that the other, although different, is not a threat but an additional way of seeing herself. As her double, this other reflects a dual vision with which she identifies: she *feels* two pairs of legs that connect to the two heads and frightened pairs of eyes that she observes. Significantly, right after Julia has this cognition, Carlos realizes that "A ti, Julia, a ti aún puedo mirarte" [You, Julia, I can still look at you] (111). He can see her because she, too, has begun to glimpse an *other* way of seeing.

Finally, when she observes her brother's death, Julia can fully comprehend the horrific angle of vision that so disturbed him: "Julia volvió la mirada hacia su hermano. Por primera vez en la vida comprendía lo que era la muerte. Inexplicable, inaprehensible, oculta tras una apariencia de fingido descanso. Veía a la Muerte, lo que tiene la muerte de horror y de destrucción, de putrefacción y abismo" [Julia turned her gaze toward her brother. For the first time in her life she understood death. Inexplicable, incomprehensible, hidden behind an appearance of feigned repose. She was seeing Death, what death holds of horror and destruction, of putrefaction and abyss] (114). Like Teresa and Nati in "El legado del abuelo," Julia is confronted by what must not be seen, by what cannot be understood. Yet the way of seeing otherwise forces her to contemplate the semblance of Death and comprehend it as the ultimate Other: "Porque ya no era Carlos quien yacía en el lecho sino Ella, la gran ladrona, burdamente disfrazada con rasgos ajenos, riéndose a carcajadas [. . .], mostrando a todos el engaño de la vida [. . .]" [Because it was no longer Carlos who lay in the bed but She, the great thief, roughly disguised with the features of another, laughing uproariously {...}, revealing to all the deceit of life {...}] (114). Julia recognizes Death as the dialogic other of life, which is also inseparable from life. Death and life mean nothing as isolated entities, for each is constituted as meaningful only in its relationship to the other.

Fernández Cubas's altered angle is horrific in the sense that it displaces the borders human beings erect to protect themselves and to create the illusion that they are encircled by life, by what they know, by the same.[6] The dialogic vision that informs all that one can see and know cannot be attained by the self alone, for the self can never perceive its completeness, its own death: "this possibility of conceiving my beginning and end as a whole life, is always enacted in the time/space of the other: I may see my death, but not in the category of my 'I.' For my 'I,' death occurs only for others, even when the death in question is my own" (Holquist 1990, 37). Carlos sees death in every other upon whom he rests his gaze. The only way to escape this totalizing vision, this constant knowledge, is to die himself, for he cannot see and be fully cognizant of his own death. Julia, when she observes her brother's death, is repositioned into the extended angle of vision that the other provides—a perspective that she eventually will pass on to her sister, a different other.

Although the siblings alternately shift into this different angle of sight, they are not able to see the larger picture of relationships that I have sketched here, for they are implicated within that picture. The view readers take of these relationships parallels that of Bakhtin's outside observer:

> If motion is to have meaning, not only must there be two different bodies in a relation with each other, but there must as well be someone to grasp the nature of such a relation: the non-centeredness of the bodies themselves requires the center constituted by an observer.... Bakhtin's observer is also, simultaneously, an active participant in the relation of simultaneity. Conceiving being dialogically means that reality is always experienced, not just perceived, and further that it is experienced from a particular position. (Holquist 1990, 21)

Positioned on the outside, readers observe but also participate in the dialogic relationship in that they experience it through their perception. Readers see the larger purview of dialogic perspectives in their position of what Bakhtin calls transgredience: "Transgredience ... is reached when the *whole* existence of others is seen from outside not only their own knowledge that they are being perceived by somebody else, but from beyond their awareness that such an other even exists" (Holquist 1990, 32). Readers' outside view in "El ángulo del horror" is integrally shaped by the "omniscient" narrative perspective of this tale, one of the few Fernández Cubas stories told in the third person. Thus the narrator's perspective parallels that of readers, outside the subject/object dynamics he purports to observe. In contrast, a first-person narration would preclude the transgredience that comprehends the full import of all the dialogic subjects and objects that it relates.

The dual meaning of "relate," as (1) to interact in the creation of meaning and (2) to tell a story, is fundamental for Bakhtin, because narration observes and weaves together the relationships among characters as subjects and objects. Thus he distinguishes the novel as a metaphor for dialogic dynamics. So too with the short story, I would argue (viewing the vaguely delineated requirement of length—the principal distinction between the two "genres" of short story and novel—as a dialogically [de]constructed border). As a narrative text, then, "El ángulo del horror" focuses on the dynamics of perspectivism that dialogically constitute subject/object relations. By constantly reversing the relationship of seer and seen, this text suggests that knowledge is achieved not dialectically, but relationally, dialogically, through ever shifting centers of vision. In this way, Fernández Cubas's narrative poses subjectivity as inherently dialogic, a relationship that, for Holquist, is liberating in its eternal postponement of closure:

> the tripartite nature of dialogue bears within it the seeds of hope: in so far as my 'I' is dialogic, it insures that my existence is not a lonely event but part of a larger whole. The thirdness of dialogue frees my existence from the very circumscribed meaning it has in the limited configuration of self/other relations available in the immediate time and particular place of my life. For in later times, and in other places, there will always be other configurations of such relations, and in conjunction with *that* other, my self will be differently understood. (Holquist 1990, 38)

If the desire for knowledge, mediated by perspective, ultimately points toward knowledge of death and the end of the story of the subject, the story is always repeated "in another time, in another place" by successive readers. Thus the story is always begun again and consumed anew in the drive toward the end and an altered vision of our others and ourselves. This, after all, is why we read.

"La Flor de España"

Fernández Cubas playfully emphasizes the effect that repositioning the subject in "another time, another place" has on the subject's visual construction of itself and its others in "La Flor de España" ["The Flower of Spain"], the last tale in this collection. The unnamed Spanish narrator/protagonist of this text, who works as a university instructor in "el país del frío" [the country of cold] (presumably a Scandinavian country), characterizes Spaniards and Northerners according to the time and space of their homelands. Feeling miserably out of place in this land, and having just been rejected by her Northern boyfriend, one day she happens upon a small shop called "La Flor de España," run by a short, blond woman named Rosita. Annoyed that a Northerner would presume to be able to transplant Spain to this land, the narrator obsessively tries to find fault with Rosita. Eventually she realizes that Rosita is actually Spanish and, furthermore, knows a whole colony of Spaniards with whom the protagonist herself begins to associate. With increasing frequency, she visits "La Flor de España" to bait Rosita into conversation, interpreting the shopkeeper's terse, apathetic replies as overtures of friendship.

Puzzled when the other workers at the shop announce that Rosa is not just very busy but also very ill, and in any case will be indisposed for months, the narrator spends her summer vacation with three Northern wives who delight in belittling Spain, the homeland of their husbands. From these women she learns that, oddly enough, the Northern boyfriend who recently left her has become romantically involved with her previous Northern boyfriend, whom she herself had rejected. At the end of her vacation, the protagonist hides herself to keep watch outside the shop door of "La Flor de España" in anticipation of its reopening. Rosa finally arrives—sun-tanned, vivacious, and in control—but seems to have some sort of collapse after the narrator enters the shop to pester her with questions once again. Unconcerned, the narrator decides that she will not abandon the country of cold after all because she has so many good friends there, the most important of whom is Rosita.

The binary opposition of North/South in this story, with the radically different cultural adaptations to space and time that characterize the respective lands, invites a consideration of the role of the "chronotope"—or "time/space"—in shaping the perspective of the subject.[7] Whereas Bakhtin's chronotope is a complex concept with multiple applications in his study of the novel, it applies to this analysis in its role as a marker of subjectivity, in the way it delineates a subject's space and structures a subject's time. Borrowing the term from mathematics and the theory of relativity, Bakhtin employs the chronotope to study space and time as a singular unit: "In the literary artistic chronotope, spatial and temporal indicators are fused into one carefully thought-out, concrete whole. Time, as it were, thickens, takes on flesh, becomes artistically visible; likewise, space becomes charged and responsive to the movements of time, plot and history" (Bakhtin 1981, 84). In "La Flor de España" the narrator's national chronotope indelibly marks the way she perceives events in the North and plots them into a coherent story, for, as Bakhtin emphasizes, one's locus in time/space indelibly shapes the angle of interpretation of all one perceives: "In literature and art itself, temporal and spatial determinations are inseparable from one another, and always colored by emotions and values. . . . Art and literature are shot through with *chronotopic values* of varying degree and scope" (Bakhtin 1981, 243). The value judgments that accompany human perception are inevitably shaded by the way subjects' respective chronotopes have conditioned them to view the world. Yet the narrator's perspective in this story is not absolute, for in the context of Bakhtin's dialogism and Fernández Cubas's fictional cosmos one chronotope achieves meaning when set in tension with another. Readers—positioned in a different chronotope altogether—undermine the narrator's plot when they interpret the interplay of angles, the viewpoints of the other characters in this tale. Thus "La Flor de España" posits a dialogue of chronotopes and perspectives to interrogate how time and space shape the subject's visual construction of others and of itself.

Feeling completely out of place in this Northern chronotope, "una ciudad de idioma incomprensible en la que anochece a las tres de la tarde y no se ve un alma por la calle a partir de las cuatro" [a city of an incomprehensible language where it gets dark at three in the afternoon and you don't see a soul on the street after four] (Fernández Cubas 1990, 119), the narrator rejects the possibility that others might viably overlap two time/spaces in order to extend and enrich their perspectives instead of belittling one or the other as she does. The most heinous violation of Spanish identity, in the narrator's eyes, is the deficient, makeshift tilde on the shop's neon sign, which at times garishly renders the shop's country of origin as "Espana:" "A medida que me aproximaba me pareció que el de La Flor era de todos el más vistoso [. . .] por los curiosos guiños a los que se entregaba la tilde y que supuse no del todo preconcebidos. Aquélla no era una tilde normal y corriente. Una onda apenas esbozada, un signo ligero, sugerente, sino un auténtico disparate, un trazo desmesurado, toscamente añadido a una inocente e indefensa ene" [As I approached it seemed that The Flower's sign was the showiest {. . .} due to the odd winks to which the tilde abandoned itself and which I guessed were not entirely preconceived. That was not a normal, typical tilde. Not a slightly sketched wave, a faint, suggestive sign, but a true absurdity, an excessive stroke, crudely added to an innocent and defenseless "n"] (120–21). This fixation on the inaccurate reproduction abroad of the tilde as the quintessential symbol of

Spanish identity is amusing in the extratextual context of Spain, which has felt pressure from the international community to repress its tilde in order to facilitate typewritten communication. Through the narrator's paranoid obsession with the tilde, Fernández Cubas playfully takes issue with the connection between language, national identity, and worldview: because the keyboards of other countries often do not reproduce the ñ, peculiar to the Spanish linguistic representation of the world, should Spain suppress its difference and assimilate itself to the technological inscription of the global community?

From the narrator's point of view, the shop owners tried to recreate *lo español* with tools from the North, futilely striving to integrate two opposing chronotopes. She judges their doomed endeavor to be epitomized by the Northern letter they had to cut up so that it could masquerade as a tilde. She assumes that this "letra mutilada" [mutilated letter] (121) cannot be an *authentic* tilde because it is not situated in the place of *origin*, the central chronotope of Spain itself. By extension, this shop in the North surely cannot boast of authentic Spanish products: "No era la primera vez que veía una tienda como aquélla. Naturalmente a lo largo de mi vida había visto cantidad de tiendas como aquélla. Pero allí, en medio de una calle desierta, en el país del frío, donde los días acaban a las tres de la tarde y no se ve un alma a partir de las cuatro. . . " [It wasn't the first time I saw a shop like that. Naturally, I had seen lots of shops like that one throughout my life. But there, in the middle of a deserted street, in the country of cold, where the days end at three in the afternoon and you don't see a soul after four. . .] (121).

"La Flor de España"—both the store and the story—thus foregrounds the problematic effort to transcribe identity in an increasingly globalized cultural realm. *To transcribe* literally means *to write over or across*, and conventionally signifies to make a written copy. This duplication, which is also a transgression, destabilizes the narrator's sense of unique and original Spanishness by challenging the foundational notions of sameness and inviolate difference that undergird her identity. What the narrator does not enunciate—what she deems too obvious to be uttered—is that the realm of one time/space *cannot* be duplicated within the realm of another. Like Angela in "Helicón," she fears the annihilation of individuality in repetition, in the reproduction of the self within another.

If the country of cold where the sun sets at three in the afternoon is an inferior chronotope that produces undesirable subjects who speak an incomprehensible language, then Spain is privileged as the chronotopic measure of all that is desirable. The narrator imagines how some past experience in Spain must have altered the shop owner's sense of identity and inflamed her desire for the better things in life: "Aquella mujer había conocido tiempos mejores—no hacía falta ser muy sagaz para averiguar *dónde*—, tiempos irrepetibles y lejanos, dorándose al sol, bebiendo ingentes cantidades de sangría, enamorándose sucesivamente del guía, del portero, del chófer del autocar. [. . .] Ante la imposibilidad de traerse al muchacho moreno—el guía, el portero, el conductor del autocar—se había traído el resto" [That woman had seen better times—one didn't have to be a genius to guess *where*—, times that could not be repeated, distant times, turning a golden tan under the sun, drinking enormous quantities of *sangría*, falling in love successively with the tour guide, the porter, the bus driver. {. . .} Given the impossibility of bringing home the dark young man—the tour guide, the porter, the bus driver—she had brought with her the rest] (Fernández Cubas 1990, 123).

In this enumeration of images, the narrator delineates Spanish subjectivity only along the most stereotypical level of sun, *sangría*, and seduction. Her Spanish chronotope—with its long days of warm relaxation and its nights of desire and revelry—radically contrasts with the darkness and deserted cold of the North. Yet *her* summation of Spanish identity is far more superficial than the stockpile in Rosita's shop. Beyond oppositions of race and nationality, the narrator also depends on the gender binary to inscribe the woman's experience in the South. Her list of possible male others precludes any distinction among Spanish men by setting them up as a chain of interchangeable substitutes. She views them all as swarthy, seductive, and servile—perhaps revealing, more than the Northern woman's experience with the Spanish man, her own relationship with them based on superficiality and all-or-nothing power plays. Unable to appreciate the subtleties of "the same yet different," the protagonist thrives on the absolutes of dialectical opposition in order to reinstate her side of various binaries as always superior.

To give due credit to Fernández Cubas's skill, I should emphasize that the self-centered obsessiveness of the narrator's perspective surfaces indirectly in the text, in a much more subtle manner than my analysis might suggest (because I endeavor to disclose the angle of her gaze). Much of the overall humor of this story depends on readers' perceiving and knowing more than just what the narrator shows and tells. The narrator's vision and voice work against her, for instance, in the scene where she initially peers into the shop window. Readers recognize how the trope of the window can dramatize the reversibility of the gaze, wherein the critical subject can become the ridiculed object. Angered by the unspoken threat of the mixture of chronotopes, the narrator notes that the faint sense of unreality that had led her to scrutinize the shop "se convirtió, con la nariz pegada al escaparate y nieve hasta las rodillas, en el más absoluto desconcierto" [became, with my nose pressed against the display window and snow up to my knees, the most absolute uneasiness] (121). She identifies only with her own perspective, looking with disdain and disturbance into the display window. She does not consider the possibility that those people inside the shop might also look out at her (not to mention that *readers* "look" at her). The narrator unwittingly depicts herself to be seen as an object: a snooping woman immersed in filthy snow, her nose smashed against the pane as she cranes her neck and squints to pass judgment on what she sees. Readers see, although she cannot, that she looks hilariously ridiculous.

As a seeing subject, the protagonist constantly passes *her* critical eye over the products in La Flor de España, in search of the most remote and insignificant flaw that would invalidate the project of transgressing borders and transposing chronotopes. Dissatisfied with the news that Rosita would stock all the traditional kinds of *turrón* for Christmas, she makes a fuss over the lack of *turrón de coco*. When she observes jars of *pimientos de pico*, she obsesses over the terrible oversight of not stocking *pimientos de piquillo* as well—although she is not really sure if there is a difference between the two. In addition to seeing the array of Spanish products in the North as lacking, the protagonist paradoxically considers them to be an excess, a grotesque distortion that Northerners could only view as the fearsome specter of otherness: "Lo que acababa de contemplar era lo más semejante a un museo de horrores; una vitrina de ídolos extraños arrancados de su origen [. . .]. Me pregunté a quién se le podía haber ocurrido la idea de montar un negocio tan grotesco e imaginé a algunos padres rubios y de ojos azules amenazando a sus hijos, también rubios y de ojos azules, con llevarles a La Flor de España si no se acababan la sopa" [What I had just seen was just like a museum of horrors; a showcase of strange idols uprooted from their place of origin {. . .}. I wondered who could have thought to start such a grotesque business and I imagined blond and blue-eyed parents threatening their children, also blond and blue-eyed, with taking them to The Flower of Spain if they didn't finish their soup] (122).

In contrast to Carlos of "En ángulo del horror," who was overwhelmed by the difference he suddenly perceived in the time/space of the same (his childhood home), the narrator of "La Flor de España" is unsettled by the specter of sameness within a chronotope of difference, for she can view the North/South dichotomy only as a sacred, dialectical opposition that must be preserved. Her attitude unveils the standard tactics by which any center marginalizes its periphery: by visualizing and inscribing it as lack, as excess, as the abject to be rejected because of its difference that must

5 / PLOTTING DESIRE: THE VISUAL CONSTRUCTION OF THE SUBJECT

never be recognized as the same—or its sameness that must always be represented as difference.

Toward this end, the protagonist identifies oppositionally in every situation she encounters, even to the point of siding against "her own" people, the colony of Spaniards in the city of the North. The first time she attends one of the colony's gatherings, she notices the importance of individual nationality: "Todos—yo misma desde que entrara por la puerta—teníamos nuestro *lugar de origen* marcado a hierro en la frente" [Everyone—even I once I stepped in the door—had their *place of origin* branded on their forehead] (Fernández Cubas 1990, 130). Whereas for the protagonist these differences are grounds for absolute division, she is amazed to learn that the other expatriates *choose* the blend of chronotopes in which they live: "Me sentí un poco en el exilio. Ninguno de los presentes se encontraba allí por razones forzosas; ganaban sueldos espléndidos y no parecía que se plantearan ni por asomo deshacer sus pisos y regresar a su 'lugar de origen'" [I felt a little bit exiled. Not a single person there was there by force; they earned wonderful salaries and there didn't seem to be even a chance that they would think about packing up their apartments and returning to their "place of origin"] (131).

In this group of compatriots who have voluntarily crossed the border of nationality and embraced an overlay of time/spaces, the protagonist feels like an exile. As a result, she identifies with the Northern wives of some of the Spaniards, women who delight in enumerating the defects of "cierta península del sur en la que casualmente yo había nacido" [a certain peninsula in the South where I happened to be born] (154). In this union with the different against the same, the protagonist seems to have rejected the national identity bestowed upon her by the mere accident of birth. She feels more affinity with those on the Northern side who, like herself, resent the transplantation of cultures and the superimposition of chronotopes.

Nonetheless, part of the subtlety of perspectivism in this story lies in the way the narrator, at times, vocalizes very enlightened opinions about definitions of national difference. When one Spanish woman in the colony voices her frustrations with the way Northerners are so unlike Spaniards, the protagonist mentally takes the opposite side: "aquello, además de una solemne estupidez, me pareció una aseveración un tanto discutible. Primero: ¿cómo éramos nosotros? O mejor: ¿era bueno o malo ser como nosotros? No seguí por ese camino porque resultaba evidente de qué lado se hallaba lo correcto, positivo y envidiable [. . .]" [that, besides being downright stupid, seemed to be a rather debatable assertion. First: what were we like? Or better yet: was it good or bad to be like us? I didn't continue down that path because it was evident which side was the correct, positive, and enviable one] (133). Yet, as her friendship with the Northern wives deepens and they begin to recognize her as "one of them," the protagonist reidentifies herself along the Spanish side of oppositional national lines: "Y supe, aunque nada dijeron, captar la profundidad de su mensaje: 'Ahora sí, por fin, ahora sí. . . Ahora empiezas a ser un poco de las nuestras.' Un poco, sí, era cierto. Pero, ¿y ellas? ¿Serían alguna vez como yo, como *nosotros*?" [And even though they didn't say anything, I managed to catch the deeper meaning of their message: "Now, at last, now. . . Now you're beginning to be one of ours a little bit." A little bit, yes, that was true. But, what about them? Would they ever be like me, like *us*?] (155). If there is any pattern at all to the oscillation of her self-definition, it may lie in the protagonist's persistent identification in *contention* with the objects of her attention, regardless of the opinions they profess.

As the protagonist doggedly pursues oppositional identification as a means of reaffirming her own power over others, the "other" that she prefers most is Rosita, whom she sarcastically describes as the true flower of the Spanish shop. In constructing Rosita as her dialectical—not dialogical—other, the protagonist insists on dividing and allocating Rosita's amalgam of diverse national characteristics onto one side or the other of the binary. Rosa is blond and fluent in the Northern language, but she also is extremely short and a native speaker of Castilian Spanish. Instead of seeing her as a hybrid, the protagonist first portrays her as solely Northern and then as purely Spanish: "Se había puesto en pie, y observé que, además de desvaída y seca, era fondona e increíblemente baja. Me pregunté cómo podía haberla confundido con una autóctona. Porque la verdad es que se había puesto en pie, pero se diría que seguía sentada" [She had stood up and I noticed that, besides being dull and curt, she was big-bottomed and incredibly short. I wondered how I could have taken her for a native. Because the truth is that she had stood up, but one would think that she was still sitting down] (Fernández Cubas 1990, 126). The narrator's gaze focuses on Rosa's stockiness as the target of her caustic humor and her criticism of all things Spanish situated in the North.

Of course, as Foucault and many others have demonstrated, the oppositional definition of the self is inseparable from the drive for power. The protagonist's unwaning passion for finding fault with the services of La Flor de España is an effort to assert her own superiority:

> Me había atrevido a pronunciar *¡qué contratiempo!*, y ahora me daba cuenta de que una de las constantes de esa magnífica y engañosa expresión estaba

precisamente en la superioridad arrogante, el tono de conmiseración o distancia con que la persona que dice *¡qué contratiempo!* califica unos hechos—la carencia de turrón de coco, por ejemplo—y coloca a los responsables en una posición dudosa e imprecisa, pero una posición, en resumidas cuentas, de simples siervos. (143)

[I had dared to utter *"How inconvenient!"* and now I realized that one of the constants of that magnificent and deceptive expression was precisely in the arrogant superiority, the tone of commiseration or distance with which the person who says *"How inconvenient!"* characterizes certain events—the lack of coconut Spanish nougat candy for example—and places those responsible in a doubtful and vague position, but to sum it up, in a position of simple servants.]

Once again, however, the narrator ignores that her gaze and her discourse are not the only ones that construct others as objects. All her efforts to defy the superimposition of chronotopes overlook the additional chronotope of readers—any of the almost infinite time spaces from which they might perceive and interpret her story. Most contemporary readers of this story in Castilian will recognize the ridiculous pettiness of her demands—who obsesses over *turrón de coco*, after all?— and subvert her, beneath their gaze, as the object of their humor.

The humor of the protagonist's blind struggle for power is intensified by her uproariously comical misinterpretations of the way other characters react to her. When she brings her homemade oxtail soup to Rosa in a gesture of friendship—and also in a demonstration of "la superioridad de cualquier sopa de rabo de buey hecha en casa, sobre el caldo del mismo nombre que aparecía machaconamente repetido y enlatado en uno de los anaqueles del establecimiento" [the superiority of any homemade oxtail soup over the broth of the same name that appeared monotonously repeated, in cans, on one of the shelves of the establishment] (148) (another obsessive attempt to assert the value of differentiation)—Rosa rejects the soup, tersely asserting that she does not eat between meals. Whereas many readers would perceive this as an excuse to discourage further overtures by her visitor, the narrator delightedly observes that "la flor volvía a mostrarse tan extrovertida y locuaz como en viejas ocasiones" [the flower was again proving to be as extroverted and loquacious as in old times] (148). Extroverted? Loquacious? Readers' astonishment at the incorrigible woman's point of view may be surpassed only by that of Rosa herself: "La flor se entregó a un curioso parpadeo y yo, sonriendo, acerqué una silla al mostrador. Pero enseguida me di cuenta de que me había precipitado. Porque durante unos segundos el azul de sus ojos había dejado paso a un blanco espectacular. [. . .] El blanco más blanco de todos los ojos que, a lo largo de mi vida, había visto ponerse fugazmente en blanco" [The flower gave in to a curious blinking and I, smiling, pulled a chair up to the counter. But I realized right away that I had acted too soon. Because for several seconds the blue of her eyes gave way to a spectacular white. {. . .} The whitest white of all the eyes that, in my whole life, I had seen go fleetingly white] (148–49). In her zeal to assert her perspective as superior, the protagonist is blind to other people's impressions of her. Yet, again, she inadvertently reveals the way others see her, this time by disclosing that Rosa is only one of many who react to her by rolling their eyes. Although the protagonist dismisses this as a "curious blinking," readers see it as a gesture of supreme annoyance and frustration, not to mention desperation.

The playfulness of perspective in "La Flor de España" demands its own game of oppositionality, then, by positioning readers against the narrator. Yet this dynamic is not reduced to dialectics, since the meaning of the text lies in the *relationship* between those two points of view: the self must take into account the vision of its other if it wants to see beyond its own limitations, for only in their cooperation do the two come to signify at all. The re-vision that dialogism requires unsettles the narrator, for it displaces her from the sphere of power she has staked out for herself. Whereas, within the text, self and other take their shape from their respective chronotopes, the integration of those time/spaces suggests a merging of difference into simultaneity that the narrator perceives as a threat to her sovereignty. Her perspective, however, in tension with other points of view, produces the dialogic vision created in the text, which spotlights the fundamental nature of subjectivity as repetition within difference and separation within simultaneity. In some ways the most horrific angle of vision in this collection of stories is the hilariously obnoxious and xenophobic perspective of this narrator, whose blindness to the way her antagonism alienates everyone she encounters isolates her from all of them, same or different. As symbolized by the truncated Northern letter that doubles as a tilde on the sign of the Spanish shop, the subject must confront the unsettling intermittence of sameness and difference when viewing its other.

Conclusion

In the stories of *El ángulo del horror*, desire for the other and the end is both the motivation and the potential undoing of the subject. Physics has demonstrated that the way in which one sees necessitates additional points of view in order to complete that vision, while psychoanalysis, myth, linguistics, and numerous other fields inscribe the dualistic interaction of the self and other in the process of identity formation. The dynamic of the gaze always functions as a crucial tactic in this construction; however, Fernández Cubas's texts persistently overturn any illusions inscribed in patriarchy that the seeing subject is necessarily male and its object female. *El ángulo del horror* highlights the fact that optical perception—so crucial to the construction of subjectivity—is a relative exercise, dependent on perspective, and a relational one, dependent on the dialogue between object and subject for its meaning.

As Fernández Cubas underscores in her stories, the subject's plotting of its desire for the dialogic other invariably confronts the conundrum of sameness and difference. If each object reflects its subject, its duality can reaffirm or invalidate, according to how repetition is perceived. Yet, even though being is, as Bakhtin holds, co-being, a simultaneous relationship between self and other, it is also one in which each person serves to differentiate the other. Such a perspective radically destabilizes the comfortably familiar lines of binary opposition along which the Western subject has traditionally drawn its identity. In the stories of *El ángulo del horror*, doubles and differences collide and repel, gazes are imposed and inverted, words and images capriciously twist toward multiple interpretations, all in a kaleidoscopic array of overlays and contradictions that displace the priority of any single angle on otherness and subvert the illusion of a unitary, superior subject. Although its visual *de*construction of the subject may seem horrific, ultimately Fernández Cubas's angle on the dynamics of identity in narrative would also incite the subject to plot (and) desire differently.

(In)conclusion

> "eché [las dos yemas] por el fregadero. Una tras otra. Una por el sumidero de la derecha; la otra por el de la izquierda. En ese punto culminante alcanzaron la felicidad. Venció la diferencia, ¿sabes?"
>
> [I tossed {the two egg yolks} down the sink. One after the other. One down the drain on the right; the other down the left. At that culminating point they attained happiness. Difference triumphed, you know?]
>
> —"Helicón" (*El ángulo del horror*)

"Venció la diferencia..." [Difference triumphed...]. This might seem a paradoxical affirmation, given that the quirky twin egg yolks are only the most frivolous (though nonetheless profound) of the unending entourage of doublets that parades across the pages of Fernández Cubas's texts. Contemporary Spain would also seem to herald the triumph of difference, disputable as that may be as an absolute condition, for as we have seen, all totalizing notions of sameness inevitably permutate into difference—even the notion of "difference" itself. Whereas Franco's proclamation that "Spain is different" aimed to separate the country as unique and inviolate from the rest of the West, democratic Spain embraces a nonisolationist notion of identity: it reconceives difference as the proliferation of otherness within the borders of the self, *Spain* itself. Fernández Cubas creates fictional worlds that reflect the postmodern understanding of this "real" world, wherein control, authority, and discourse constitute transitory conditions instead of absolute stasis. Far from being unmitigated, her texts suggest, power permeates all relations and is perhaps the most fundamental element of subjectivity. Its changeable nature ensures that subjectivity need never be completed, but can engage itself and its others in an ongoing process. By unveiling absolute power as an illusion, Fernández Cubas's narrative also refutes the notion of inviolate authority. In this author's work every discourse is recognized as intertextual by nature, for it always transmutes from and refers back to what has gone before. This gives rise to a crisis over originality/duplication for many characters in her texts. Inevitably, the issue condenses to the unsettling paradox of sameness and difference, for—as with innumerable other binary oppositions—Fernández Cubas inverts, subverts, and subsumes these poles to show that they both repel and dwell in one another. As a result, her characters discover that the very borders they depend upon to define their subjectivity also delineate the subjectivity of their others, both similarly and oppositionally. In the end, it is precisely the difference and repetition imbued in oppositionality that establish, destabilize, and expand the identity of the subject who is open to diverse angles on otherness.

Mi hermana Elba [My Sister Elba], the author's debut work, lays out the struggle for power between individuals in their efforts to define themselves as they play out their attractions and repulsions to difference in one another. Here Fernández Cubas investigates discursive constructs of the self imposed by society and explores ways in which the subject can maneuver around its given roles. One major social marker of identity is the concept of gender, which emerges in her works as a discursive matrix that precedes and predicts the individual. Although it is a paradigm that is inevitably reckoned with and repeated by all, gender is manipulated by some for the ends of agency. Hence *Los altillos de Brumal* [The Attics of Brumal] serves as the author's forum for contesting both feminist and patriarchal notions of gender that are founded on a sex-based dichotomy. Like the characters in her stories, the author wields the creative power of language, a primary strategy for challenging and transforming the discourse of gender: "As for me, when I write is precisely when I have the least sexual identity" (Fernández Cubas 1996). Fernández Cubas's texts deconstruct and devalue the unidirectional power dynamics of any binary structure, striving toward an alternative subjectivity that appropriates, manipulates, and maneuvers among diverse modes of being.

Similar to the subversion of the male/female opposition, in *El año de Gracia* [The Year of Grace] the revisionist portrayal of the colonizer as a weakened and distorted "other" of the colonized parodies the colonial tendency to denigrate the double as less than worthy, while it demonstrates the potential for the duplicate to deconstruct the origin by repeating it with a difference. The literary and ultimately political polarization of center/margin denounced in *El año de Gracia* neatly juxtaposes with *El columpio* [The Swing], a novel that defies the efforts of another discursive construction—the history of the Franco era—to freeze the present in an immobilized repetition of the past. Far from a monolithic moment, Fernández Cubas's novel proclaims, history is a time-dependent phenomenon, which, while often repeated, is also inevitably altered in its reiteration. In addition to the temporal influence, spatial considerations are intrinsic to subjectivity, for apart from the outside there can be no inside, and without the other there can be no self. *Con Agatha en Estambul* [With Agatha in Istanbul], therefore, projects the spatial construction of the subject in opposition to other subjects and other spaces. Seeing the other in a different place foregrounds the impact of distinct perspectives. *El ángulo del horror* [The Angle of Horror] highlights the issue of vision and its role in dialogism, a concept that in many ways elucidates the paradox of duality/difference that consistently figures as the defining mark of Fernández Cubas's fiction. As the shifting angles in her metaphorically titled collection reveal, the subject/object relationship is a symbiotic one, wherein each depends on the other to augment its personal vision; moreover, neither can exist without the perspective of its double, for each comes to have meaning only in relation to the other.

The theoretical issues that mark the contours of this study reemerge—in their own repetitions of sameness and difference—in nearly all of Fernández Cubas's texts. Although I selected concepts to help explain the intricacies involved with the reconstruction of identity in each work, the theories and fictional texts could be reconfigured. For instance, power relations infuse the mediation of identity in *El ángulo del horror*, whereas *El columpio* posits contradictory constructs of gender invested with power. *Mi hermana Elba* and *Con Agatha en Estambul* consider subjectivity as it is inscribed in many discursive fields such as literature, concepts of nationality, and religion. *El año de Gracia* alters temporal and spatial markers that individuals take for granted, and blurs the chronotopic boundaries that contour their existence. Finally, the tension of perspectives in *Los altillos de Brumal* demonstrates that, while the power of vision imparts knowledge, knowledge is at most partial and may be just illusory. Hence the author's works present multiple angles in the dialogue on subjectivity, reflecting one another in repetition only to refract off one another in difference.

As I engaged Fernández Cubas's fiction and various theoretical approaches in dialogue with one another, I found that one of the key contributions of the Spanish author is that she takes these issues farther or considers them from an angle that is slightly altered from that of the theories themselves. For instance, Foucault demonstrates power to be a two-way phenomenon that pervades all levels of social interaction, and he theorizes how objects, resistant to absolute control, may also perform as acting subjects. His analyses of specific power dynamics—such as torture, the panopticon, the examination, and the gaze—tend to focus on how one wields control or resistance, on how one *dominates*, whether one is the "subject" or the "object." Yet Fernández Cubas considers the opposite side of the equation by exploring how and why subjects *long to be dominated*, why they want to be objects that are berated or belauded, beguiled or beloved by a subject of power. She posits subjectivity as a dynamic process wherein each individual simultaneously negotiates the roles of subject and object. In her fictional paradigm, playing the role of the object is intrinsic to the formation of the subject. With this understanding, her stories depict an array of pleasures that seduce the subject out of the role of dominator: the yearning to be watched, the urge to purge through confession, and the need to be known emerge as prime motivators for the subject to submit as an object.

In addition, Fernández Cubas's tales show that those who defy our desires for domination—those who watch us with disdain or disinterest, those who edit, censure, or invalidate our stories, those who disregard our bodies and our selves as immaterial—those are the ones we resist, reject, and if possible expel from the boundaries of our identity as active subjects. Nonetheless, they still hover on the outside, contouring and contesting the selfhood we construct. If feminists have long criticized men's propensity to erase or devalue women's identity in this process, frequently in Fernández Cubas's tales the violators of male subjectivity are women— they are the Ulla Goldbergs, the Clara Sonia Galván Kraskowas, the Angelas, the Yasmines, the Teresas, the women who distort and defy men's desired image of themselves. Hence these women are denounced by men as monstrous, excessive, insufficient, abnormal, impossible, and unimportant: "un ser inhumano fuera de toda posible lógica" [an inhuman being outside all possible logic] (Fernández Cubas 1988, 95). Yet this logic of seeking the desirable other is not just men's logic, but women's. Equally, then—or perhaps even more frequently—the author's texts spawn disruptive women who contort the ideal self-image cultivated by other women: the Mother Perús, the Evas, the Lúnulas, the Jezabels, the Elbas, the Rositas, the Dina Dachs's, all stymie their nemeses' efforts to attain a comfortable sense of self. More importantly, as seen through Elena Vila Gastón in "Ausencia" ["Absence"; *Con Agatha en Estambul*], the principal object that inhibits a woman's full realization of subjectivity is often, in the end, the woman herself. In a parallel manner, the author's well-known novel *El año de Gracia* depicts the subject-object dichotomy as man against man, Daniel against Grock. In all these scenarios the antagonists are fundamental to the development of the subject, male or female, for without their defiance and difference, the protagonist would sink into stagnation.

Although self and other constitute essential players in subjectivity, an equally key aspect of identity is the disturbing duality that the subject perceives not just in the other, but in itself. When undesirable difference originates in the self, the subject may well seek to spurn and split from that part which it cannot or will not acknowledge as its own. Hence it strives to defer and distance what is abject in *itself* as what is *other*. After all, the most rabid rejection of difference in the other often stems from the suspicion of sameness, the fear that the other touches a chord of recognition and repetition in ourselves. We see this when the music of "Helicón" ["Helicon"; *El ángulo del horror*] inspires the composition of Cosme, where the controlled and cautious Marcos invents a twin brother to account for the side of himself that flails about in filth and euphony. If such dissonance occurs in men, a similar disparity may be seen in women such as Clara Sonia Galván Kraskowa, who has a mental crisis of disassociation from half of her identity in "En el hemisferio sur" ["In the Southern Hemisphere"; *Los altillos de Brumal*]. Yet are these stories truly alike? One could point out that Marcos/Cosme ultimately embraces his helicon, whereas Clara Galván cannot cope with the overwhelming domination of the Voice that drives her to write unceasingly and be the best-selling novelist, Sonia Kraskowa. When Clara separates herself in two, she identifies with her Spanish, Southern heritage and distances her Northern heritage, the half that characterizes the smash-hit writer. In the end, though, Clara/Sonia may achieve the greatest feat of all by vanquishing both the Voice and the art it inspires, when she writes a text that reflects her dreams and dictates the real-life events to follow.

The Voice that is the bane of Clara's existence repeats in other stories as other kinds of voices, which are in turn demanding, delusional, subversive, inspiring, or simply mischievous. An archetypal figure pertaining to identity, the voice perturbs and disturbs; it speaks to create disorder and to generate change. At times it is an echo of those long gone, the figuration of a present absence, such as the voice of Elba haunting her sister in "Mi hermana Elba" or the ghostly Clarisa conversing with her husband in "El lugar" ["The Place"; *Con Agatha en Estambul*], or the childhood playmates calling to "Anairda" in "Los altillos de Brumal." These voices beckon the protagonists to recognize some part of themselves that was erased or eclipsed, or perhaps never confronted at all. On other occasions the voice may well be the instigator of mischief, such as the "forty-year-old voice of wisdom" that prods the protagonist to search for clues in "Con Agatha en Estambul" and seek out mystery where there is none, other than the mystery of subjectivity itself. Alternately, in a tale like "La mujer de verde" ["The Woman in Green"; *Con Agatha en Estambul*], the voice seems to thunder the will of destiny as it drives the protagonist to commit murder in defiance of an impossible identity. Otherwise it might resonate as condemnation, like the oleanders that resist the closure of power in Carolina's "Mundo" ["World"; *Con Agatha en Estambul*] and steadfastly proclaim the realities of change. Whether emanating from the other or echoing somewhere inside the self, the voice ultimately speaks from a perspective of difference that destabilizes identity and propels the subject onward in pursuit of resolution.

The voice is such a prevalent trope in the author's work that even when its function is horrific, it constantly repeats and refers back to the other voices in a way that is quite amusing. Hence the author's reiteration of this and many other tropes serves another strategy: humor. Indeed, the great attraction of Fernández Cubas's tales is that, while they are profound, they also tend to be quite funny, displaying a subtle and strange sense of humor that never ceases to entertain, no matter how often one has read the stories. What is the root and role of this humor? Part of me hesitates to answer this, for fear that an analysis might somehow eradicate the magic. Yet the question merits consideration. I know that in each of my many readings of these works I inevitably laughed aloud in sheer enjoyment of what I read. Far from becoming predictable, the pleasure of reading Fernández Cubas only intensified as I found myself anticipating the twists and turns, the endless doubling and idiosyncrasies that characterize her stories. With each tale I found that this pattern was suddenly disrupted by a "strange loop" (to borrow a metaphor from Robert Spires), a perturbing perversion that skewed the whole story and made me rethink everything that I thought I knew about it. If repetition and subversion, difference and deconstruction, irony and erosion are the hallmarks of the postmodern world in which Fernández Cubas writes, her humor communicates these tenets in ways that unsettle and enlighten and—even better, I might say—bring more pleasure to the text. Such strategies of humor and their place in postmodernist writing are a subject of valuable study, but one that exceeds the borders I have had to construct to contain this particular text. Others, no doubt, will soon fill the gap in this and other areas of Fernández Cubas criticism. Ultimately, the proliferation in her texts of humor, twin images, and bizarre subversions through difference all undermine the patriarchal privileging of absolute centrality, of logic, and of cause-and-effect relations, in order to reveal that a richer experience is often gained by losing oneself in the unexpected and the inexplicable.

The constant repetition of strategies and double images in Fernández Cubas's fiction brings into question what duality *itself* excludes in order to constitute the terms of its own existence. Why does the self always depend on its other to reflect and complete its image? Despite the endless inversions and subversions of power that typify subjectivity, each subject is still defined by its object, each center mapped by its margin. The constant shifts of perspective in her texts suggest that no viewpoint can ever be total in and of itself, hence the need for reflection, repetition, supplementation, alteration, and so on, in a chain that could extend indefinitely. If the nature of subjectivity necessitates an other in the quest for completion, an augmented perspective from outside that relationship affords even greater vision and knowledge. Thus the visual optics of subjectivity in her work ultimately surpass duality to create multiplicity, extending out to the textual level. Fernández Cubas's works are marked by prominent themes that coalesce to advance her underlying design: to change the way *readers* see the world and, ultimately, to change the way they desire to be. More than dialectical, this model is dialogic in its search for supplementation.

Her texts always implicate readers in the dialogic process, for she sets up and subverts their expectations in order to induce them to change their perspectives. At times the author posits such a dynamic in terms of theatricality: if the characters are like actors on a stage (both performing subjects and seen objects), they are also objects of the gaze of others (spectators or readers). Hence Fernández Cubas's depiction of subjectivity as performativity traces an implicit path to agency for those beyond the stage (those supposedly denied the opportunity to act), by enlisting the critical power of their gaze into the performance. This interpretive role, bestowed by theater, fiction, and literature in general, dramatizes subjectivity and power as mutable processes that can be manipulated by all. Rather than mere repetition designed to reify some "original," constructed identity, Fernández Cubas's narrative discourse elicits the *interpretation*—the reading and acting out—of subjectivity in order to challenge the performance of identity both within and outside the text.

My own readings of these works, while designed to be cohesive, do not pretend to stand as the only viable interpretation of Fernández Cubas's texts. I recite and respond to the analyses of critics who have preceded me. Hence, my reading is one more repetition with a difference, which other readers may well unravel as they weave the threads of Fernández Cubas's tales into the fabric of their own discourse. The ingenious complexity of her fiction is such that, even if readers believe that they perceive a message and attempt to illustrate it through textual analyses, the stories themselves threaten to destabilize the certainty of their interpretations. This leads to the invention of more and more texts in response to those that the author initially created. In exploring the dynamic of subjects/objects and the ways they distinguish one another, her texts invert and ultimately subvert their definition to show that identity is ever in creation, never in conclusion. So, too, is it with the analyses in this book. One could view such a critical endeavor pessimistically, as a constant chain of supplementation that drives one farther and farther from the origin, from the "truth," whatever that may be. Yet I prefer to see it another way, as would, I suspect, Fernández Cubas: creating texts is a productive undertaking, for it spurs the subject to interrogate his or her own discursive constructions by searching for their abject zone—what was left out in order to present the work as a cohesive entity. Thus we, as subjects, seek out the similarity and difference in the excluded other to glimpse, within the discourses we construct, those discourses that construct us. By interpreting our texts and ourselves from diverse angles on otherness, then, we continue plotting the story of subjectivity as one whose ending is yet unwritten.

Notes

INTRODUCTION: SUBJECTIVITY AND DIFFERENCE IN POST-FRANCO SPAIN

1. Cristina Fernández Cubas, "Los altillos de Brumal," in *Mi hermana Elba y Los altillos de Brumal* (Fernández Cubas 1988, 157); "The Attics of Brumal," translated by Phyllis Zatlin (Fernández Cubas 1990b, 55). Fernández Cubas's fiction has been translated into numerous languages, but this is one of her few texts that have been translated into English. Unless otherwise indicated, the translations of all Spanish citations in this book are my own. In the interest of space, I use my English translations in place of the original Spanish when citing interviews and critical analyses.

Fernández Cubas frequently employs ellipses in her writing; to distinguish them from the ones I introduce in my quotations of her fiction, I place brackets around my ellipses. For all quoted material, I use ellipses without brackets.

2. The study of subjectivity has been developed by a host of theorists far too numerous to name here. The reader in search of an introduction and overview might consult Silverman (1983), Moi (1985), and Smith (1988).

3. See, for example, Constantino Bértolo's "Le nouveau pacte narratif" (1995) in France's *Magazine littéraire*.

4. See Fernando Valls's interview with Cristina Fernández Cubas, Ignacio Martínez de Pisón, Juan Miñana, Enrique Vila-Matas, and Pedro Zarraluki (Valls 1994b).

5. It is not my intention to suggest that 1975 was a magical year that triggered sudden, absolute changes in Spain. I see it more as a symbolic marker of a transformation that was well on its way in the 1960s. Critics have long debated over the time and the degree of the change from Francoism to Post-Francoism. See, for example, the Introduction to *La cultura española en el posfranquismo*, edited by Samuel Amell and Salvador García Castañeda. What is undeniable, however, is that major alterations have occurred. My particular study is concerned with the literary representation of altered Spanish identity, not with the actual timing of when it took place.

6. Balfour (1995) and Fox (1999) provide useful overviews of the historical development and mythologization of national identity in Spain. This identity is fundamentally altered with the end of Franco's dictatorship, which Spires correlates with the initiation of a "worldwide trend away from dictatorship and centralized power" (Spires 1996, 51). This alteration necessitated a reconstruction of the Spanish subject to allow for multiplicity, diversity, and flux instead of imposing pure homogeneity and hegemony.

7. For information on the development of feminism in Spain in the contemporary period, González (1979) and Folguera (1988) provide a starting point for investigation, in addition to various publications by the Instituto de la Mujer such as Ortiz Corulla's (1987). For perspectives on feminism in contemporary Spanish narrative, see Zatlin (1987b); Ciplijauskaité (1988); Manteiga, Galerstein, and McNerney (1988); Brown (1991); Ordóñez (1991); Jones (1992); and Nichols (1992).

8. Stephanie Seiburth studies the effect of uneven modernization on Spain as shown in its novel, drawing a parallel between the social and literary situations of the late nineteenth and late twentieth centuries. For an understanding of this phenomenon in the late dictatorship and early democracy years, see pages 1–26, 137–214, and 231–44 (Seiburth 1994).

9. For basic texts that set up and debate the phenomenon of postmodernism, readers might consult Hassan (1987), Hutcheon (1988 and 1989), Lyotard (1989), Jameson (1991), and McHale (1987 and 1992). For a sampling of the debate over the validity of the term "postmodern" when applied to Spain and Latin America, see the issue entitled "Fragmented Identities: Postmodernism in Spain and Latin America" in the *Journal of Interdisciplinary Literary Studies* (Herrero-Olaizola 1995b). Navajas gives a postmodern analysis of specifically Spanish novels (Navajas 1987).

10. Paul Smith's *Discerning the Subject* provides a lucid explanation of "agents" and "agency." For him, agency may be seen as a form of subjectivity where "the possibility (indeed, the actuality) of resistance to ideological pressure is allowed for (even though that resistance too must be produced in an ideological context)" (Smith 1988, xxxv).

11. In addition to the works already cited, readers may consult the following for an overview of general trends in post-Franco narrative: Alonso (1983), Basanta (1990), de Castro and Montejo (1990), Barrero Pérez (1992), Monleón (1995), and Labanyi (1999). Furthermore, special issues of *Ínsula*, numbers 464–65 and 512–13, focus on the status of the contemporary Spanish novel.

12. Although I agree with the intertextual parallels that Bellver lucidly draws in this article, our distinct conclusions are probably a reflection more of slightly different interpretations of postmodernity as a creative versus limiting force. These alternate emphases draw from the debate over postmodernism alluded to above.

13. It is also possible that, as a child of parents from Aragon who was raised speaking Castilian, Fernández Cubas does not feel that the Catalan identity is hers to embrace. She has been criticized by those who feel that *lo catalán* should be expressed by texts written in that tongue, yet her professional formation was not constructed in that language. Interestingly, she observes of her childhood years that "Catalan, in those days, was a language for playing" (Nichols 1993, 57). The contrast between the Catalan expression of free playtime and the Castilian expression of daily life presents an interesting duality of exclusion/inclusion, although it is one that the author herself has chosen not to incorporate into her fiction. For a discussion of manifestations of "feminism" in the author's work, see my study of the representation of gender in *Los altillos de Brumal* in chap. 2.

14. In addition to the novels and short story collections that I have mentioned, Fernández Cubas's prose fiction includes a short story, "Omar, amor," in the anthology *Doce relatos de mujeres*, edited by Ymelda Navajo, and two works of children's literature, *El vendedor de sombras* (1982) and *Cris y Cros* (1988). In selecting among her works of short fiction for my study, I have chosen to focus on her collections of stories because they imply an interrelationship among the tales within each collection. Nonetheless, the author's tales for children reflect many of the themes—such as the double, identity, and difference—that I discuss in relation to her adult fiction in this book. See Glenn (1996) for an interesting analysis of the author's stories for children.

15. Spires discusses the representation of power as "all-pervasive and contradictory" in post-Franco Spanish fiction (Spires 1989, 286).

Chapter 1: Looking Objectively at the Subject

1. In his introduction to *La cultura española en el posfranquismo*, Samuel Amell discusses the arguments of numerous critics on this issue (Amell and García Castañeda 1988, 7–10).

2. Foucault's account reads,

> On 2 March 1757 Damiens the regicide was condemned "to make the *amende honorable* before the main door of the Church of Paris." . . . Bouton, an officer of the watch, left us his account: "The sulphur was lit, but the flame was so poor that only the top skin of the hand was burnt, and that only slightly. Then the executioner, his sleeves rolled up, took the steel pincers, which had been especially made for the occasion, and which were about a foot and a half long, and pulled first at the calf of the right leg, then at the thigh, and from there at the two fleshy parts of the right arm; then at the breasts. Though a strong, sturdy fellow, this executioner found it so difficult to tear away the pieces of flesh that he set about the same spot two or three times, twisting the pincers as he did so, and what he took away formed at each part a wound about the size of a six-pound crown piece." (Foucault 1979, 3–4)

When the horses were unable to pull the limbs off the prisoner, the executioner had to assist by hacking at them:

> After two or three attempts, the executioner Samson and he who had used the pincers each drew out a knife from his pocket and cut the body at the thighs instead of severing the legs at the joints; the four horses gave a tug and carried off the two thighs after them, namely, that of the right side first, the other following; then the same was done to the arms, the shoulders, the arm-pits and the four limbs; the flesh had to be cut almost to the bone, the horses pulling hard carried off the right arm first and the other afterwards. (5)

3. Fernández Cubas extends the ramifications of binary struggles for power in this text by introducing the European/New World power struggle that will inform later works such as *El año de Gracia* [The Year of Grace] and *Con Agatha en Estambul* [With Agatha in Istanbul]. In this early story, the author foregrounds the issue through the image of the jacaranda, which figures in Lúnula's storytelling as a tyrannical tropical plant from the Americas imbued with the magical ability to carry out one's wishes, but also to deny them and drastically alter the supplicant's destiny if he or she does not obey the proper rituals for wishing. Lúnula sows the seeds of this plant in her garden, and Violeta is sure that if anyone can make a tropical plant grow in an inhospitable climate, Lúnula can. Through its metonymical association with Lúnula, the mythical power of the jacaranda implicitly underscores the inversion of power in which a formerly subjugated object (Lúnula, the Americas) wields power over the one who would control it.

4. Lúnula's ability to "provoke images" as a tactic of power links her to other great manipulators in *Mi hermana Elba*, the characters of "El provocador de imágenes" ["The Provoker of Images"].

5. This translation can be only partial, at best, because the passage depends upon word plays with homonyms and synonyms for its humorous meaning.

6. Rueda observes that this ambiguous identity merges the two women into one, thereby fusing the opposition of power between them. In effect, they become a single identity, a single body, and a single text (Rueda 1988, 262).

7. My thanks go to Robert Spires for pointing out the complexities that the mirror introduces into the theatrical subjectivity of this scene.

8. The semantic confusion of *luna* in this story also harks back to the previous story, with ambiguity of the word *luna* in relation to the *luna del espejo* and to Lúnula, who did not reflect power or knowledge according to the expectations of Violeta's logic.

9. I draw here on Stanzel's distinction between the narrating self and the experiencing self (Stanzel 1971, 59–70).

10. Pérez discusses the uncertainty created by the phenomenon of the unreliable narrator, which recurs frequently in Fernández Cubas's texts (Pérez 1998).

11. The difference in perception that a displacement in time imposes on the subject serves as the focus of my analysis of *El columpio* [The Swing] in chap. 3.

12. Although "Mi hermana Elba" was not technically the first story Fernández Cubas wrote, she identifies this tale as a watershed in her writing career: "My first story was 'The Garden Window.' I know it doesn't seem at all like a first story, but it was. The thing is, if I hadn't written 'My Sister Elba' I might possibly have been an author of just one story. Because in 'My Sister Elba' I got a ton of things off my chest, things that I needed to tell and that allowed me to continue writing" (Heymann and Mullor-Heymann 1991, 120).

13. In *Cosas que ya no existen*, Fernández Cubas recalls that, as a child, she was locked up in a freezing convent classroom for an entire day by a vengeful nun, to await heinous punishment for a small infraction she had committed (Fernández Cubas 2001, 17–32). In contrast, "Mi hermana Elba" features a labyrinthine convent where the young girls can penetrate closed spaces at will and escape any authoritarian detection of their covert deeds. *Cosas que ya no existen* reveals abundant parallels such as this between the author's fiction and her real experiences. Indeed, she wrote her memoirs in order to dismantle the masquerade of truth and fiction in her work: "Estaba empezando a cansarme de los préstamos que la realidad—mi realidad—concedía a menudo a la ficción—mi ficción—. De disfrazar recuerdos" [I was beginning to tire of the loans that reality—my reality—often conceded to fiction—my fiction. To tire of masking memories.] (Fernández Cubas 2001, 12).

14. Fernández Cubas recasts the oppositions of Spanish/Northern and normal/monstrous as the focus of the story "La Flor de España" ("The Flower of Spain") in the collection *El ángulo del horror* [The Angle of Horror], which I discuss in chap. 5.

CHAPTER 2: PERFORMING AND REFORMING GENDER

1. See Bretz (1988), Glenn (1990), and Zatlin (1996).

2. Paul Smith distinguishes between the "subject" and the "agent," for the latter can resist compliance with the discourses that abound in society to mold the subject a certain way:

> [T]he state of being a "subject"' is best conceived of in something akin to a temporal aspect—the "subject" as only a moment in a lived life. Along with this it can be said that ideological interpellations may *fail* to produce "a subject" or even a firm subject-position. Rather, what is produced by ideological interpellation is

contradiction, and through a recognition of the contradictory and dialectical elements of subjectivity it may be possible to think a concept of the agent. (Smith 1988, 37)

3. In Fernández Cubas's own life, Olvido parallels Antonia García Pegés, the woman who raised the author and her siblings. Described in "Elba: El origen de un cuento" (Elba: The Origin of a Story), Antonia was a marvelous storyteller whose "dominion . . . began in the kitchen, in her fief of casseroles and cooking pots, to extend then up the icy stairs and arrive at its zenith in the second floor bedrooms" (Fernández Cubas 1991, 115). Moreover, Antonia, too, shunned the clock and had a special relationship with the spirits: "Antonia always bragged about not needing in the least the services of an alarm clock. The grateful spirits more than complied with this task and Antonia woke up everyday, fresh as a rose, at seven a.m. on the dot" (115). Further parallels between Olvido and Antonia can be found in the author's description of the latter in *Cosas que ya no existen* (Fernández Cubas 2001, 33–49).

4. Fernández Cubas's childhood memories provide wonderfully fertile sources for the imagery of the clock and of objects infused with life, in addition to the figure of Antonia: "En realidad, en aquellos tiempos, casi todos los objetos tenían vida. Las casas respiraban también—de ahí la necesidad de ventanas, azoteas y balcones—, y en un lugar secreto, o por lo menos no siempre conocido, se encontraba el corazón. Todas las viviendas tenían corazón, aunque muchas veces sus habitantes no se dieran cuenta. El de la nuestra era fácil de detectar. A la vista estaba. En la escalera. Exactamente en el primer descansillo. El gran reloj de pie y sus inconfundibles latidos" [In reality, in those days, almost all the objects had life. The houses breathed, too—hence the need for windows, flat roofs, and balconies—and in a place that was secret, or at least not always known, was found the heart. All the dwellings had a heart, although many of their inhabitants did not realize it. Ours was easy to find. It was in plain view. On the stairway. Exactly on the first landing. The great upright clock and its unmistakable heartbeats.] (Fernández Cubas 2001, 42). The author goes on to recall her childhood feelings about the clock, which clearly form the seeds of the tale "El reloj de Bagdad."

5. In this power struggle, Olvido eclipses the children's actual mother, who is a flighty, self-centered, and largely absent figure. This nonideal mother also serves to detract from any perceived elevation of the feminine as a solely positive realm.

6. Rueda analyzes "En el hemisferio sur" and "La noche de Jezabel" ["Jezabel's Night"] in her study of the tension between orality and the written word in Fernández Cubas's fiction (Rueda 1988).

7. See Althusser's essay "Ideology and Ideological State Apparatuses," particularly pp. 170–177 (Althusser 1971, 127–186).

8. Cristina Fernández Cubas, "En el hemisferio sur," in *Mi hermana Elba y Los altillos de Brumal* (Fernández Cubas 1988, 137); "In the Southern Hemisphere," translated by Phyllis Zatlin (Fernández Cubas 1992, 85–86). Subsequent quotes from both the original and the translation will be from these editions and noted in the text.

9. Glenn argues that this story inverts the binomial of masculine/feminine, thereby installing woman at the center of power and authority (Glenn 1990). On one level this tactic does seem to take place, but I am not sure that Clara maintains domination or "has the last word." I see the story more as an implicit questioning of the validity of the gender binary itself. In my view, this work erodes authority as a locus of originating power for male or female, by showing that both genders, like the text itself, are discursive constructions.

10. Butler rethinks theories of constructivism that displace human subjects from power and install notions such as "Power" or "Discourse" as the metaphysical and grammatical

forces that control and act on humans. Rejecting the subject-verb-object paradigm as the *effect* and not the *cause* or *creator* of subjectivity, Butler argues that construction neither produces nor is produced by subjects. Rather, subjects come to exist at all only through a process of materialization (Butler 1993, 4–12).

11. In this respect, Clara/Sonia's feat evokes Butler's analysis of Irigaray's penetration of patriarchal philosophy. Butler describes Irigaray's repetition of male-centered philosophy as a resurgence of the excluded into the center:

> Irigaray's response to this exclusion of the feminine from the economy of representation is effectively to say, Fine, I don't want to be in your economy anyway, and I'll show you what this unintelligible receptacle can do to your system; I will not be a poor copy in your system, but I will resemble you nevertheless by *miming* the textual passages through which you construct your system and showing that what cannot enter it is already inside it (as its necessary outside), and I will mime and repeat the gestures of your operation until this emergence of the outside within the system calls into question its systematic closure and its pretension to be self-grounding. (Butler 1993, 45)

12. Butler points out the inconsistency of Lacan's theorization that the phallus is both (1) the law of the father that originates the masculine versus feminine binary, and (2) the prototype of any body that is thus exempt from strict gendered associations. Butler stresses that the phallus cannot be both origin and prototype, or symptom, of the origin. This contradiction unveils the contrived nature of the privileged penis:

> [W]e can read here the phantasmatic rewriting of an organ or body part, the penis, as the phallus, a move effected by a transvaluative denial of its substitutability, dependency, diminutive size, limited control, partiality. The phallus would then emerge as a symptom, and its authority could be established only through a metaleptic reversal of cause and effect. Rather than the postulated origin of signification or the signifiable, the phallus would be the effect of a signifying chain summarily suppressed. (Butler 1993, 81)

Playing on the instability of the foundation of gendered roles in the law of the father, Butler then posits that the phallus is fundamentally transferable: as an idealization that can never be realized through any body part, the phallus is intrinsically tied to none, which makes it exchangeable. This displacement of the phallus from the origin is key to a concept of agency, for it frees the feminine from the moorings of mere reflection or exclusion, and it liberates the masculine from the illusion of its own centrality as the originator of power:

> Inasmuch as the phallus signifies, it is also always in the process of being signified and resignified. In this sense, it is not the incipient moment or origin of a signifying chain, as Lacan would insist, but part of a reiterable signifying practice and, hence, open to resignification: signifying in ways and in places that exceed its proper structural place within the Lacanian symbolic and contest the necessity of that place. If the phallus is a privileged signifier, it gains that privilege through being reiterated. And if the cultural construction of sexuality compels [*sic*] a repetition of that signifier, there is nevertheless in the very force of repetition, understood as resignification or recirculation, the possibility of depriviliging that signifier. (89)

See Butler's deconstruction of the phallus as the paradigm for sexual signification in her chapter entitled "The Lesbian Phallus and the Morphological Imaginary" (57–91).

13. Cristina Fernández Cubas, "Los altillos de Brumal," in *Mi hermana Elba y Los altillos de Brumal* (Fernández Cubas 1988, 157); "The Attics of Brumal," translated by Phyllis Zatlin (Fernández Cubas 1990b, 55). Subsequent quotes from both the original and the translation will be from these editions and noted in the text.

14. Phyllis Zatlin gives a sexual, psychoanalytical reading of the space and discourse of Brumal in this story: "The retreat to the semiotic–that is, to the enclosure of a world that through inverted language resists communication with the other, outside world—points to a rejection of her own sexuality, not unrelated to the rejection of her mother" (Zatlin 1996, 39).

15. Fernández Cubas often allows for a "logical" explanation of events in characters' altered mind states caused by alcohol, drugs, and insanity, as part of a ludic resistance to absolute closure in her stories, as well as a questioning of the nature of reality and reason. See, for example, "La mujer de verde" ["The Woman in Green"] and "Con Agatha en Estambul" ["With Agatha in Istanbul"], both from *Con Agatha en Estambul*, as well as "El ángulo del horror" ["The Angle of Horror"] from the collection by that title.

16. In her fiction Fernández Cubas repeatedly plays with the image of a closed space that is also paradoxically open. Adriana in the attic of Brumal evokes the young girls of "Mi hermana Elba" ["My Sister Elba"], who discovered invisible spaces of freedom within their convent. Of course, Lewis Carroll's *Alice in Wonderland* is another obvious allusion. Brumal is an enclosure that implodes to virtually infinite openness, reminiscent of Borges's "El aleph" and Fernández Cubas's own image of a trunk within the convent of "Mundo" ("World") in *Con Agatha en Estambul* [With Agatha in Istanbul]. In a 1991 interview with Glenn, three years before "Mundo" is published in *Con Agatha en Estambul*, Fernández Cubas comments on the similarity of the image of a trunk to the image of the attic in "Los altillos de Brumal":

> It is possible that attics, as closed and somewhat mysterious spaces in houses, have always interested me.... [They have elements] of mystery, of memories, of discoveries, of nostalgia. They are places where somehow life has stopped, has been enclosed in old chests. By the way, I don't know if you know that in some parts of Spain a chest or a trunk is called a "world." ... I've always loved storerooms, since I was a child. Closed places, wardrobes, rooms in shadow where, suddenly, things appear, things from another time or things that you had come to forget. (Glenn 1993, 358–59)

In chap. 5 of this study, I examine in detail the author's representations of space as configured in *Con Agatha en Estambul*.

17. I draw on Judith Butler's *Bodies That Matter* for my use of the term "abject." In contrast, Pérez provides an interesting application of Julia Kristeva's psychoanalytical study of abjection to Fernández Cubas's *El ángulo del horror* (Pérez 1995–96).

18. If "agency" can be seen as the ability to maneuver among the constraints of the sociopolitical and cultural norms that construct humans, it does not mean overcoming or escaping the system of discursive control within which all subjects operate. On the contrary, as Butler points out, individuals come into being as "subjects" only when they come into existence in the discursive paradigm of society. Subjects cannot exist outside of discourse and, correspondingly, agency can occur only within the discursive system "as a reiterative or rearticulatory practice, immanent to power, and not a relation of external opposition to power" (Butler 1993, 15).

19. For further explanation of "Performativity as Citationality," see the section by that title in the Introduction of *Bodies That Matter* (Butler 1993, 12–16).

20. Zatlin (1987a) and Talbot (1989) analyze in detail the fantastic elements in this and other short stories by Fernández Cubas. Ortega (1992) also examines the fantastic in her work, although he does not include "La noche de Jezabel" in his analysis. Exploring a related genre, Glenn (1992) discusses the Gothic elements in the author's work. For a more detailed explanation of the distinctions between the fantastic, the marvelous, and the uncanny as literary genres, see Todorov's influential work, *The Fantastic: A Structural Approach to a Literary Genre*, especially pages 24–57 (Todorov 1975).

CHAPTER 3: RE-CITING AND RE-SITING

1. Spires draws a parallel between Spain and this island, for the latter is revealed at the end of the novel to have been chosen as a site for biological experimentation: "An island designated for wartime chemical experimentation clearly echoes the Spanish peninsula and its role just prior to World War II as a laboratory for new German and Russian weaponry" (Spires 1997, 136). In fact, with this novelistic Island of Gruinard, Fernández Cubas sets up the fictionalization of history that she explores furthur in *El columpio*. In 1942 the British indeed dropped an experimental anthrax bomb on the sheep-inhabited Island of Gruinard off the coast of Scotland. Officially quarantined until 1990, the island is still generally shunned for fear of continued contamination. The 1985 novel depicts anthrax as the devastating weapon of a formerly imperialistic power, a weapon which in 2001 is being wielded by an apparently marginalized (and to date, unidentified) power to contaminate the United States from within. Hence Fernández Cubas presciently points to the quintessential ambiguity of biological warfare, which joins the war on terrorism to illustrate a key feature of the late twentieth and twenty-first centuries: the blurred borders of national identities, alliances, and enemies in a globalized realm.

2. Numerous critics have noted the importance of the *Robinson Crusoe* referent in *El año de Gracia*. For analyses of this and other intertextual elements of the novel, see Bellver (especially 1992 and 1995), Gleue (1992), Margenot (1993), Spires (1996, particularly pages 156–72), and Zatlin (1987b).

3. Spires perceptively notes the repetitious, cyclical nature of the numbers of time and dates in Daniel's life (Spires 1996, 158).

4. Using Yasmine as an example, Spires argues that this novel, published on the eve of Spain's integration into the European Union, implicitly criticizes the way communities propagate limiting constructs, such as gender, through repetition:

> As represented in this novel, social bodies serve to construct and reinforce gender roles. Whereas iteration plays a creative role in Goytisolo's novelistic project, in Fernández Cubas's it has a normative and enervating effect. Communities perpetuate historical gender constructs responsible at least in part for a global state of entropy. This novel suggests that even the most radical centrifugal movement is inadequate to the task of dismantling a construct so securely anchored by social systems. (Spires 1997, 138)

The paradox of iteration is that it can ingrain an idea even as it undermines it by repeating it with a difference. Although Fernández Cubas exploits both elements of this duality in her fiction, my study focuses on her tactics of subversion in repetition.

5. Pérez threads together the many motifs of narrative unreliability in *Con Agatha en Estambul* [With Agatha in Istanbul] and *El columpio* (Pérez 1998). To date, no other studies have been published on *El columpio*.

6. Bellver (1992), Zatlin (1987a), Alborg (1987), and Spires (1996) discuss various metafictional elements in *El año de Gracia*.

7. Interestingly, in *The End of Modernity*, Vattimo argues that the experience of the work of art offers one of the few opportunities to experience truth in the postmodern world: "We may then say that the work of art is a 'setting-into-work of truth' because it sets up historical worlds; it inaugurates and anticipates, as an original linguistic event, the possibility of historical existence–but always shows this only in reference to mortality" (Vattimo 1991, 126). The work of art is subject to differing interpretations according to the influence of history–of the passage of time–on the viewer. This idea is borne out in *El columpio*, as the niece and her uncles, effectively living in different historical moments, see radically different truths in their interpretations of the painting of Eloísa.

8. As Pérez points out, theatricality permeates this novel: "theatricality constitutes an extended metaphor, as the uncles are several times termed actors and references made to performance" (Pérez 1998, 36).

9. Fernández Cubas plays further with the concept of intertextuality by incorporating within *El columpio* numerous allusions to images in other texts that she herself has written. The compartmentalized, secret nature of Eloísa's desk and other furniture in the house, as well as the closed spaces of the rooms, the attic, the tower, and the house itself, all in turn repeat similar images in other Fernández Cubas works such as *Con Agatha en Estambul* [With Agatha in Istanbul]; (see my analysis in chap. 4) and *Los altillos de Brumal* [The Attics of Brumal]; (see chap. 2). Such spaces sometimes represent closure and prohibition, while at other times they implode into paradoxically infinite openness, depending on the use ordained by the person associated with that space. Indirectly, *El columpio* also repeats the intertext of *Mi hermana Elba* [My Sister Elba]. With its characterization of a little girl who possesses the uncanny ability to manipulate time and space, this novel might well be called "Mi madre Eloísa." The treatment of time itself in *El columpio* is alternately foregrounded in the seemingly infinite span of one year in *El año de Gracia*.

Moreover, Fernández Cubas's second novel projects a plane of suspended time that depicts a perspective of things from an "angle of horror." In a play on dual meaning of the word *ángulo* as "corner" and "angle," this passage shows how Eloísa's manipulation of the diabolo affected the viewer's angle of vision:

> La penumbra que señoreaba la cocina ayudaba a creerla allí. En cualquiera de los ángulos. O en un ángulo de otra dimensión, que se superponía de pronto a cualquiera de aquellos ángulos, ejecutando las maravillas que pregonaba Lucas, como . . . un circo en el que el maestro de ceremonias pudiera, con la sola fuerza de la palabra, convocar imágenes, personajes, decorados. (Fernández Cubas 1995, 71)

> [The shadows that ruled the kitchen helped to make her seem there. In any of the corners. Or in a corner of another dimension, that suddenly superimposed itself on any of those corners, performing the wonders that Lucas announced, like . . . a circus in which the master of ceremonies could, with merely the power of his word, convoke images, people, scenery.]

Even the reference to *convocar imágenes* points to a Fernández Cubas intertext, recalling the discursive power of "El provocador de imágenes" ["The Provoker of Images"] in *Mi hermana Elba*. So many references, condensed into two pages of *El columpio*, underscore Fernández Cubas's reiteration of the act of writing as a repetition of other texts that have gone before.

Chapter 4: The Space of Oppositional Subjectivity

1. This displacement of the "original" text and its author by the translator may be an ironic acknowledgment of the slipperiness of language, the writing profession, and authority itself. Once again, Fernández Cubas focuses on repetition as a destabilizer of authority: translation, as reiteration, is a reinscription that writes over and often replaces the original, even as it reaffirms and disseminates that original.

2. It is not my intention to associate imagistic communication solely with the feminine or to ally the written word only with patriarchy. "Patriarchy" may be the term to describe a culture in which men have dominated textual and hence ideological inscription; however, women participate in that process as well. Likewise, both genders perform in the deconstruction of logocentrism, as Fernández Cubas's fiction depicts. For my analysis of the author's treatment of binary positions specifically related to gender, see chap. 2.

3. Julie Gleue has posed an alternate interpretation of this story by reading the protagonist's confrontation with Dina Dachs as a hallucination, not an actual event (Gleue 1995). By allowing for numerous interpretations, the rich complexity of this tale escapes any definitive interpretation; indeed, its elusivity argues for the impossibility and pointlessness of absolute delineations in language, in literature, and by extension, in life.

4. In the figure of Aunt Ricarda, who exploited the resources of the Americas for her own enrichment, Fernández Cubas takes issue with the Old World/New World binary, a thread that she also weaves into texts such as "Mundo" *(Con Agatha en Estanbul),* "Lúnula y Violeta" *(Mi hermana Elba),* and *El año de Gracia.* While Mother Perú falls victim to the system of power in the Old World in "Mundo," Lúnula's otherness triumphs with her discursive obliteration of the subject of enunciation in her story. In *El año de Gracia* and "El lugar," the author explores otherness as a spatial inversion and resituates the subject as the object in the realm of the outside, which becomes a new center.

5. The color of this suitcase recalls the titular character of "La mujer de verde," who similarly serves as a spatial repository. The woman in green encompasses all that the narrator could not tolerate in her own identity–both sameness (the futility of an impossible subjectivity) and difference (the ideal of perfection). Similarly, the narrator of "El lugar" attempts to encase his otherness in the green suitcase to facilitate his acceptance in the other world.

6. His dilemma recalls the narrator of "La mujer de verde," who found the ideal feminine to be impossibly "other" than her own reality.

7. In an interview, Derrida is reported to have emphasized, "First of all, I didn't say that there was no center, that we could get along without the center. I believe that the center is a function, not a being–a reality, but a function. And this function is absolutely indispensable. The subject is absolutely indispensable. I don't destroy the subject; I situate it" (Derrida 1970, 271–72).

8. In Althusser's view, subjects are inevitably and inescapably defined by the discourses of ideology: "[Ideology] 'transforms' the individuals into subjects (it transforms them all) by that very precise operation which I have called *interpellation* or hailing, and which can be imagined along the lines of the most commonplace everyday police (or other) hailing: 'Hey, you there!'" (Althusser 1971, 174).

9. Pritchett lists a number of possible symbolic referents for the fish. In addition, she posits Tinkerbell as representative of the protagonist's immaturity prior to the transformation that she undergoes on this trip (Pritchett 1996, 253).

10. Imagining Flora as the dastardly antagonist in a crime novel, the narrator again casts herself as the detective and protagonist. Moreover, as Pritchett demonstrates, this

woman parallels her adventures in Istanbul with the real-life mysterious adventures of Agatha Christie (Pritchett 1996, 248–49).

11. This story points to other fictional worlds as well through its intertextuality. Zatlin observes that, in addition to the most obvious intertext of Agatha Christie–particularly her disappearance and attack of amnesia in Istanbul in 1926–the Fernández Cubas story may well be an implicit response to Antonio Gala's *La pasión turca* (1993) (Zatlin 1996, 40–41).

12. Zatlin argues that this tale comments on the infidelity that is often part of female experience: "It suggests that Agatha Christie's fabled disappearance and amnesia were her response to her husband's infidelity; by analogy, the narrator's impulsive choice of vacation spot and her runaway imagination stem from marital malaise" (Zatlin 1996, 41).

13. The humor of this passage is lost in the translation, due to the play on words of *asunción* as "assumption," (as in the assumption or ascension of the Virgin Mary) and of *aventuras* as "love affairs." Knowing the sexually dichotomous meanings of the terms makes it hilarious to imagine the confused, disconcerted gentleman on the plane overhear the protagonist jabber to herself about "assumptions" and "affairs," not about accepting things or having adventures.

CHAPTER 5: THE VISUAL CONSTRUCTION OF THE SUBJECT

1. Critics have taken diverse approaches to *El ángulo del horror*. For further discussion of doubling in "Helicón" and other Fernández Cubas stories, see Glenn (1992). Ortega (1992) and Zatlin (1996) have noted the play of the fantastic mixing with reality in this text. Taking a different perspective, Spires views this collection as emblematic of the contemporary subversion of cause-and-effect relationships in narrative, wherein "symmetry yields to aberrancy [and] the Euclidean straight lines bend into fractal strange loops" (Spires 1992b, 1). He also examines how the work "addresses a dimension of the illogic of logic" (Spires 1995, 234). Valls (1993) also refers to the collection in the introduction to his anthology of Spanish short fiction. Finally, Pérez studies the collection in light of Kristeva's theory of abjection, whereby the child excludes "those parts of itself which society deems unclean or otherwise unacceptable" (Pérez 1995–96, 160).

2. Throughout *Alice Doesn't*, de Lauretis traces the Oedipal logic of narrativity as presented by numerous critics. This paradigm involves

> the inscription of desire in the very *movement* of narrative, the unfolding of the Oedipal scenario as *drama* (action). Can it be accidental, I ask, that the semantic structure of all narrative is the movement of an actant-subject toward an actant-object (Greimas), that in fairy tales the object of the hero's quest (action) is "a *princess* (a sought-for person) and *her father*" (Propp), that the central Bororo myth in Lévi-Strauss's study of over eight hundred North and South American myths is a variant of the Greek myth of Oedipus? (de Lauretis 1984, 79)

Her intriguing discussion of theories that engage the Oedipal foundations of narrative includes, among others, Lévi-Strauss (1967 and 1969), Freud (1955, particularly the essay "Femininity" in vol. 22), Propp (1968), Lacan (1975 and 1977), and Lotman (1979).

3. Bataille asserts: "eroticism is assenting to life even in death. Indeed, although erotic activity is in the first place an exuberance of life, the object of this psychological quest, independent as I say of any concern to reproduce life, is not alien to death" (Bataille

1986, 11). He further explains, "We are discontinuous beings, individuals who perish in isolation in the midst of an incomprehensible adventure, but we yearn for our lost continuity" (15). This "lost continuity" is reachieved through death, or through sexual union with the other. Interestingly, when Bataille fleshes out the details of this drive toward continuity, he, too, founds his explication on the binary opposition of male/female:

> In the process of dissolution, the male partner has generally an active role, while the female partner is passive. The passive, female side is essentially the one that is dissolved as a separate entity. But for the male partner that dissolution of the passive partner means one thing only: it is paving the way for a fusion where both are mingled, attaining at length the same degree of dissolution. (17)

Whereas "the same degree of dissolution" may be the end goal, it is realized by the female eradicating herself and being subsumed by the male. Despite the limitations of this reductive foray into the intricate workings of subject formation, I believe that Bataille signals an inescapable element of subjectivity: the impetus to define oneself in relation to an other. Moreover, he draws an important parallel between the desire for the other and the inevitable drive toward death.

4. Spires interprets the symbolism of the pipe ironically:

> The ugly corroded pipe serves as a sign of corrupted family and moral values, a sign reinforced by the visual images of the grandfather's children. These are the old man's legacy to his grandson: keepsakes that reify the older generation's avaricious, hypocritical, tyrannical, and illogical essence. The grandson not only inherits these qualities, but contributes an act of sadistic parricide to pass along to his own eventual heirs. (Spires 1995, 236)

5. For an explanation of the distinction between the experiencing self and the narrating self in first-person narrations, see Franz Stanzel, "The First Person Novel" (Stanzel 1971, 59–70).

6. In his analysis of the subversion of logic in this story, Spires comments: "Rationality itself constitutes the horrific angle from which we join Julia to view this stranger than fantasy world called reality" (Spires 1995, 235). In displacing the angle from which reason views reality, the author defamiliarizes readers' view of reason itself.

7. For a discussion of the ambiguity of signs in this story, see Glenn (1992).

Works Cited

Alborg, Concha. 1987. Cuatro narradoras de la transición. In *Nuevos y novísimos: algunas perspectivas críticas sobre la narrativa española desde la década de los '60*. Edited by Ricardo Landeira and Luis T. González del Valle, 11–28. Boulder, Colo.: Society of Spanish and Spanish American Studies.

Alonso, Santos. 1983. *La novela en la transición (1976–1981)*. Madrid: Puerta del Sol/Ensayo.

Althusser, Louis. 1971. *Lenin and Philosophy and Other Essays*. Translated by Ben Brewster. New York: Monthly Review Press.

Amell, Samuel, and Salvador García Castañeda, eds. 1988. *La cultura española en el posfranquismo: Diez años de cine, cultura y literatura (1975–1985)*. Madrid: Editorial Playor.

Ashcroft, Bill, Gareth Griffiths, and Helen Tiffin. 1989. *The Empire Writes Back: Theory and Practice in Post-Colonial Literatures*. New York: Routledge.

Bakhtin, Mikhail. 1981. *The Dialogic Imagination: Four Essays*. Edited by Michael Holquist. Translated by Caryl Emerson and Michael Holquist. Austin: University of Texas Press.

Balfour, Sebastian. 1995. The Loss of Empire, Regenerationism, and the Forging of a Myth of National Identity. In *Spanish Cultural Studies: An Introduction*. Edited by Helen Graham and Jo Labanyi, 25–31. Oxford: Oxford University Press.

Barrero Pérez, Oscar. 1992. *Historia de la literatura española contemporánea (1939–1990)*. Madrid: Istmo.

Basanta, Angel. 1990. *La novela española de nuestra época*. Madrid: Anaya.

Bataille, Georges. 1986. *Erotism: Death and Sensuality*. Translated by Mary Dalwood. San Francisco: City Lights Books.

Bellver, Catherine G. 1992. *El año de Gracia* and the Displacement of the Word. *Studies in Twentieth Century Literature* 16, no. 2: 221–32.

———. 1993–94. *El año de Gracia*: El viaje como rito de iniciación. *Explicación de Textos Literarios* 22, no. 1: 3–10.

———. 1995. *Robinson Crusoe* Revisited: *El año de Gracia* and the Postmodern Ethic. *Journal of Interdisciplinary Literary Studies* 7, no. 1: 105–18.

Benveniste, Émile. 1971. *Problems in General Linguistics*. Translated by Mary Elizabeth Meek. Coral Gables, Fla.: University of Miami Press.

Bértolo, Constantino. 1995. Le nouveau pacte narratif. *Magazine littéraire*. March: 33–36.

Bhabha, Homi K. 1985. Signs Taken for Wonders: Questions of Ambivalence and Authority under a Tree Outside Delhi, May 1817. *Critical Inquiry* 12, no. 1 (Autumn): 144–65.

———. 1994. Of Mimicry and Man: The Ambivalence of Colonial Discourse. In *The Location of Culture*, 85–92. New York: Routledge.

Bretz, Mary Lee. 1988. Cristina Fernández Cubas and the Recuperation of the Semiotic in *Los altillos de Brumal*. *Anales de la Literatura Española Contemporánea* 13: 177–88.

Brooks, Peter. 1984. *Reading for the Plot: Design and Intention in Narrative*. Cambridge: Harvard University Press.

Brown, Joan Lipman, ed. 1991. *Women Writers of Contemporary Spain: Exiles in the Homeland*. Newark: University of Delaware Press.

Butler, Judith. 1990a. *Gender Trouble: Feminism and the Subversion of Identity*. New York: Routledge.

———. 1990b. Performative Acts and Gender Constitution: An Essay in Phenomenology and Feminist Theory. In *Performing Feminisms: Feminist Critical Theory and Theatre*. Edited by Sue-Ellen Case, 270–82. Baltimore: Johns Hopkins University Press.

———. 1993. *Bodies That Matter: On the Discursive Limits of Sex*. New York: Routledge.

Carmona, Vincent, Jeffrey Lamb, Sherry Velasco, and Barbara Zecchi. 1991. Conversando con Mercedes Abad, Cristina Fernández Cubas y Soledad Puértolas: "Feminismo y literatura no tienen nada que ver." *Mester* 20, no. 2 (Fall): 157–65.

Chambers, Iain. 1990. *Border Dialogues: Journeys in Postmodernity*. New York: Routledge.

Chambers, Ross. 1991. *Room for Maneuver: Reading (the) Oppositional (in) Narrative*. Chicago: University of Chicago Press.

Ciplijauskaité, Biruté. 1988. *La novela femenina contemporánea (1970–1985)*. Barcelona: Anthropos.

de Castro, Isabel, and Lucía Montejo. 1990. *Tendencias y procedimientos de la novela española actual (1975–1988)*. Madrid: UNED.

de Lauretis, Teresa. 1984. *Alice Doesn't: Feminism, Semiotics, Cinema*. Bloomington: Indiana University Press.

———. 1987. *Technologies of Gender: Essays on Theory, Film and Fiction*. Bloomington: Indiana University Press.

Derrida, Jacques. 1970. Structure, Sign and Play in the Discourse of the Human Sciences. In *The Structuralist Controversy*. Edited by Richard Macksey and Eugenio Donato, 247–72. Baltimore: Johns Hopkins University Press.

Epps, Bradley S. 1996. *Significant Violence: Oppression and Resistance in the Narratives of Juan Goytisolo, 1970–1990*. Oxford: Clarendon Press.

Fernández Cubas, Cristina. 1985. *El año de Gracia*. Barcelona: Tusquets.

———. 1988. *Mi hermana Elba y Los altillos de Brumal*. Barcelona: Tusquets.

———. 1990a. *El ángulo del horror*. Barcelona: Tusquets.

———. 1990b. "The Attics of Brumal." Translated by Phyllis Zatlin. *Short Story International* 14, no. 8 (June): 53–75.

———. 1991. Elba: el origen de un cuento. *Lucanor* 6 (September): 113–16.

———. 1992. "In the Southern Hemisphere." Translated by Phyllis Zatlin. *Kansas Quarterly* 23, no. 1–2: 83–93.

———. 1994. *Con Agatha en Estambul*. Barcelona: Tusquets.
———. 1995. *El columpio*. Barcelona: Tusquets.
———. 1996. Interview by author. Barcelona. 25 July.
———. 2001. *Cosas que ya no existen*. Barcelona: Lumen.
Folguera, Pilar, ed. 1988. *El feminismo en España: Dos siglos de historia*. Madrid: Pablo Iglesias.
Foucault, Michel. 1979. *Discipline and Punish: The Birth of the Prison*. Translated by Alan Sheridan. New York: Vintage.
———. 1980. *Power/Knowledge: Selected Interviews and Other Writings (1972–1977)*. Edited by Colin Gordon. Translated by Colin Gordon, Leo Marshall, John Mepham, and Kate Soper. New York: Pantheon Books.
———. 1990. *The History of Sexuality*. Vol. 1. Translated by Robert Hurley. New York: Vintage.
———. 1994. *The Order of Things: An Archaeology of the Human Sciences*. New York: Vintage.
Fox, E. Inman. 1999. Spain as Castile: Nationalism and National Identity. In *The Cambridge Companion to Modern Spanish Culture*. Edited by David T. Gies, 21–36. New York: Cambridge University Press.
Freud, Sigmund. 1955. *The Standard Edition of the Complete Psychological Works of Sigmund Freud*. Translated by James Strachey. New York: Hogarth.
García Lorca, Federico. 1985. *Bodas de sangre*. Madrid: Austral.
Glenn, Kathleen M. 1990. Authority and Marginality in Three Contemporary Spanish Narratives. *Romance Languages Annual* 2: 426–30.
———. 1992. Gothic Indecipherability and Doubling in the Fiction of Cristina Fernández Cubas. *Monographic Review/Revista Monográfica* 8: 125–41.
———. 1993. Conversación con Cristina Fernández Cubas. *Anales de la Literatura Española Contemporánea* 18, no. 2: 355–63.
———. 1996. Fantastic Doubles in Cristina Fernández Cubas' Tales for Children. In *Visions of the Fantastic: Selected Essays from the Fifteenth International Conference on the Fantastic in the Arts*. Edited by Allienne R. Becker, 57–62. Westport, Conn.: Greenwood Press.
———. 1998. Narrative Designs in Cristina Fernández Cubas's "Mundo." *Romance Languages Annual* 9: 501–4.
Gleue, Julie L. 1992. The Epistemological and Ontological Implications in Cristina Fernández Cubas' *El año de Gracia*. *Monographic Review/Revista Monográfica* 8: 142–56.
———. 1995. Narrative as Knowledge in Cristina Fernández Cubas's *Con Agatha en Estambul*. Paper presented at Mid-America Conference on Hispanic Literature, 13 October, at the University of Colorado, Boulder.
González, Anabel. 1979. *El feminismo en España, hoy*. Bilbao: Zero.
Hassan, Ihab. 1987. *The Postmodern Turn: Essays in Postmodern Theory and Culture*. Columbus: Ohio University Press.
Herrero-Olaizola, Alejandro. 1995a. Cuestiones preliminares: Las enseñanzas del postmodernismo. *Journal of Interdisciplinary Literary Studies* 7, no. 2: 119–30.
———, ed. 1995b. Fragmented Identities: Postmodernism in Spain and Latin America. Special issue of the *Journal of Interdisciplinary Studies* 7, no. 2.

Herzberger, David K. 1995. *Narrating the Past: Fiction and Historiography in Postwar Spain*. Durham, N.C.: Duke University Press.

Heymann, Jochen, and Montserrat Mullor-Heymann. 1991. *Retratos de escritorio: Entrevistas a autores españoles*. Frankfurt: Vervuert.

Holquist, Michael. 1990. *Dialogism: Bakhtin and His World*. New York: Routledge.

Hooper, John. 1995. *The New Spaniards*. New York: Penguin.

Hutcheon, Linda. 1988. *A Poetics of Postmodernism: History, Theory, Fiction*. New York: Routledge.

———. 1989. *The Politics of Postmodernism*. New York: Routledge.

Insula. 1985. 464–65 (July-August).

———. 1989. 512–13 (August-September).

Jameson, Frederic. 1991. *Postmodernism, or, The Cultural Logic of Late Capitalism*. Durham, N.C.: Duke University Press.

Jones, Margaret. 1992. Different Wor(l)ds: Modes of Women's Communication in Spain's *Narrativa Femenina*. *Monographic Review/Revista Monográfica* 8: 57–69.

Kristeva, Julia. 1980. *Desire in Language: A Semiotic Approach to Literature and Art*. Edited by Leon S. Roudiez. Translated by Thomas Gora, Alice Jardine, and Leon S. Roudiez. New York: Columbia University Press.

———. 1984. *Revolution in Poetic Language*. Translated by Margaret Waller. New York: Columbia University Press.

Labanyi, Jo. 1995. Postmodernism and the Problem of Cultural Identity. In *Spanish Cultural Studies: An Introduction*. Edited by Helen Graham and Jo Labanyi, 396–406. Oxford: Oxford University Press.

———. 1999. Narrative in Culture, 1975–1996. In *The Cambridge Companion to Modern Spanish Culture*. Edited by David T. Gies, 147–62. New York: Cambridge University Press.

Lacan, Jacques. 1975. *Encore: Le seminaire livre XX*. Paris: Seuil.

———. 1977. *Ecrits: A Selection*. Translated by Alan Sheridan. London: Norton.

Lévi-Strauss, Claude. 1967. *Structural Anthropology*. Garden City, N.Y.: Doubleday.

———. 1969. *The Elementary Structures of Kinship*. Boston: Beacon Press.

Lotman, Jurij M. 1979. The Origin of Plot in the Light of Typology. Translated by Julian Graffy. *Poetics Today* 1, no. 1–2 (Autumn): 161–84.

Lyotard, Jean-François. 1989. *The Postmodern Condition: A Report on Knowledge*. Translated by Geoff Bennington and Brian Massumi. Minneapolis: University of Minnesota Press.

Manteiga, Roberto C., Carolyn Galerstein, and Kathleen McNerney, eds. 1988. *Feminine Concerns in Contemporary Spanish Fiction by Women*. Potomac, Md.: Scripta Humanistica.

Margenot, John B., III. 1993. Parody and Self-Consciousness in Cristina Fernández Cubas' *El año de Gracia*. *Siglo XX/Twentieth Century* 11: 71–87.

Martín Gaite, Carmen. 1987. *Usos amorosos de la postguerra española*. Barcelona: Anagrama.

McHale, Brian. 1987. *Postmodernist Fiction*. New York: Methuen.

———. 1992. *Constructing Postmodernism*. New York: Routledge.

Mitchell, W. J. T. 1994. *Picture Theory*. Chicago: University of Chicago Press.

Moi, Toril. 1985. *Sexual/Textual Politics*. New York: Methuen.

Monleón, José B., ed. 1995. *Del franquismo a la posmodernidad: Cultura española 1975–1990*. Madrid: Ediciones Akal.

Montero, Rosa. 1995. The Silent Revolution: The Social and Cultural Advances of Women in Democratic Spain. In *Spanish Cultural Studies: An Introduction*. Edited by Helen Graham and Jo Labanyi, 381–85. Oxford: Oxford University Press.

Navajas, Gonzalo. 1987. *Teoría y práctica de la novela española postmoderna*. Barcelona: Ediciones del Mall.

———. 1997. España/Europa: Reconfiguración de un paradigma cultural. *Revista de Estudios Hispánicos* 31, no. 2 (May): 235–48.

Nichols, Geraldine C. 1992. *Des/cifrar la diferencia: Narrativa femenina de la España contemporánea*. Madrid: Siglo XXI.

———. 1993. Entrevista a Cristina Fernández Cubas. *España Contemporánea* 6, no. 2: 55–71.

Ordóñez, Elizabeth J. 1991. *Voices of Their Own: Contemporary Spanish Narrative by Women*. Lewisburg, Pa.: Bucknell University Press.

Ortega, José. 1992. La dimensión fantástica en los cuentos de Fernández Cubas. *Monographic Review/Revista Monográfica* 8: 157–63.

Ortiz Corulla, Carmen. 1987. *La participación política de las mujeres en la democracia (1979–1986)*. Madrid: Instituto de la Mujer.

Pérez, Janet. 1988. *Contemporary Women Writers of Spain*. Boston: Twayne.

———. 1995–96. Fernández Cubas, Abjection, and the 'retórica del horror.' *Explicación de Textos Literarios* 24, no. 1–2: 159–71.

———. 1998. Cristina Fernández Cubas: Narrative Unreliability and the Flight from Clarity, or, The Quest for Knowledge in the Fog. *Hispanófila* 122 (January): 29–39.

Pritchett, Kay. 1996. Cristina Fernández Cubas's "Con Agatha en Estambul": Traveling into Mist and Mystery. *Monographic Review/Revista Monográfica* 12: 247–57.

Propp, Vladimir. 1968. *Morphology of the Folktale*. Edited by Louis A. Wagner. Austin: University of Texas Press.

Rueda, Ana. 1988. Cristina Fernández Cubas: Una narrativa de voces extinguidas. *Monographic Review/Revista Monográfica* 4: 257–67.

Said, Edward. 1995. Orientalism. In *The Post-Colonial Studies Reader*. Edited by Bill Ashcroft, Gareth Griffiths, and Helen Tiffin, 87–91. New York: Routledge.

Schaefer-Rodríguez, Claudia. 1990. On the Waterfront: Realism Meets the Postmodern in Post-Franco Spain's *Novela Negra*. *Hispanic Journal* 11, no. 1 (Spring): 133–46.

Seiburth, Stephanie. 1994. *Inventing High and Low: Literature, Mass Culture, and Uneven Modernity in Spain*. Durham, N.C.: Duke University Press.

Silverman, Kaja. 1983. *The Subject of Semiotics*. New York: Oxford University Press.

Smith, Paul. 1988. *Discerning the Subject*. Minneapolis: University of Minnesota Press.

Sobejano, Gonzalo. 1985. La novela poemática y sus alrededores. *Insula* 464–65 (July-August): 1 and 26.

Spires, Robert C. 1989. A Play of Difference: Fiction after Franco. *Letras Peninsulares* 1, no. 3: 285–98.

———. 1992a. El concepto de antisilogismo en la novelística del posfranquismo. *España Contemporánea* 5, no. 2 (Fall): 9–16.

———. 1992b. From Angles to "Strange Loops": *El ángulo del horror* by Cristina Fernández Cubas. Paper presented at the Modern Language Association of America Convention, December, New York.

———. 1995. Postmodernism/Paralogism: *El ángulo del horror* by Cristina Fernández Cubas. *Journal of Interdisciplinary Literary Studies* 7, no. 2: 233–45.

———. 1996. *Post-Totalitarian Spanish Fiction*. Columbia: University of Missouri Press.

———. 1997. Discursive Constructs and Spanish Fiction of the 1980s. *Journal of Narrative Technique* 27.1 (Winter): 128–46.

Stanzel, Franz. 1971. The First Person Novel. In *Narrative Situations in the Novel: Tom Jones, Moby-Dick, The Ambassadors, Ulysses*. Translated by James P. Pusack, 59–70. Bloomington: Indiana University Press.

Subirats, Eduardo. 1995. Postmodern Modernity: España y los felices ochenta. *Journal of Interdisciplinary Literary Studies* 7, no. 2: 207–17.

Suñén, Luis. 1984. La realidad y sus sombras: Las obras de Rosa Montero y Cristina Fernández Cubas. *Insula* 446 (June): 5.

Talbot, Lynn K. 1989. Journey into the Fantastic: Cristina Fernández Cubas's "Los altillos de Brumal." *Letras Femeninas* 15, no. 1–2: 37–47.

Todorov, Tzvetan. 1975. *The Fantastic: A Structural Approach to a Literary Genre*. Translated by Richard Howard. Ithaca: Cornell University Press.

Valls, Fernando. 1993. El renacimiento del cuento en España (1975–1993). In *Son cuentos: Antología del relato breve español, 1975–1993*, 9–78. Madrid: Espasa Calpe.

———. 1994a. De las certezas del amigo a las dudas del héroe: Sobre "La ventana del jardín" de Cristina Fernández Cubas. *Insula* 568 (April): 18–19.

———. 1994b. De últimos cuentos y cuentistas. *Insula* 568 (April): 3–6.

Vattimo, Gianni. 1991. *The End of Modernity*. Translated by Jon R. Snyder. Baltimore: Johns Hopkins University Press.

Zatlin, Phyllis. 1987a. Tales from Fernández Cubas: Adventure in the Fantastic. *Monographic Review/Revista Monográfica* 3, no. 1–2: 107–18.

———. 1987b. Women Novelists in Democratic Spain: Freedom to Express the Female Perspective. *Anales de la Literatura Española Contemporánea* 12, no. 1–2: 29–44.

———. 1996. Amnesia, Strangulation, Hallucination and Other Mishaps: The Perils of Being Female in Tales of Cristina Fernández Cubas. *Hispania* 79, no. 1 (March): 36–44.

Index

abject, the. *See* otherness: exclusion of
agency, 24, 29, 44, 66, 68, 74, 76, 77, 81–83, 91, 99–100, 137, 139, 143, 156–57, 158, 166, 173, 184, 190, 192, 225, 230, 233 n. 10, 235 n. 2, 237 n. 12, 238 n. 18
Alborg, Concha, 24, 104, 115, 240 n. 6
Almodóvar, Pedro, 20–21
Alonso, Santos, 233 n. 11
Althusser, Louis, 77, 151, 172, 236 n. 7, 241 n. 8
altillos de Brumal, Los, 15, 19, 27, 66, 67–100, 102, 127, 157–58, 225–26, 240 n. 9
"altillos de Brumal, Los," 85–91, 112, 157, 228, 232 n. 1, 238 nn. 13 and 16
Amell, Samuel, 232 n. 5, 234 n. 1
ángulo del horror, El, 15, 17, 24, 28, 185, 186–223, 226, 238 n. 17
"ángulo del horror, El," 207–13, 218, 238 n. 15, 240 n. 9
año de Gracia, El, 15, 21, 24, 25, 27, 101–17, 119, 127, 135, 137–38, 161, 175, 225–27, 234 n. 3, 240 n. 9, 241 n. 4
anthrax, 239 n. 1
Ashcroft, Bill, 107
"Ausencia," 165–74, 176, 184, 188, 227
authority, 27, 30, 97, 112, 142; destabilization of, 21, 31, 42–44, 64, 77, 84, 86, 104–6, 115, 119, 127, 144–48, 156, 208, 224–25, 236 n. 9, 237 n. 12, 241 n. 1. *See also* repetition

Bakhtin, Mikhail, 94, 190, 193, 28, 208, 212–13, 214–15, 223. *See also* chronotope; dialogism

Balfour, Sebastian, 232 n. 6
Barrero Pérez, Oscar, 233 n. 11
Basanta, Angel, 15, 233 n. 11
Bataille, Georges, 188, 242–43 n. 3
Bellver, Catherine G., 24, 25, 104, 106, 112–13, 233 n. 12, 239 n. 2, 240 n. 6
Benet, Juan, 23
Benveniste, Émile, 166, 171
Bértolo, Constantino, 232 n. 3
Bhabha, Homi, 27, 104–5, 108–9, 112, 116, 117, 129
body, the, 42, 77, 79, 81–82, 85–86, 98, 114, 193, 227, 235 n. 6, 237 n. 12. *See also* Butler, Judith
Borges, Jorge Luis, 40, 43, 52, 130, 238 n. 16
Bretz, Mary Lee, 24, 29, 69, 70, 75–76, 157, 235 n. 1
Brooks, Peter, 28, 186, 200, 207
Brown, Joan Lipman, 233 n. 7
Butler, Judith, 27, 71–72, 76, 77, 79, 80–82, 85–86, 93, 96–97, 101, 126, 129, 160, 190, 210, 236 n. 10, 237 nn. 11 and 12, 238 nn. 17–19

Carmona, Vincent, 68
Carroll, Lewis, 238 n. 16
Cela, Camilo José, 23
center, the, 14, 16, 32, 56, 84, 86–88, 90, 100, 101, 102, 104–5, 123–25, 137–38, 144, 159, 164, 168, 174, 188, 194, 204, 210, 213, 218–19, 225, 229–30, 237 n. 12, 241 nn. 4 and 7; shift away from, 20, 21, 22, 27, 82, 115–17
Chambers, Iain, 137

Chambers, Ross, 28, 143–44, 146, 156, 162–63, 173, 184
chronotope (time/space), 208–10, 213–23, 226; *See also* Bakhtin, Mikhail
Ciplijauskaité, Biruté, 233 n. 7
columpio, El, 15, 18, 27, 101, 117–38, 202, 225–26, 235 n. 11
Con Agatha en Estambul, 15, 28, 138, 139–85, 226, 234 n. 3, 239 n. 5, 240 n. 9
"Con Agatha en Estambul," 170, 174–84, 228, 238 n. 15
Cosas que ya no existen, 15, 235 n. 13, 236 nn. 3–4
Cris y Cros, 233 n. 14

de Castro, Isabel, 233 n. 11
de Lauretis, Teresa, 71, 76, 160, 164, 187–88, 192, 198, 242 n. 2
Derrida, Jacques, 86, 129, 168, 241 n. 7
desire, 17, 28, 62, 72, 86, 105, 115, 141–43, 145–46, 148, 158, 164, 182, 184, 186–223, 227, 230
dialogism, 28, 208, 212–13, 215, 220, 222, 226, 230. *See also* Bakhtin, Mikhail; Holquist, Michael
difference, 13, 14–15, 16–18, 21, 22, 25–26, 28, 29, 65, 86–87, 89, 105, 114, 116, 125–26, 148, 184, 187, 189, 191–92, 196–98, 205, 208–9, 211, 216–19, 222–23, 224–25, 229; logic/illogic, 45–47, 52, 55, 66, 75, 89–91, 156, 157, 161, 167–68, 174, 177–78, 180, 238 n. 15, 242 n. 1, 243 n. 6; normal/abnormal, 39, 43, 48, 54, 56, 59–60, 62, 64, 111, 156, 188, 194–97, 227, 235 n. 14; Old World/New World, 102, 144, 234 n. 3, 241 n. 4; South/ North, 17, 78, 83, 84–85, 213–23, 235 n. 14; West/East, 71–72, 110. *See also* gender; otherness; repetition; sameness; subject, the: and object
discourse, 23–24, 27, 29, 31, 33–35, 63, 65–66, 72–74, 77, 79, 81–84, 85–86, 91–100, 101–2, 104–5, 109, 118, 119, 126–27, 135, 137, 143, 164, 184, 192, 195, 198, 211, 221, 224–26, 235 n. 2, 236 n. 10, 238 n. 18, 241 n. 8; and manipulation of language, 25, 39–41, 45–47, 50–52, 54, 58, 60, 76, 88–90, 107, 131, 141, 145–48, 154, 155, 160–61, 165–74, 176, 179, 200–201, 204–6, 208, 225, 230, 235 n. 8, 238 n. 14, 241 n. 1; direct, 36–37; indirect, 94, 193
doubles, trope of, 17, 28, 105, 109, 119, 187–98, 211, 223, 224–26, 228–30, 242 n. 1. *See also* hybrid; repetition: with a difference

ekphrasis, 144, 148
"En el hemisferio sur," 19, 76–85, 91, 130, 228, 236 nn. 6 and 8
Epps, Bradley, 126, 131, 134

fantastic, the, 23–24, 29, 97, 104, 135, 239 n. 20, 242 n. 1
feminism, 19, 26, 68, 225, 227, 233 n. 7
"Flor de España, La," 17, 213–23, 235 n. 14
Folguera, Pilar, 233 n. 7
Foucault, Michel, 26, 30–45, 47–48, 61–62, 66, 72, 129, 220, 226, 234 n. 2. *See also* power
Fox, E. Inman, 232 n. 6
Franco, Francisco, 15, 16, 18, 24, 27, 29, 122–23, 125–27, 129, 133
Freud, Sigmund, 174, 242 n. 2

Galerstein, Carolyn, 233n. 7
García Castañeda, Salvador, 232 n. 5, 234 n. 1
García Lorca, Federico, 94
gender, 17–19, 26, 66, 67–100, 104, 166–67, 173–74, 184, 207, 217, 225–26, 239 n. 4; male/female dichotomy, 14, 19, 27, 102, 110, 114, 140–41, 146, 158, 161–65, 187–98, 203, 227, 236 nn. 5 and 9, 237 nn. 11 and 12, 241 nn. 2 and 6, 242 n. 2, 243 n. 3; social role of women, 18, 62–63, 143, 149–57, 178. *See also* Butler, Judith; de Lauretis, Teresa; difference; feminism; performativity; subject, the.
generation of '68, 15
Glenn, Kathleen, 25, 68, 139, 147, 192, 233 n. 14, 235 n. 1, 236 n. 9, 238 n. 16, 239 n. 20, 242 n. 1, 243 n. 7
Gleue, Julie, 104, 115, 239 n. 2, 241n. 3
González, Anabel, 233 n. 7

Goytisolo, Juan, 23, 24
Goytisolo, Luis, 23, 239 n. 4
Griffith, Gareth. *See* Ashcroft, Bill
Guelbenzu, José María, 15

Hassan, Ihab, 233 n. 9
Heidegger, Martin, 125
"Helicón," 17, 187–98, 216, 228
Hermanas de sangre, 15
Herrero-Olaizola, Alejandro, 21, 233 n. 9
Herzberger, David, 122–23, 126–27, 129
Heymann, Jochen, 235 n. 12
history, 18, 23, 26, 27, 101, 112, 116–38, 146–47, 188, 207, 215, 225–26, 239 n. 1, 240 n. 7
Holquist, Michael, 208–9, 212–13
Hooper, John, 16
Hutcheon, Linda, 21, 22–23, 233 n. 9
hybrid, the, 102, 104–5, 119, 220. *See also* Bhabha, Homi; doubles; repetition: with a difference

identity, 14–15, 18, 25–26, 28, 31, 41, 43–44, 62–63, 71, 78, 82, 86, 91, 93, 104, 114–15, 119, 126, 139–40, 141–42, 145, 152–53, 155, 158–59, 182, 187, 205, 230; national, 15, 17–18, 22, 27, 215–16, 219–20, 224, 232n. 6, 239. 1; regional, 17, 26, 233 n. 13. *See also* subject, the; subjectivity
Irigaray, Luce, 80, 86, 129, 237 n. 11

Jameson, Fredric, 130, 233 n. 9
Jones, Margaret, 233 n. 7

Kristeva, Julia, 28, 69–72, 157–58, 160–61, 164, 195, 238n. 17, 242 n. 1

Labanyi, Jo, 18, 22, 233 n. 11
Lacan, Jacques, 25, 69, 72, 165–66, 174, 237 n. 12, 242 n. 2
Lamb, Jeffrey. *See* Carmona, Vincent
"legado del abuelo, El," 198–207, 211
Lévi-Strauss, Claude, 242 n. 2
Lotman, Jurij, 188, 242 n. 2
"lugar, El," 157–65, 177, 184, 228
"Lúnula y Violeta," 19, 31–45, 47–48, 51, 54, 56, 62, 66, 70, 112, 234 n. 3, 235 n. 8, 241 n. 4

Lyotard, Jean-François, 233 n. 9

Manteiga, Roberto, 233 n. 7
Margenot, John, 24, 104, 239 n. 2
Martín Gaite, Carmen, 23, 122
McHale, Brian, 28, 174–76, 180, 233 n. 9
McNerney, Kathleen, 233 n. 7
memory, 23, 60, 64, 74–75, 89–90, 114, 134, 165, 170, 206, 235 n. 13
Mendoza, Eduardo, 15, 23, 24
metafiction, 23, 104, 119, 240 n. 6; metatheatre, 49–51
Mi hermana Elba, 14, 15, 19, 20, 26–27, 28, 29–66, 67, 102, 225–26
"Mi hermana Elba," 56–60, 64, 228, 235 n. 12, 235 n. 13, 238 n. 16, 240 n. 9
Millás, Juan José, 15, 23
Mitchell, W. J. T., 144, 148
modernity, 21, 27, 118, 136–37, 174, 233 n. 8
Moi, Toril, 232 n. 2
Moix, Ana María, 15
Monleón, José, 233 n. 11
Montejo, Lucía, 233 n. 11
Montero, Rosa, 18–19
"mujer de verde, La," 149–57, 173, 178, 184, 228, 238 n. 15, 241nn. 5 and 6
Mullor-Heymann, Montserrat. *See* Heymann, Jochen
"Mundo," 140–49, 161, 184, 228, 238 n. 16, 241n. 4

Navajas, Gonzalo, 17, 233 n. 9
Navajo, Ymelda, 233 n. 14
Nichols, Geraldine, 233 n. 7 and 13
"noche de Jezabel, La," 91–99, 236 n. 6, 239 n. 20

"Omar, amor," 233 n. 14
oppositionality, 26, 28, 66, 141, 143–49, 162–63, 184, 225. *See also* otherness; subject: and object
Ordóñez, Elizabeth, 233 n. 7
Ortega, José, 24, 29, 239 n. 20, 242 n. 1
Ortiz, Lourdes, 15, 23
Ortiz Corulla, Carmen, 233 n. 7
otherness, 14–15, 16, 26, 28, 32, 65, 71, 73, 89, 104–5, 109–10, 115, 117, 127, 137, 141–42, 144–45, 148, 150–52, 163,

166, 169–70, 173, 176, 179, 186, 188, 202, 211–12, 218–23, 241 nn. 4 and 5; exclusion of, 25–26, 27, 79, 84–87, 90–91, 94, 101–2, 125, 136, 157–58, 160–61, 164–65, 194–98, 210, 227–28, 231, 233 n. 13, 237 nn. 11 and 12. *See also* subject: and object

Pérez, Janet, 25, 139, 175, 195, 235 n. 10, 238 n. 17, 239 n. 5, 240 n. 8, 242 n. 1
performativity, 27, 66, 67–100, 238 n. 19; performance and theatricality, 31, 45, 47–51, 53, 91, 95–97, 99, 126, 170–71, 230, 240 n. 8. *See also* Butler, Judith; gender
Pombo, Alvaro, 15
postcolonialism, 27, 101–17, 207, 225
postmodernism, 21–24, 26, 118, 136–37, 175, 224, 229, 233 nn. 9 and 12, 240 n. 7
power, 14–19, 26–67, 71–73, 81–82, 101–2, 104–7, 109–14, 116–17, 119, 124–27, 137–38, 141, 143–46, 148, 156, 157, 160–65, 184, 191, 193–94, 197–98, 207, 220–22, 224–27, 229–30, 234 n. 3, 236 nn. 9–10, 237 n. 12, 239 n. 1, 241 n. 4; and confession, 33–35, 45, 56, 60, 61, 64, 227; and examination, 38–39, 47–48, 59, 61–65, 192, 226; and panopticon, 37, 42, 226; and torture, 36–39, 226. *See also* Foucault, Michel; vision: and the gaze
Pritchett, Kay, 139, 181, 241 nn. 9 and 10
Propp, Vladimir, 242 n. 2
"provocador de imágenes, El," 60–65, 66, 192, 234 n. 4, 240 n. 9
Puértolas, Soledad, 15

"reloj de Bagdad, El," 68–76, 84, 85, 88, 91, 236 n. 3, 236 n. 4
repetition, 141, 161, 189–90, 208, 216, 228, 238 n. 18, 240 n. 9, 241 n. 1; with a difference, 24, 27, 79, 81–82, 91–92, 95, 97–99, 101–39, 141, 192, 222, 225–26, 229–30, 237 nn. 11–12, 239 n. 4. *See also* doubles, trope of; sameness
Rueda, Ana, 25, 29, 235 n. 6, 236 n. 6

Said, Edward, 27, 102

sameness, 22, 105, 114, 116–17, 119, 121, 123, 126–27, 129, 136, 161, 167, 212, 241 n. 5. *See also* difference; doubles; repetition
Saussure, Ferdinand de, 25, 52
Schaefer-Rodríguez, Claudia, 23
Seiburth, Stephanie, 233 n. 8
Silverman, Kaja, 171–72, 232 n. 2
Smith, Paul, 14, 143, 232 n. 2, 233 n. 10, 235 n. 2
Sobejano, Gonzalo, 23–24
space, 14, 18, 26–28, 56, 58, 117, 123, 125, 128, 133–35, 138–85, 208, 210–11, 213, 226, 235 n. 13, 238 nn. 14 and 16, 240 n. 9. *See also* otherness: exclusion of
Spires, Robert, 24, 30, 104, 113–15, 229, 232 n. 6, 234 n. 15, 235 n. 7, 239 nn. 1–4, 240 n. 6, 242 n. 1, 243 nn. 4 and 6
Stanzel, Franz, 235 n. 9, 243 n. 5
Subirats, Eduardo, 21
subject, the, 26, 68–69, 77, 81–86, 94, 116–17, 125–26, 151–56, 165–74, 176–77, 182–83, 235 n. 2, 236 n. 10, 238 n. 18, 241 nn. 7 and 8; and object, 14–15, 26–28, 30–34, 36–41, 45, 49, 56, 59, 61–66, 140–49, 157, 164–65, 186–98, 203–6, 208–10, 213, 217–23. *See also* identity; otherness; sameness; subjectivity
subjectivity, 13–15, 17, 25–26, 28, 29, 45, 59, 66, 71–72, 76, 91, 99–100, 102, 135, 137, 149, 159–62, 184–85, 214, 224–31, 232 n. 2, 233 n. 10, 243 n. 3. *See also* identity; otherness; sameness; subject, the
Suñén, Luis, 24

Talbot, Lynn, 24, 29, 239 n. 20
Tiffin, Helen. *See* Ashcroft, Bill
time, 18, 21, 43, 56, 70–71, 90, 108, 117–18, 120–23, 125, 127–29, 131–39, 145–46, 154–55, 167, 188, 200, 205–8, 213, 225–26, 235 n. 11, 239 n. 3, 240 nn. 7 and 9. *See also* chronotope (time/space)
Todorov, Tzvetan, 239 n. 20

Valls, Fernando, 25, 29, 48, 232 n. 4, 242 n. 1

Vattimo, Gianni, 27, 118, 122, 125, 136, 240 n. 7
Vázquez Montalbán, Manuel, 15, 23
Velasco, Sherry. *See* Carmona, Vincent
vendedor de sombras, El, 233 n. 14
"ventana del jardín, La," 20, 45–56, 58, 59, 66, 89, 112, 167–68, 178, 235 n. 12
vision, 14, 19, 20, 26, 45, 115, 152, 175, 186–223, 230; and the gaze, 31–32, 36–39, 41–42, 44, 47–50, 52–56, 59–66, 108–9, 114, 140–41, 145, 147, 226, 230 (*see also* power); and perspective, 26–28, 52–56, 94, 101–2, 105–6, 109, 111, 115–16, 118–19, 121, 123, 127, 131–41, 149, 155–57, 160, 162, 165, 168, 185, 198–207, 226, 229–30

Zatlin, Phyllis, 24, 29, 104, 139, 157, 232 n. 1, 233 n. 7, 235 n. 1, 236 n. 8, 238 nn. 13 and 14, 239 n. 20, 239 n. 2, 240 n. 6, 242 nn. 11 and 12, 242 n. 1
Zecchi, Barbara. *See* Carmona, Vincent